Contents

1 Introduction   **1**
- 1.1 Glitch (music) 1
    - 1.1.1 History 1
    - 1.1.2 Production techniques 1
    - 1.1.3 Notable artists 2
    - 1.1.4 Glitch hop 2
    - 1.1.5 See also 2
    - 1.1.6 References 2
    - 1.1.7 Further reading 3

2 Further Reading   **4**
- 2.1 Ableton Live 4
    - 2.1.1 History 4
    - 2.1.2 Features 4
    - 2.1.3 Versions 6
    - 2.1.4 See also 6
    - 2.1.5 References 6
    - 2.1.6 External links 7
- 2.2 AudioMulch 7
    - 2.2.1 History 7
    - 2.2.2 Features 8
    - 2.2.3 Musicians that use or have used AudioMulch 8
    - 2.2.4 See also 9
    - 2.2.5 Notes 9
    - 2.2.6 References 9
    - 2.2.7 External links 9
- 2.3 Bidule 9
    - 2.3.1 References 10
    - 2.3.2 External links 10
- 2.4 ChucK 10

	2.4.1	Language features	10
	2.4.2	Code example	10
	2.4.3	Uses	11
	2.4.4	See also	11
	2.4.5	References	11
	2.4.6	Further reading	11
	2.4.7	External links	12
2.5	Circuit bending		12
	2.5.1	Experimental process	12
	2.5.2	Innovators	13
	2.5.3	See also	13
	2.5.4	References	14
	2.5.5	External links	14
2.6	Clicks & Cuts Series		14
	2.6.1	Volumes	14
	2.6.2	See also	14
	2.6.3	External links	14
2.7	Crash (computing)		14
	2.7.1	Application crashes	15
	2.7.2	Web server crashes	15
	2.7.3	Operating system crashes	16
	2.7.4	Security implications of crashes	16
	2.7.5	See also	16
	2.7.6	References	16
	2.7.7	External links	16
2.8	Data compression		16
	2.8.1	Lossless	16
	2.8.2	Lossy	17
	2.8.3	Theory	17
	2.8.4	Uses	18
	2.8.5	Outlook and currently unused potential	22
	2.8.6	See also	22
	2.8.7	References	22
	2.8.8	External links	23
2.9	Distortion		24
	2.9.1	Electronic signals	24
	2.9.2	Correction of distortion	25
	2.9.3	Teletypewriter or modem signaling	25

	2.9.4	Distortion in art	26
	2.9.5	Audio distortion	26
	2.9.6	Optics	26
	2.9.7	Map projections	26
	2.9.8	See also	26
	2.9.9	References	27
2.10	Electronica	27
	2.10.1	Regional definitions	27
	2.10.2	A wave of diverse acts	27
	2.10.3	New York City	27
	2.10.4	Effect on mainstream popular music	27
	2.10.5	Included in contemporary media	28
	2.10.6	See also	28
	2.10.7	References	28
2.11	FL Studio	29
	2.11.1	History	29
	2.11.2	Software overview	30
	2.11.3	Plug-ins	31
	2.11.4	Version history	32
	2.11.5	Support	32
	2.11.6	Notable users	33
	2.11.7	See also	33
	2.11.8	References	33
	2.11.9	External links	35
2.12	Generative music	35
	2.12.1	Theory	35
	2.12.2	Software	35
	2.12.3	Other notes	36
	2.12.4	See also	37
	2.12.5	Footnotes	37
	2.12.6	References	37
2.13	Jeskola Buzz	38
	2.13.1	Development	38
	2.13.2	Plugin system	38
	2.13.3	Notable users	38
	2.13.4	See also	38
	2.13.5	References	38
	2.13.6	External links	39

2.14	Max (software)	39
	2.14.1 History	39
	2.14.2 Language	40
	2.14.3 See also	41
	2.14.4 References	41
	2.14.5 External links	41
2.15	Microsound	41
	2.15.1 See also	41
	2.15.2 References	41
	2.15.3 Sources	41
2.16	Music software	42
	2.16.1 History	42
	2.16.2 Effects	42
	2.16.3 Humans/education	42
	2.16.4 The future	42
	2.16.5 See Also	42
	2.16.6 References	43
	2.16.7 External links	43
2.17	Noise music	43
	2.17.1 Development	43
	2.17.2 Postmodern developments: Noise as genre	47
	2.17.3 Definitions	49
	2.17.4 Characteristics	50
	2.17.5 Compilations	50
	2.17.6 See also	50
	2.17.7 Footnotes	50
	2.17.8 References	53
	2.17.9 Further reading	55
	2.17.10 External links	57
2.18	Pure Data	58
	2.18.1 Similarities to Max	58
	2.18.2 Language features	58
	2.18.3 Language limitations	59
	2.18.4 Projects using Pure Data	59
	2.18.5 Code examples	59
	2.18.6 See also	59
	2.18.7 Notes	60
	2.18.8 References	60

- 2.18.9 Further reading 60
- 2.18.10 External links 60
- 2.19 Raster-Noton 60
  - 2.19.1 Artists 61
  - 2.19.2 Catalogue 62
  - 2.19.3 References 62
  - 2.19.4 External links 62
- 2.20 Reaktor 62
  - 2.20.1 Development History 62
  - 2.20.2 Functionality 63
  - 2.20.3 Reaktor Ensembles 64
  - 2.20.4 See also 64
  - 2.20.5 References 64
  - 2.20.6 External links 64
- 2.21 Reason (software) 64
  - 2.21.1 Overview 65
  - 2.21.2 Devices 67
  - 2.21.3 ReFills 69
  - 2.21.4 Demo songs 70
  - 2.21.5 References 70
  - 2.21.6 External links 71
- 2.22 Renoise 71
  - 2.22.1 History 71
  - 2.22.2 Features 71
  - 2.22.3 Versions 72
  - 2.22.4 Development 72
  - 2.22.5 See also 72
  - 2.22.6 References 72
  - 2.22.7 External links 73
- 2.23 Software bug 73
  - 2.23.1 Etymology 73
  - 2.23.2 History 74
  - 2.23.3 Prevalence 74
  - 2.23.4 Mistake metamorphism 74
  - 2.23.5 Prevention 74
  - 2.23.6 Debugging 75
  - 2.23.7 Bug management 76
  - 2.23.8 Security vulnerabilities 78

- 2.23.9 Common types of computer bugs 78
- 2.23.10 Well-known bugs 79
- 2.23.11 In popular culture 79
- 2.23.12 See also 79
- 2.23.13 Notes 80
- 2.23.14 Further reading 80
- 2.23.15 External links 80
- 2.24 Sonic artifact 80
  - 2.24.1 Types 80
  - 2.24.2 See also 81
  - 2.24.3 References 81
- 2.25 SuperCollider 81
  - 2.25.1 Architecture 81
  - 2.25.2 Interfacing and system support 82
  - 2.25.3 Code examples 83
  - 2.25.4 Live coding 83
  - 2.25.5 See also 83
  - 2.25.6 References 83
  - 2.25.7 External links 84
- 2.26 The Art of Noises 84
  - 2.26.1 The evolution of sound 84
  - 2.26.2 Six Families of Noises for the Futurist Orchestra 85
  - 2.26.3 Conclusions 86
  - 2.26.4 Musicians/Artists influenced by *The Art of Noises* 86
  - 2.26.5 See also 86
  - 2.26.6 External links 87
  - 2.26.7 References 87

3 Text and image sources, contributors, and licenses   **88**
- 3.1 Text 88
- 3.2 Images 94
- 3.3 Content license 97

Chapter 1

Introduction

1.1 Glitch (music)

Glitch is a genre of electronic music that emerged in the late 1990s. It has been described as a genre that adheres to an "aesthetic of failure," where the deliberate use of glitch-based audio media, and other sonic artifacts, is a central concern.[1]

Sources of glitch sound material are usually malfunctioning or abused audio recording devices or digital electronics, such as CD skipping, electric hum, digital or analog distortion, bit rate reduction, hardware noise, software bugs, crashes, vinyl record hiss or scratches and system errors.[2] In a *Computer Music Journal* article published in 2000, composer and writer Kim Cascone classifies glitch as a subgenre of electronica, and used the term *post-digital* to describe the glitch aesthetic.[1]

1.1.1 History

The origins of the glitch aesthetic can be traced to the early 20th century, with Luigi Russolo's Futurist manifesto *The Art of Noises*, the basis of noise music. He also constructed noise generators, which he named *intonarumori*. Later musicians and composers made use of malfunctioning technology, such as Michael Pinder of The Moody Blues in 1968's "The Best Way to Travel," and Christian Marclay, who used mutilated vinyl records to create sound collages beginning in 1979. The title track of OMD's popular 1981 album *Architecture & Morality* makes use of invasive computer- and industrial noise snippets, and has been cited as an early incarnation of glitch.[3] Yasunao Tone used damaged CDs in his *Techno Eden* performance in 1985, while Nicolas Collins's 1992 album *It Was a Dark and Stormy Night* included a composition that featured a string quartet playing alongside the stuttering sound of skipping CDs.[4] Yuzo Koshiro's electronic soundtrack for 1994 video game *Streets of Rage 3* used automatically randomized sequences to generate "unexpected and odd" experimental sounds.[5]

Glitch originated as a distinct movement in Germany with the musical work and labels (especially Mille Plateaux) of Achim Szepanski.[6][7] While the movement initially slowly gained members (including bands like Oval),[8] the techniques of Glitch later quickly spread around the world as many artists followed suit. Trumpeter Jon Hassell's 1994 album *Dressing for Pleasure*—a dense mesh of funky trip hop and jazz—features several songs with the sound of skipping CDs layered into the mix.

Oval's *Wohnton*, produced in 1993, helped define the genre by adding ambient aesthetics to it.[9]

The mid-nineties work of Warp Records artists Aphex Twin (*Richard D. James Album*, *Windowlicker*, *Come to Daddy* EP) *chan-EL*, and Autechre (Tri Repetae, Chiastic Slide) were also influential in the development of the digital audio manipulation technique and aesthetic.

1.1.2 Production techniques

Glitch is often produced on computers using modern digital production software to splice together small "cuts" (samples) of music from previously recorded works. These cuts are then integrated with the signature of glitch music: beats made up of glitches, clicks, scratches, and otherwise "erroneously" produced or sounding noise. These glitches are often very short, and are typically used in place of traditional percussion or instrumentation. Skipping CDs, scratched vinyl records, circuit bending, and other noise-like distortions figure prominently into the creation of rhythm and feeling in glitch; it is from the use of these digital artifacts that the genre derives its name. However, not all artists of the genre are working with erroneously produced sounds or are even using digital sounds. Some artists also use digital synthesizer such as the Clavia Nord Modular G2 and Elektron Machinedrum and Monomachine.

Popular software for creating glitch includes trackers like Jeskola Buzz and Renoise, as well as modular software like Reaktor, Ableton Live, Reason, AudioMulch, Bidule, SuperCollider, FLStudio, Max/MSP, Pure Data, and ChucK. Circuit bending, the intentional modification of low power electronic devices to create new musical devices, also plays a significant role on the hardware end of glitch music and its creation.

1.1.3 Notable artists

- Alva Noto (Carsten Nicolai)
- Farmers Manual
- Frank Bretschneider
- Kid606
- Kim Cascone
- Mokira (Andreas Tilliander)
- OMFG
- Oval
- Pan Sonic
- Pole
- Prefuse 73
- Ryoji Ikeda
- The Glitch Mob
- Tipper
- Death Grips
- TheFatRat

1.1.4 Glitch hop

Glitch hop is a subgenre of glitch and fuses it with hip hop elements. While it does not necessarily include rap it fuses funky hip hop beats with glitchy effects and techniques[10] such as beat repeaters, sweeps cutting, skipping, repeating, chopping and bit crush reduction.[11] The genre took shape at about the year 2001 with the early works of Prefuse 73 on Warp Records and became popular at about the year 2004.[11][12] While it was once based on heavily twisted, sliced and distorted glitchy hip hop beats modern glitch hop has become a more defined standalone genre, quite detached from its hip hop origins and also takes increased influence of dubstep and the drum and bass subgenre neurofunk with whose neurohop variant it shares many similarities.[13][14] Popular artists of the genre include edIT, Bassnectar, KOAN Sound, Pretty Lights, GRiZ, Opiuo, Mr. Bill, Skope, Shurk, and The Glitch Mob.

1.1.5 See also

- Circuit bending
- Clicks & Cuts Series
- Generative music
- Microsound
- Noise music
- Raster-Noton

1.1.6 References

[1] "The glitch genre arrived on the back of the electronica movement, an umbrella term for alternative, largely dance-based electronic music (including house, techno, electro, drum'n'bass, ambient) that has come into vogue in the past five years. Most of the work in this area is released on labels peripherally associated with the dance music market, and is therefore removed from the contexts of academic consideration and acceptability that it might otherwise earn. Still, in spite of this odd pairing of fashion and art music, the composers of glitch often draw their inspiration from the masters of 20th century music who they feel best describe its lineage." *THE AESTHETICS OF FAILURE: 'Post-Digital' Tendencies in Contemporary Computer Music*, Kim Cascone, Computer Music Journal 24:4 Winter 2000 (MIT Press)

[2] Cox, Christoph and Warner, Daniel, eds. (2004). *Audio Culture: Readings in Modern Music*. Continuum Books. p. 393.

[3] *The Pioneers of Electropop*. 23 September 2001. 17 minutes in. Channel 4. Channel Four Television Corporation. Paul Gambaccini: There's even a track on there [*Architecture & Morality*]—the title cut, in fact—that, when you listen to [it], is really like an early incarnation of glitch techno."

[4] 1995 Interview with Nicolas Collins, by Brian Duguid

[5] Horowitz, Ken (February 5, 2008). "Interview: Yuzo Koshiro". *Sega-16*. Archived from the original on 21 September 2008. Retrieved 6 August 2011.

[6] "First championed by the ideological German techno figure Achim Szepanski and his stable of record labels—Force Inc, Mille Plateaux, Force Tracks, Ritornell—this tight-knit scene of experimental artists creating cerebral hybrids of experimental techno, minimalism, digital collage, and noise glitches soon found themselves being assembled into a community."Allmusic

[7] "Random Inc.", "Allmusic"

[8] "Glitch", "Allmusic"

[9] "Although Oval are perhaps more well-known for how they make their music than for the music they actually make, the German experimental electronic trio have provided an intriguing update of some elements of avant-garde composition in combination with techniques of digital sound design.[...]" Allmusic

[10] *FutureMusic - Issues 178-182*. Future Pub. 2006. Even when it's beautiful, Glitch Hop is disturbing. It's the wrinkle in the bedsheet, the sand in the vaseline. Artists like Prefuse 73, Telefon Tel Aviv, Matmos, Kid606, and others fuse hip hop beats with clicky, digital tones that are as gorgeous as they are defective. Glitch Hop producers are not content to make mathematical abstractions. Instead they combine this with funky, head-nodding beats to make a music that is both challenging and instinctively booty-shakin'. And now Big Fish Audio and producer Brian Saitzyk have distilled the essence of this sound into Glitch Hop.

[11] Michael, John (1 July 2010). "What is Glitch Hop?". Retrieved 5 July 2015.

[12] Duthel, C. *Pitbull - Mr. Worldwide*. p. 155. ISBN 9781471090356. Retrieved 5 July 2015.

[13] "Glitch Hop Guide". TheDanceMusicGuide. Retrieved 5 July 2015.

[14] "What Is Neurohop? Its Beginnings, Pioneers and Future". BassGorilla. Retrieved 26 August 2015.

1.1.7 Further reading

- Andrews, Ian, *Post-digital Aesthetics and the return to Modernism*, MAP-uts lecture, 2000, available at author's website.

- Bijsterveld, Karin and Trevor J. Pinch. "'Should One Applaud?': Breaches and Boundaries in the Reception of New Technology in Music." *Technology and Culture*. Ed. 44.3, pp. 536–559. 2003.

- Byrne, David. "What is Blip Hop?" *Lukabop*, 2002. Available here.

- Collins, Adam, "Sounds of the system: the emancipation of noise in the music of Carsten Nicolai", *Organised Sound*, 13(1): 31–39. 2008. Cambridge University Press.

- Collins, Nicolas. Editor. "Composers inside Electronics: Music after David Tudor." *Leonardo Music Journal*. Vol. 14, pp. 1–3. 2004.

- Krapp, Peter, Noise Channels: Glitch and Error in Digital Culture. Minneapolis: University of Minnesota Press 2011.

- Prior, Nick, "Putting a Glitch in the Field: Bourdieu, Actor Network Theory and Contemporary Music", *Cultural Sociology*, 2: 3, 2008: pp. 301–319.

- Thomson, Phil, "Atoms and errors: towards a history and aesthetics of microsound", *Organised Sound*, 9(2): 207–218. 2004. Cambridge University Press.

- Sangild, Torben: "Glitch—The Beauty of Malfunction" in *Bad Music*. Routledge (2004, ISBN 0-415-94365-5)

- Young, Rob: "Worship the Glitch", *The Wire* 190/191 (2000)

- Noah Zimmerman, "Dusted Reviews, 2002"

Chapter 2

Further Reading

2.1 Ableton Live

Ableton Live is a software music sequencer and digital audio workstation for OS X and Windows. The latest major release of Live, Version 9, was released on March 5, 2013. In contrast to many other software sequencers, Live is designed to be an instrument for live performances as well as a tool for composing, recording, arranging, mixing and mastering. It is also used by DJs, as it offers a suite of controls for beatmatching, crossfading, and other effects used by turntablists, and was one of the first music applications to automatically beatmatch songs.

2.1.1 History

Ableton Live is written in C++, with the first version released in 2001 as commercial software. Contrary to popular belief, Live itself was not prototyped in Max/MSP, although most of the audio devices were.[2]

2.1.2 Features

Live does now support latency compensation for plug-in and mixer automation.

Much of Live's interface comes from being designed for use in live performance as well as for production.[17] As such the interface is more compact than most sequencers and clearly designed for use on a single screen. There are few pop up messages or dialogs. Portions of the interface are hidden and shown based on arrows which may be clicked to show or hide a certain segment (e.g. to hide the instrument/effect list or to show or hide the help box).

Views

Live is composed of two 'views' – the arrangement view and the session view. The session view is primarily used to organize and trigger sets of MIDI and audio called clips. These clips can be arranged into scenes which can then be triggered as a unit. For instance a drum, bass and guitar track might comprise a single scene. When moving on to the next scene, which may feature a synth bassline, the artist will trigger the scene, activating the clips for that scene. As of Live 6, "device racks" have been implemented which allow the user to easily group instruments and effects, as well as map their controls to a set of 'macro' controls.

The other view is the arrangement view, which is used for recording tracks from the session view and further manipulating their arrangement and effects. It is also used for manual MIDI sequencing, something for which a classical composer would have a greater affinity. This view is fairly similar to a traditional software sequencer interface.

Clips may either be an audio sample or MIDI sequence. MIDI triggers notes on Live's built in instruments, as well as third party VST instruments or external hardware.

Instruments

Built-In By default, Live comes with two instruments - Impulse and Simpler.

- **Impulse** is a traditional drum triggering instrument which allows the user to define a kit of up to eight drum sounds, each based on a single sample. There are a number of effects available such as basic equalization, attack, decay, pitch shift, etc. Once the kit is defined, rhythms and beats are created through Live's MIDI sequencer.

- **Simpler** is a relatively easy-to-use sampling instrument. It works using a single sample, applying some simple effects, envelopes, and timing, and then applying pitch transformations in the form of Granular synthesis. In this case, incoming MIDI does not trigger drums as it does in *Impulse*, but selects the final pitch of the sample, with C3 playing the sample at its original pitch.

- **Drum Rack** Is a sampler for drums. Midi notes trigger individual "Simplers" so rather than triggering one sample at multiple pitches, individual samples are triggered at predefined pitches, as is suitable for midi drum programming. As is usual with Ableton almost anything can be drag dropped to or from the drum racks, for example you can drop a clip or part of a clip into the drum rack to isolate drum parts from audio.

Dedicated Hardware Instruments

Akai Professional makes the APC40, a MIDI controller designed to work solely with Ableton Live. A smaller version, the APC20, was released in 2010. Though there are hundreds of MIDI controllers compatible with Ableton, these Akai units try to closely map the actual Ableton Live layout onto physical space. Novation Digital Music Systems has created the "Launchpad" which is a pad device that has been designed for use with Ableton. Ableton has also released their own MIDI controller, the Push, which is the first pad-based controller that embraces scales and melody.[18]

Add-ons

There are a number of additional instruments which may be purchased separately or as part of the Ableton Suite.[19]

- **Amp** - a device that delivers the sounds of various amplifiers and cabinet combos. It is the newest add-on and a part of Suite 8.2.
- **Sampler** - an enhanced sampler.
- **Operator** - an FM synthesizer.
- **Electric** - an electric piano instrument.
- **Tension** - a string physical modelling synthesizer.
- **Collision** - a mallet percussion physical modelling synthesizer.
- **Analog** - simulates an analog synthesizer.
- **Drum Machines** - a collection of emulators for classic drum machines.
- **Session Drums** - a collection of sampled drum kits.
- **Latin Percussion** - a collection of sampled latin percussion hits and loops.
- **Essential Instruments Collection** - a large collection of acoustic and electric instrument samples.
- **Orchestral Instrument Collection** - a collection of four different orchestral libraries, which can be purchased individually or as a bundle: Orchestral Strings, Orchestral Brass, Orchestral Woodwinds and Orchestral Percussion. The Orchestral Instrument Collection is not included in Live Suite.

Effects

Most of Live's effects are already common effects in the digital signal processing world which have been adapted to fit Live's interface. They are tailored to suit Live's target audience – electronic musicians and DJs - but may also be used for other recording tasks such as processing a guitar rig. The effects featured in Ableton Live are grouped into two categories - MIDI effects and audio effects.

Live is also able to host VST plugins and, on the OS X version, Audio Unit plug-ins.

Working with audio clips

Sasha playing a DJ set using Ableton Live.

In addition to the instruments mentioned above, Live can work with samples. Live attempts to do beat analysis of the samples to find their meter, number of bars and the number of beats per minute. This makes it possible for Live to shift these samples to fit into loops that are tied into the piece's global tempo.

Additionally, Live's Time Warp feature can be used to either correct or adjust beat positions in the sample. By setting warp markers to a specific point in the sample, arbitrary points in the sample can be pegged to positions in the measure. For instance a drum beat that fell 250 ms after the midpoint in measure may be adjusted so that it will be played back precisely at the midpoint.

Some artists and online stores, such as The Covert Operators and Puremagnetik, now make available sample packs that are pre-adjusted, with tempo information and warp markers added. The audio files are accompanied with an "analysis file" in Live's native format.[20][21]

Envelopes

Almost all of the parameters in Live can be automated by envelopes which may be drawn either on clips, in which case they will be used in every performance of that clip, or on the entire arrangement. The most obvious examples are volume or track panning, but envelopes are also used in Live to control parameters such as the root note of a resonator or, more commonly, a filter's cutoff frequency. Clip envelopes may also be mapped to MIDI controls, which can also control parameters in real-time using sliders, faders and such.

2.1.3 Versions

Live Intro and Live LE

As of version 6, Ableton also offers a stripped-down version of Live targeted at the non-professional market. It has limitations on the number of audio channels and effects and does not feature some of the synchronization (MIDI Clock, ReWire) utilities the full version has to offer. The current Live LE version is 8.1.4.[22]

As part of the Able10 celebrations, Ableton introduced Live Intro as an effective replacement to LE. Registered users of Live LE can now receive a free upgrade to Live Intro.[23] The current version is 8.3.3.

Ableton Live 8 Launchpad Edition and Ableton Live 8 Akai Professional APC Edition

Specially packaged versions of Ableton that are custom-tailored for the controllers they are bundled with. (Novation Launchpad, Akai APC20/40) These versions of the software are less limited than the LE and intro versions but still don't have all the features of the full version. This version is known as Live lite.

Live 8

On 17 January 2009 Ableton announced version 8 of Live. Live 8 includes a wealth of new features, including an integrated Max/MSP platform, internet collaboration features, and many new effects and workflow enhancements, as well as a refined piracy protection system. Also announced was a dedicated hardware controller developed in collaboration with Akai, called the APC40. Live 8 was released on April 2 of 2009.[24] Max for Live was released on November 23 of 2009.[25]

Suite 8

Suite 8 includes all the features of Live 8 plus a new Library with new sounds and resources. Suite 8 contains 10 Ableton instruments including synths, a sampler, electric and acoustic drums, mallets, numerous sampled instruments, reworked Operator and two completely new instruments, Collision and Tension.

Live 9

On October 25, 2012, Ableton hosted a preview event for Live 9. New features such as integration of Max for Live and the Push hardware controller were announced and demonstrated. Later announced features in Live 9 include a Glue Compressor as well the ability to add curves and shapes to track automation among many other updates.[26] Live 9 and the Push hardware were released on March 5, 2013.

Suite 9

A major addition to the Live 9 suite offering was the inclusion of Max For Live for all Live 9 Suite customers. This dramatically increases the size of the Max for Live community and holds significant promise toward grass roots enhancements in Live by community members creating their own Max For Live devices. Live 9 Suite also expanded the "sound-ware" included over Suite 8.

2.1.4 See also

- Category:Ableton Live users
- Ableton Push
- Commercial digital audio workstations
- List of music software

2.1.5 References

[1] "Ableton Live End Use License Agreement". Retrieved August 18, 2014.

[2] "Prototyping explained by Live co-creator Robert Henke". Archived from the original on 2010-11-18. Retrieved 2010-11-18.

[3] "Find the Latest in Music Gear News and More | Harmony Central". News.harmony-central.com. Archived from the original on 7 May 2010. Retrieved 2010-05-04.

[4] "Find the Latest in Music Gear News and More | Harmony Central". News.harmony-central.com. Retrieved 2010-05-04.

[5] "Find the Latest in Music Gear News and More | Harmony Central". News.harmony-central.com. Retrieved 2010-05-04.

[6] "Find the Latest in Music Gear News and More | Harmony Central". News.harmony-central.com. Retrieved 2010-05-04.

[7] "Harmony Central". Aes.harmony-central.com. Retrieved 2010-05-04.

[8] "Harmony Central". Namm.harmony-central.com. Archived from the original on 18 April 2010. Retrieved 2010-05-04.

[9] "Harmony Central". Namm.harmony-central.com. Retrieved 2010-05-04.

[10] "Find the Latest in Music Gear News and More | Harmony Central". News.harmony-central.com. Retrieved 2010-05-04.

[11] "Find the Latest in Music Gear News and More | Harmony Central". News.harmony-central.com. Retrieved 2010-05-04.

[12] "Find the Latest in Music Gear News and More | Harmony Central". News.harmony-central.com. Archived from the original on 24 May 2010. Retrieved 2010-05-04.

[13] "Find the Latest in Music Gear News and More | Harmony Central". News.harmony-central.com. Archived from the original on 16 April 2010. Retrieved 2010-05-04.

[14] "Ableton Forum • View topic - Current Version: Live 8.2". Forum.ableton.com. Retrieved 2010-09-22.

[15] "Ableton Blog". ableton.com/blog. 2012-04-02.

[16] "Ableton Blog". ableton.com/blog. 2012-10-25.

[17] Tusa, Scott. "Getting Started with Ableton Live". O'Reilly Digital Media. Archived from the original on 9 April 2009. Retrieved 2009-04-19. This user-friendly program was designed for live performances by musicians who wanted to use the recording studio like a musical instrument. As performers and recording engineers, they felt stymied by the non-real-time nature of typical audio programs, so they wrote their own.

[18] https://www.ableton.com/en/manual/using-push/

[19] Ableton - Ableton Suite

[20] "The Covert Operators - Ableton Live Packs". Retrieved 2011-08-05.

[21] "Puremagnetik". Archived from the original on 16 December 2008. Retrieved 2008-12-17.

[22] Ableton - Live 7 LE Features

[23] "Live Intro". Ableton. Retrieved 2010-05-04.

[24] Ableton - Live 8 - What's New

[25] Max for Live

[26] https://www.ableton.com/en/live/new-in-9/

Ableton vs. FL Studio

2.1.6 External links

- Ableton's official website
- Lastfm website
- Ableton Live how-to database
- Ableton Live tutorials, tips & news
- macableton.com Free tutorials & resources for Ableton Live users—updated daily! Beginner to advanced.

2.2 AudioMulch

AudioMulch is modular audio software for making music and processing sound. The software can synthesize sound and process live and pre-recorded sound in real-time.

AudioMulch has a patcher-style graphical user interface, in which modules called *contraptions* can be connected together to route audio and process sounds. Included are modules used in electronic dance music such as a bassline-style synthesizer and a drum machine, effects like ring modulation, flanging, reverb and delays, and other modules such as a delay-line granulator and stereo spatializer.[1] As well as these internal contraptions, AudioMulch supports VST and VSTi plugins.

2.2.1 History

Origins of AudioMulch

AudioMulch grew out of musician Ross Bencina's performance practice in the mid-1990s. At this time, live, computer-based sound processing systems were often expensive and restricted to use within research institutions.

By 1995 however, the processing capabilities of the personal computer were sufficient that Bencina was able to create OverSYTE, a real-time performance granulator. OverSYTE was used by Bencina to process sound in his real-time performances with vocalists and instrumental musicians. AudioMulch grew out of the limitations of OverSYTE, which could process only one sound at a time. In contrast, AudioMulch can process multiple sounds sources at once.[2]

Development of AudioMulch

AudioMulch has been in development since 1997. The first release made available for download on the Internet was Beta version 0.7b1, in March 1998. There were 36 Beta releases prior to Version 1.0 of the software, which was released in February 2006.[3] AudioMulch 1.0 was developed for Microsoft Windows in the C++ programming language, using the Borland C++ Builder development environment.[4]

Version 1.0

Version 1.0 was released on 21 February 2006.

Version 2.0

AudioMulch 2.0 was released June 5, 2009. According to the website, this version is available for both Windows and Macintosh computers.[5]

Version 2.1

Version 2.1 was released August 4, 2010. Version 2.1 supports custom time signatures, Audio Unit plugin support on Mac OS X, dynamic processing contraptions, and an alternate light grey color scheme.[6]

2.2.2 Features

AudioMulch 1.0 features

- An interactive user-interface with three main panes:

1. a patcher for routing audio between contraptions
2. a pane containing control panels for each contraption
3. an automation time line supporting automation of contraption parameters

- Support for real-time sound-processing and performance.
- 24 channels of real-time input/output.
- Multi-channel recording and playback of multiple sound files.
- Contraptions including signal generators, effects, filter and mixers.
- Input sound can be taken from sound files or real-time audio input.
- Output is heard in real-time and can be simultaneously recorded to a sound file.
- Any processing parameter in AudioMulch can be controlled by MIDI. This includes the use of external hardware such as knob boxes, gaming controllers, virtual reality gloves and custom control devices.[7]

AudioMulch 2.0 features

- A new Patcher with advanced drag-and-drop patching and MIDI routing
- MIDI and automation control for Clock transport (tempo, stop, start) and Metasurface interpolation.
- Enhanced Drums contraption with 8 channels and a new pattern editor supporting arbitrary length high-resolution patterns
- Expanded multichannel audio I/O capability to support up to 256 channels in each direction and improved compatibility with consumer multichannel audio interfaces using DirectSound and Windows Multimedia drivers.

Future

As outlined in AudioMulch's road map, future versions should bring new sound mangling, filtering and resonating contraptions, an overhauled undo system, 3rd party host integration and performance modulation, as well as further enhancements to existing sound and keyboard controls.

2.2.3 Musicians that use or have used AudioMulch

- Nine Inch Nails
- Girl Talk
- Four Tet

- Lackluster
- Erdem Helvacioglu
- Shitmat
- Pimmon

The discography on the AudioMulch website has a list of other artists that have used AudioMulch in commercial releases.[8]

2.2.4 See also

- granular synthesis
- modular synthesizer
- computer music

2.2.5 Notes

[1] Bencina, R. (1998), "Oasis Rose the Composition - Real-Time DSP with AudioMulch," *Proceedings of the Australasian Computer Music Conference*, ANU Canberra, pp. 85-92.

[2] Bencina, R. (2006) "Creative Software Development: Reflections on AudioMulch Practice." In *Digital Creativity*, Routledge, Vol. 17, no. 1, pp. 12-13

[3] AudioMulch website - resources page. Retrieved on 2009-01-28

[4] Clatterbox. Retrieved on 2009-01-28

[5] AudioMulch website – homepage. Retrieved on 2009-11-20

[6] AudioMulch website – news. Retrieved on 2011-12-31

[7] AudioMulch website – info page. Retrieved on 2009-01-28

[8] AudioMulch website – discography Retrieved on 2009-01-28

2.2.6 References

- AudioMulch website – info page. Retrieved on 2009-01-28
- AudioMulch website – discography. Retrieved on 2009-01-28
- Clatterbox website. Retrieved on 2009-01-28
- Dugan, S. (2006), "Girl Talk". In *Remix Magazine*, December 1, 2006. Retrieved on 2009-01-28
- (2008) "Girl Talk/Gregg Gillis on New Album/Music Industry". In *The Washington Post*, July 29, 2008. Retrieved on 2009-01-28
- Inglis, S. (2003), "FourTet – Kieran Hebden: Recording Rounds". In *Sound on Sound*, July 2003. Retrieved on 2009-01-28
- Hsieh, C. (2005), "Audio Anarchy". In *Remix Magazine*, June 1, 2005. Retrieved on 2009-01-28
- Interview with the Nine Inch Nails by Greg Rule, *Keyboard Magazine*, February 2000. Retrieved on 2009-01-28
- Gallagher, M. (2004), "Between the Lines." In *Electronic Musician Magazine*, February 1, 2004.
- Bencina, R. (2006) "Creative Software Development: Reflections on AudioMulch Practice." In *Digital Creativity*, Routledge, Vol. 17, no. 1, pp. 11 – 24.
- Bencina, R. (1998), "Oasis Rose the Composition - Real-Time DSP with AudioMulch," *Proceedings of the Australasian Computer Music Conference*, ANU Canberra, pp. 85–92.
- Cleveland, B. (2007), "Erdem Helvacioglu". In *Guitar Player*, September 2007, pp. 32–33.
- Frere-Jones, S. (2008), "Re-Start: Laptops go Live". In *The New Yorker*, September 15, 2008, pp. 94–95.

2.2.7 External links

- AudioMulch Interactive Music Studio website
- Interview with Ross Bencina, creator of AudioMulch
- Live performance of protofuse artist made exclusively with AudioMulch

2.3 Bidule

Bidule is a commercial software application for the creation of interactive computer music and multimedia produced by the Canadian company Plogue Arts and Technology.[1] It runs on both Windows and Mac computers.[2]

Bidule uses a modular structure based on a patch cord metaphor much like AudioMulch, Reaktor, Pure Data, and Max/MSP. Individual modules are called bidules (the Plogue web site states that the word "Bidule" is French for "thingy" or "gadget"). A set of bidules and connections is called a layout, and sub-patches called groups can be built within layouts and saved for use elsewhere. The program features real time audio, MIDI, Open Sound Control (OSC), and spectral processing. With other audio DAW software ReWire, Bidule can run as a ReWire mixer or device. Bidule can run standalone or as a VST, VSTi or AU plugin, and can host the same. ASIO/CoreAudio is supported for low latency audio. Bidule can use multithread processing, and there is a beta build for discreet processing. Parameters can be linked to MIDI or OSC input or to other module parameters. Over one hundred modules and groups come with the software, including modules that can perform high-level math on signals.

2.3.1 References

[1] http://www.softsea.com/review/Plogue-Bidule.html

[2] http://www.computermusicjournal.org/reviews/31-2/regan-bidule.html

2.3.2 External links

- Bidule home page.

2.4 ChucK

For other uses, see Chuck (disambiguation).

ChucK is a concurrent, strongly timed audio programming language for real-time synthesis, composition, and performance,[2] which runs on Linux, Mac OS X, Microsoft Windows, and iOS. It is designed to favor readability and flexibility for the programmer over other considerations such as raw performance. It natively supports deterministic concurrency and multiple, simultaneous, dynamic control rates. Another key feature is the ability to live code; adding, removing, and modifying code on the fly, while the program is running, without stopping or restarting. It has a highly precise timing/concurrency model, allowing for arbitrarily fine granularity. It offers composers and researchers a powerful and flexible programming tool for building and experimenting with complex audio synthesis programs, and real-time interactive control.[3]

ChucK was created and chiefly designed by Ge Wang as a graduate student working with Perry R. Cook.[1] ChucK is distributed freely under the terms of the GNU General Public License on Mac OS X, Linux and Microsoft Windows. On iPhone and iPad, ChiP (ChucK for iPhone) is distributed under a limited, closed source license, and is not currently licensed to the public. However, the core team has stated that it would like to explore "ways to open ChiP by creating a beneficial environment for everyone".[4]

2.4.1 Language features

The ChucK programming language is a loosely C-like object-oriented language, with strong static typing.

ChucK is distinguished by the following characteristics:[5]

- Direct support for real-time audio synthesis

- A powerful and simple concurrent programming model

- A unified timing mechanism for multi-rate event and control processing.

- A language syntax that encourages left-to-right syntax and semantics within program statements.

- Precision timing: a strongly timed sample-synchronous timing model.

- Programs are dynamically compiled to ChucK virtual machine bytecode.

- A runtime environment that supports on-the-fly programming.

ChucK standard libraries provide:

- MIDI input and output.

- Real-time control via the Open Sound Control protocol.

- Synthesis Toolkit unit generators.

2.4.2 Code example

The following is a simple ChucK program that generates sound and music:

// our signal graph (patch) SinOsc f => dac; // set gain .3 => f.gain; // an array of pitch classes (in half steps) [0, 2, 4, 6, 9, 10] @=> int hi[]; // infinite loop while(true) { // choose a note, shift registers, convert to frequency Std.mtof(65 + Std.rand2(0,1) * 43 + hi[Std.rand2(0,hi.cap()−1)]) => f.freq; // advance time by 120 ms 120::ms => now; }

2.4.3 Uses

ChucK has been used in performances by the Princeton Laptop Orchestra (PLOrk) and for developing Smule applications, including their ocarina emulator.[6] PLOrk organizers attribute some of the uniqueness of their performances to the live coding they can perform with ChucK.[7]

2.4.4 See also

- Comparison of audio synthesis environments

2.4.5 References

[1] Dean, R. T. (2009). *The Oxford handbook of computer music*. Oxford Handbooks in Music Series. Oxford University Press US. p. 57. ISBN 0-19-533161-3.

[2] Wang, Ge (2008). *The ChucK Audio Programming Language: A Strongly-timed and On-the-fly Environ/mentality* (Ph.D.). Princeton University.

[3] "ChucK : Strongly-timed, Concurrent, and On-the-fly Music Programming Language". Retrieved 2013-09-06. ...offers composers, researchers, and performers a powerful programming tool for building and experimenting with complex audio synthesis/analysis programs, and real-time interactive music.

[4] Wang, Ge. "ChucKian greetings and updates!". *chuck-users mailing list*. Princeton University. Retrieved 2011-05-24.

[5] Wang, G. and P. Cook (2003). "ChucK: A concurrent, on-the-fly audio programming language" (PDF). *Proceedings of the International Computer Music Conference*.

[6] Kirn, Peter (July 22, 2009). "Interview: Smule's Ge Wang on iPhone Apps, Ocarinas, and Democratizing Music Tech". *Create Digital Music*. Retrieved 2011-05-24.

[7] Petersen, Brittany (2008-06-11). "Laptop Orchestra Makes (Sound) Waves". PC Magazine. The other thing that set PLOrk apart from the beginning was its use of a text-based program called ChucK, developed by a Princeton graduate student. ChucK allows the user to code quickly—similar to live coding—and "on the fly" for a performance, allowing for the spontaneity and real-time interaction that is important in live music performance. "ChucK is the only language that I know of that was designed from the outset to facilitate that," Trueman says. The program is also "concurrent," meaning that it can handle many different processes going on at once. Its "innate sense of time" allows performers to communicate during live rehearsals and performances, he says, adding that many other laptop musicians probably use a program like Max/MSP (which PLOrk uses in addition to ChucK) or another widely available commercial program. Today some other laptop orchestras—including the Stanford Laptop Orchestra (SLOrk), which was directly inspired by PLOrk—also employ ChucK.

2.4.6 Further reading

Literature by its authors

- Wang, G. (2008). "The ChucK Audio Programming Language". *PhD Thesis, Princeton University*.

- Wang, G.; Cook, P. (2003). "ChucK: A concurrent, on-the-fly audio programming language" (PDF). *Proceedings of the International Computer Music Conference*.

- Wang, G.; Cook, P. (2004). "On-the-fly programming: Using code as an expressive musical instrument" (PDF). *Proceedings of the International Conference on New Interfaces for Musical Expression*.

- Wang, G.; Cook, P. (2004). "The Audicle: A context-sensitive, on-the-fly audio programming environ/mentality" (PDF). *In Proceedings of the International Computer Music Conference*.

- Wang, G; Misra, A.; Kapur, A; Cook, P (2005). "Yeah ChucK it! => Dynamic, controllable, interface mapping" (PDF). *Proceedings of the International Conference on New Interfaces for Musical Expression*.

- Wang, G.; Cook, P.; Misra, A (2005). "Designing and implementing the ChucK programming language" (PDF). *Proceedings of the International Computer Music Conference*.

- Wang, G; Fiebrink, R; Cook, P (2007). "Combining analysis and synthesis in the ChucK programming language" (PDF). *Proceedings of the International Computer Music Conference*.

- Wang, G. (2007). Nicholas Collins, Julio d'Escriván, ed. *The Cambridge companion to electronic music*. Cambridge University Press. p. 69. ISBN 978-0-521-86861-7.

Seemingly independent coverage

- Graham Morrison, (2009) *Generate choons with Chuck*. Tired of the same old music in the charts, we create our own music from a series of pseudo random numbers. *Linux Format* issue 125

- Alan Blackwell and Nick Collins, *The Programming Language as a Musical Instrument* in P. Romero, J. Good, E. Acosta Chaparro & S. Bryant (Eds). Proc. PPIG 17, pp. 120–130

- R. T. Dean, ed. (2009). *The Oxford Handbook of Computer Music*. Oxford University Press. pp. 27 and 580. ISBN 978-0-19-533161-5.

2.4.7 External links

- ChucK homepage
- Graham Coleman's ChucK page
- Ge Wang lecture at Stanford

2.5 Circuit bending

Probing for "bend" using a jeweler's screwdriver and alligator clips

Circuit bending is the creative, chance-based customization of the circuits within electronic devices such as low voltage, battery-powered guitar effects, children's toys and digital synthesizers to create new musical or visual instruments and sound generators.

Emphasizing spontaneity and randomness, the techniques of circuit bending have been commonly associated with noise music, though many more conventional contemporary musicians and musical groups have been known to experiment with "bent" instruments. Circuit bending usually involves dismantling the machine and adding components such as switches and potentiometers that alter the circuit.

2.5.1 Experimental process

Circuit bending is often practiced by those with no formal training in circuit theory or design, experimenting with second-hand electronics in a DIY fashion. Inexpensive keyboards, drum machines, and electronic children's toys (not necessarily designed for music production) are commonly used. Haphazard modifications can result in short circuits, resulting in the risk of fire, burning, or electrocution.

Aesthetic value, immediate usability and highly randomized results are often factors in the process of successfully bending electronics. Although the history of electronic music

A 1989 Kawasaki toy guitar used in a circuit bending project

is often associated with unconventional sonic results, such innovators as Robert Moog[1] and Léon Theremin[2] were electrical engineers, and more concerned with the consistency and sound design of their instruments. Circuit bending is typified by inconsistencies in instruments built in an unscientific manner. While many pre-fitted circuit bent machines are on offer for sale at auction sites such as eBay, this somewhat contravenes the intention of most practitioners. Machines bent to a repeated configuration are more analogous to the well known practice of "mods", such as the Devilfish mod for the Roland TB-303, the famous Speak and Spell toys or various Analogman or Pedaldoc guitar pedal circuit modifications.

Circuit bending an audio device typically involves removing the rear panel of the device and connecting any two circuit locations with a "jumper" wire, sending current from one part of the circuit into another. Results are monitored through either the device's internal speaker or by connecting an amplifier to the speaker output. If an interesting effect is achieved, this connection would be marked for future reference or kept active by either soldering a new connection or bridging it with crocodile clips. Often other components are inserted at these points such as pushbuttons or switches, to turn the effect on or off; or components such as resistors or capacitors, to change the quality of the audio output. This is repeated on a trial and error basis. Other components added into the circuit can give the performer more expressiveness, such as potentiometers, photoresistors (for reaction to light) and pressure sensors.

The simplest input, and the one most identified with circuit bending, is the body contact,[3] where the performer's touch causes the circuit to change the sound. Often metal knobs, plates, screws or studs are wired to these circuit points to give easier access to these points from the outside the case of the device.

Since creative experimentation[4] is a key element to the practice of circuit bending, there is always a possibility

2.5. CIRCUIT BENDING

A Yamaha PSR-6 used in a circuit bending project.

that short circuiting may yield undesirable results, including component failure. In particular, connecting the power supply or a capacitor directly to a computer chip lead can destroy the chip and make the device inoperable. Before beginning to do circuit bending, a person should learn the basic risk factors about working with electrical and electronic products, including how to identify capacitors (which can give a person a serious shock due to the electrical charge that they store), and how to avoid risks with AC power. For safety reasons, a circuit bender should have a few basic electronics tools, such as a multimeter (an electronic testing device which measures voltage, resistance and other factors). It is advised that beginner circuit benders should *never* "bend" any device that gets its power from mains electricity (household AC power), as this would carry a serious risk of electrocution.

2.5.2 Innovators

Although similar methods were previously used by other musicians and engineers, this method of music creation is believed to have been pioneered by Reed Ghazala in the 1960s. Ghazala's experience with circuit-bending began in 1966 when a toy transistor amplifier, by chance, shorted-out against a metal object in his desk drawer, resulting in a stream of unusual sounds.[5] While Ghazala says that he was not the first circuit bender, he coined the term Circuit Bending [6] and whole-heartedly promoted the proliferation of the concept and practice through his writings and internet site, earning him the title "Father of Circuit Bending".

Serge Tcherepnin, designer of the Serge modular synthesizers, discussed[7] his early experiments in the 1950s with the transistor radio, in which he found sensitive circuit points in those simple electronic devices and brought them out to "body contacts" on the plastic chassis. Prior to Mark's and Reed's experiments other pioneers also explored the body-contact idea, one of the earliest being Thaddeus Cahill (1897) whose telharmonium, it is reported, was also touch-sensitive.

Since 1984, Swiss duo Voice Crack created music by manipulating common electronic devices in a practice they termed "cracked everyday electronics." [8]

2.5.3 See also

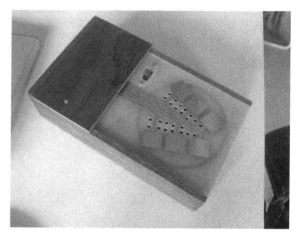

Kraakdoos.

- Atari Punk Console
- Axesynth (Known as the "Atari", as used by the rock band MuteMath, and Velva (Chicago)
- Bent Festival
- Casper Electronics
- Chiptunes
- Electronic art music
- Glitch (music)
- Kraakdoos (CrackleBox)
- MIDIbox
- MOS Technology SID
- Music Tech Fest
- NIME
- No-Fi
- Noise music
- List of music software

2.5.4 References

Alexandre Marino Fernandez, Fernando Iazzetta, Circuit-Bending and DIY Culture

[1] "Robert Moog: Music Pioneer". *NPR.org*. 23 August 2005. Retrieved 3 June 2015.

[2] "No. 1818: Leon Theremin". Retrieved 3 June 2015.

[3] Reed Ghazala: http://www.anti-theory.com/soundart/circuitbend/cb14.html

[4] "circuit-bending". Retrieved 3 June 2015.

[5] Reed Ghazala: *Circuit-Bending, Build Your Own Alien Instruments*, Extreme Tech, 2006

[6] Reed Ghazala: "Circuit-Bending and Living Instruments," EMI Volume VIII #1, 1992

[7] Vail, Mark: *Vintage Synthesizers: Pioneering Designers, Groundbreaking Instruments, Collecting Tips, Mutants of Technology*, Backbeat Books; 2.00 edition (March 15, 2000)

[8] "YULE 2008". Retrieved 3 June 2015.

2.5.5 External links

- oddmusic.com's circuit bending section - Gallery of some of Reed Ghazala's work, facts, history, tutorial, benders guide, tools of the trade and more
- Q.R. Ghazala's How-To Ghazala's official website tutorial
- GetLoFi a circuit bending blog with a lot of circuit bending tips and resources

2.6 Clicks & Cuts Series

Clicks & Cuts Series is a compilation series from the German music label Mille Plateaux. It features various experimental electronic artists to give an example of the sound and variety of the glitch music movement of the early 2000s. So far, six volumes have been released.

The term "clicks & cuts" was first used by an English journalist writing about glitch music and the Mille Plateaux label.

2.6.1 Volumes

1. Clicks & Cuts
2. Clicks & Cuts 2
3. Clicks & Cuts 3
4. Clicks & Cuts 4
5. Clicks & Cuts 5.0 - Paradigm Shift
6. Clicks & Cuts 5.1 - Paradigm Shift (The Bonus Package)

- *Clicks & Cuts, Vol. 2*

(2001)

Mille Plateaux

2.6.2 See also

- Mille Plateaux (Label)
- Glitch music
- Minimal techno
- Intelligent dance music
- Microhouse

2.6.3 External links

- Official label website
- Article on Clicks + Cuts Compilation at Salon.com

2.7 Crash (computing)

A **crash** (or **system crash**) in computing is when a computer program (such as a software application or an operating system) stops functioning properly. Often it will exit the affected program after encountering this type of error. The program responsible may appear to freeze until a crash reporting service reports the crash and potentially any details relating to it. If the program is a critical part of the operating system, the entire computer may crash, often resulting in a kernel panic or fatal system error, or in rare cases, an unstable network.

Many crashes are the result of single or multiple machine instructions running incorrectly. Typical causes are when the program counter is set to an incorrect address or a buffer overflow overwrites a portion of the affected program code due to an earlier bug. In either case, it is common for the CPU to attempt to access data or random memory values. Since all data values are possible to select but not always valid for the request, this often results in an illegal

2.7. CRASH (COMPUTING)

A public payphone that has experienced a fatal error causing a crash and is displaying the Blue Screen of Death.

A display at Frankfurt Airport running a program under Windows XP that has crashed due to a memory read access violation

instruction exception. By chance, such data or random values could be valid (though unplanned) instructions. The original program problem (software bug) is considered as what "caused" the crash, but the actual fault may be an illegal instruction. The process of debugging such crashes is connecting the actual cause of the crash with the code that started the chain of events. This is often far from obvious; the original bug is usually perfectly valid code presented to the processor.

In earlier personal computers, it was possible to cause hardware damage through attempting to write data to hardware addresses outside of the system's main memory.

The execution of arbitrary data on a system will result in a breakup of screen display. This is widely considered a severe system crash.

2.7.1 Application crashes

An application typically crashes when it performs an operation which is not allowed by the operating system. The operating system then triggers an exception or signal in the application. Unix applications traditionally responded to the signal by dumping core. Most Windows and Unix GUI applications respond by displaying a dialogue box (such as the one shown to the right) with the option to attach a debugger if one is installed. This behavior is called "crashing". Some applications attempt to recover from the error and continue running instead of crashing.

Typical errors that result in application crashes include:

- attempting to read or write memory that is not allocated for reading or writing by that application (segmentation fault) or x86 specific (general protection fault)

- attempting to execute privileged or invalid instructions

- attempting to perform I/O operations on hardware devices to which it does not have permission to access

- passing invalid arguments to system calls

- attempting to access other system resources to which the application does not have permission to access (bus error)

- attempting to execute machine instructions with bad arguments (depending on CPU architecture): divide by zero, operations on denorms or NaN values, memory access to unaligned addresses, etc.

2.7.2 Web server crashes

The software running the web server behind a website may crash, rendering it inaccessible entirely or providing only an error message instead of normal content.

For example: if a site is using an SQL database (such as MySQL) for a script (such as PHP) and that SQL database server crashes, then PHP will display a connection error.

2.7.3 Operating system crashes

An operating system crash commonly occurs when a hardware exception occurs that cannot be handled. Operating system crashes can also occur when internal sanity-checking logic within the operating system detects that the operating system has lost its internal self-consistency.

Modern multi-tasking operating systems, such as Windows NT, Linux, and Mac OS X usually remain unharmed when an application program crashes.

2.7.4 Security implications of crashes

Many software bugs which cause crashes are also exploitable for arbitrary code execution and other types of privilege escalation.[1][2] For example, a stack buffer overflow can overwrite the return address of a subroutine with an invalid value, which will cause a segmentation fault when the subroutine returns. However, if an exploit overwrites the return address with a valid value, the code in that address will be executed.

2.7.5 See also

- Blue Screen of Death
- Crash reporter
- Crash to Desktop
- Data loss
- Debugging
- Guru Meditation
- Kernel panic
- Memory corruption
- Reboot
- Safe Mode
- Segmentation fault
- SystemRescueCD
- Undefined behaviour

2.7.6 References

[1] "Analyze Crashes to Find Security Vulnerabilities in Your Apps". Msdn.microsoft.com. 2007-04-26. Retrieved 2014-06-26.

[2] "Jesse Ruderman » Memory safety bugs in C++ code". Squarefree.com. 2006-11-01. Retrieved 2014-06-26.

2.7.7 External links

- Computer Crash
- Picking Up The Pieces After A Computer Crash
- Why do computers crash?

2.8 Data compression

"Source coding" redirects here. For the term in computer programming, see Source code.

In digital signal processing, **data compression**, **source coding**,[1] or **bit-rate reduction** involves encoding information using fewer bits than the original representation.[2] Compression can be either lossy or lossless. Lossless compression reduces bits by identifying and eliminating statistical redundancy. No information is lost in lossless compression. Lossy compression reduces bits by identifying unnecessary information and removing it.[3] The process of reducing the size of a data file is referred to as data compression. In the context of data transmission, it is called source coding (encoding done at the source of the data before it is stored or transmitted) in opposition to channel coding.[4]

Compression is useful because it helps reduce resource usage, such as data storage space or transmission capacity. Because compressed data must be decompressed to use, this extra processing imposes computational or other costs through decompression; this situation is far from being a free lunch. Data compression is subject to a space–time complexity trade-off. For instance, a compression scheme for video may require expensive hardware for the video to be decompressed fast enough to be viewed as it is being decompressed, and the option to decompress the video in full before watching it may be inconvenient or require additional storage. The design of data compression schemes involves trade-offs among various factors, including the degree of compression, the amount of distortion introduced (when using lossy data compression), and the computational resources required to compress and decompress the data.[5][6]

2.8.1 Lossless

Lossless data compression algorithms usually exploit statistical redundancy to represent data more concisely without losing information, so that the process is reversible. Lossless compression is possible because most real-world data have statistical redundancy. For example, an image may have areas of colour that do not change over several

2.8. DATA COMPRESSION

pixels; instead of coding "red pixel, red pixel, ..." the data may be encoded as "279 red pixels". This is a basic example of run-length encoding; there are many schemes to reduce file size by eliminating redundancy.

The Lempel–Ziv (LZ) compression methods are among the most popular algorithms for lossless storage.[7] DEFLATE is a variation on LZ optimized for decompression speed and compression ratio, but compression can be slow. DEFLATE is used in PKZIP, Gzip and PNG. LZW (Lempel–Ziv–Welch) is used in GIF images. Also noteworthy is the LZR (Lempel-Ziv–Renau) algorithm, which serves as the basis for the Zip method. LZ methods use a table-based compression model where table entries are substituted for repeated strings of data. For most LZ methods, this table is generated dynamically from earlier data in the input. The table itself is often Huffman encoded (e.g. SHRI, LZX). A current LZ-based coding scheme that performs well is LZX, used in Microsoft's CAB format.

The best modern lossless compressors use probabilistic models, such as prediction by partial matching. The Burrows–Wheeler transform can also be viewed as an indirect form of statistical modelling.[8]

The class of grammar-based codes are gaining popularity because they can compress *highly repetitive* input extremely effectively, for instance, a biological data collection of the same or closely related species, a huge versioned document collection, internet archival, etc. The basic task of grammar-based codes is constructing a context-free grammar deriving a single string. Sequitur and Re-Pair are practical grammar compression algorithms for which software is publicly available.

In a further refinement of the direct use of probabilistic modelling, statistical estimates can be coupled to an algorithm called arithmetic coding. Arithmetic coding is a more modern coding technique that uses the mathematical calculations of a finite-state machine to produce a string of encoded bits from a series of input data symbols. It can achieve superior compression to other techniques such as the better-known Huffman algorithm. It uses an internal memory state to avoid the need to perform a one-to-one mapping of individual input symbols to distinct representations that use an integer number of bits, and it clears out the internal memory only after encoding the entire string of data symbols. Arithmetic coding applies especially well to adaptive data compression tasks where the statistics vary and are context-dependent, as it can be easily coupled with an adaptive model of the probability distribution of the input data. An early example of the use of arithmetic coding was its use as an optional (but not widely used) feature of the JPEG image coding standard. It has since been applied in various other designs including H.264/MPEG-4 AVC and HEVC for video coding.

2.8.2 Lossy

Lossy data compression is the converse of lossless data compression. In these schemes, some loss of information is acceptable. Dropping nonessential detail from the data source can save storage space. Lossy data compression schemes are designed by research on how people perceive the data in question. For example, the human eye is more sensitive to subtle variations in luminance than it is to the variations in color. JPEG image compression works in part by rounding off nonessential bits of information.[9] There is a corresponding trade-off between preserving information and reducing size. A number of popular compression formats exploit these perceptual differences, including those used in music files, images, and video.

Lossy image compression can be used in digital cameras, to increase storage capacities with minimal degradation of picture quality. Similarly, DVDs use the lossy MPEG-2 video coding format for video compression.

In lossy audio compression, methods of psychoacoustics are used to remove non-audible (or less audible) components of the audio signal. Compression of human speech is often performed with even more specialized techniques; speech coding, or voice coding, is sometimes distinguished as a separate discipline from *audio compression*. Different audio and speech compression standards are listed under audio coding formats. *Voice compression* is used in internet telephony, for example, audio compression is used for CD ripping and is decoded by the audio players.[8]

2.8.3 Theory

The theoretical background of compression is provided by information theory (which is closely related to algorithmic information theory) for lossless compression and rate–distortion theory for lossy compression. These areas of study were essentially forged by Claude Shannon, who published fundamental papers on the topic in the late 1940s and early 1950s. Coding theory is also related to this. The idea of data compression is also deeply connected with statistical inference.[10]

Machine learning

See also: Machine learning

There is a close connection between machine learning and compression: a system that predicts the posterior probabilities of a sequence given its entire history can be used for optimal data compression (by using arithmetic coding on the output distribution) while an optimal compressor can be used for prediction (by finding the symbol that compresses best, given the previous history). This equivalence has been used as a justification for using data compression as a benchmark for "general intelligence."[11]

Data differencing

Main article: Data differencing

Data compression can be viewed as a special case of data differencing:[12][13] Data differencing consists of producing a *difference* given a *source* and a *target*, with patching producing a *target* given a *source* and a *difference*, while data compression consists of producing a compressed file given a target, and decompression consists of producing a target given only a compressed file. Thus, one can consider data compression as data differencing with empty source data, the compressed file corresponding to a "difference from nothing." This is the same as considering absolute entropy (corresponding to data compression) as a special case of relative entropy (corresponding to data differencing) with no initial data.

When one wishes to emphasize the connection, one may use the term *differential compression* to refer to data differencing.

2.8.4 Uses

Audio

See also: Audio codec and Audio coding format

Audio data compression, as distinguished from dynamic range compression, has the potential to reduce the transmission bandwidth and storage requirements of audio data. Audio compression algorithms are implemented in software as audio codecs. Lossy audio compression algorithms provide higher compression at the cost of fidelity and are used in numerous audio applications. These algorithms almost all rely on psychoacoustics to eliminate less audible or meaningful sounds, thereby reducing the space required to store or transmit them.[2]

In both lossy and lossless compression, information redundancy is reduced, using methods such as coding, pattern recognition, and linear prediction to reduce the amount of information used to represent the uncompressed data.

The acceptable trade-off between loss of audio quality and transmission or storage size depends upon the application. For example, one 640MB compact disc (CD) holds approximately one hour of uncompressed high fidelity music, less than 2 hours of music compressed losslessly, or 7 hours of music compressed in the MP3 format at a medium bit rate. A digital sound recorder can typically store around 200 hours of clearly intelligible speech in 640MB.[14]

Lossless audio compression produces a representation of digital data that decompress to an exact digital duplicate of the original audio stream, unlike playback from lossy compression techniques such as Vorbis and MP3. Compression ratios are around 50–60% of original size,[15] which is similar to those for generic lossless data compression. Lossless compression is unable to attain high compression ratios due to the complexity of waveforms and the rapid changes in sound forms. Codecs like FLAC, Shorten and TTA use linear prediction to estimate the spectrum of the signal. Many of these algorithms use convolution with the filter $[-1\ 1]$ to slightly whiten or flatten the spectrum, thereby allowing traditional lossless compression to work more efficiently. The process is reversed upon decompression.

When audio files are to be processed, either by further compression or for editing, it is desirable to work from an unchanged original (uncompressed or losslessly compressed). Processing of a lossily compressed file for some purpose usually produces a final result inferior to the creation of the same compressed file from an uncompressed original. In addition to sound editing or mixing, lossless audio compression is often used for archival storage, or as master copies.

A number of lossless audio compression formats exist. Shorten was an early lossless format. Newer ones include Free Lossless Audio Codec (FLAC), Apple's Apple Lossless (ALAC), MPEG-4 ALS, Microsoft's Windows Media Audio 9 Lossless (WMA Lossless), Monkey's Audio, TTA, and WavPack. See list of lossless codecs for a complete listing.

Some audio formats feature a combination of a lossy format and a lossless correction; this allows stripping the correction to easily obtain a lossy file. Such formats include MPEG-4 SLS (Scalable to Lossless), WavPack, and OptimFROG DualStream.

Other formats are associated with a distinct system, such as:

- Direct Stream Transfer, used in Super Audio CD
- Meridian Lossless Packing, used in DVD-Audio, Dolby TrueHD, Blu-ray and HD DVD

Lossy audio compression Lossy audio compression is used in a wide range of applications. In addition to the direct applications (mp3 players or computers), digitally compressed audio streams are used in most video DVDs, digital television, streaming media on the internet, satellite and cable radio, and increasingly in terrestrial radio broadcasts. Lossy compression typically achieves far greater compression than lossless compression (data of 5 percent to 20 per-

2.8. DATA COMPRESSION

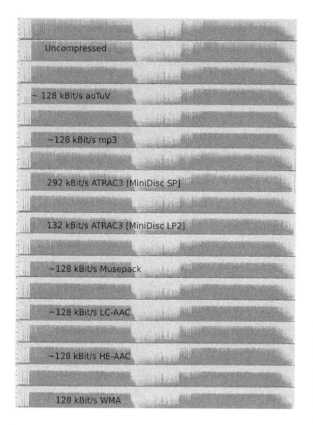

Comparison of acoustic spectrograms of a song in an uncompressed format and lossy formats. That the lossy spectrograms are different from the uncompressed one indicates that they are, in fact, lossy, but nothing can be assumed about the effect of the changes on perceived quality.

Coding methods To determine what information in an audio signal is perceptually irrelevant, most lossy compression algorithms use transforms such as the modified discrete cosine transform (MDCT) to convert time domain sampled waveforms into a transform domain. Once transformed, typically into the frequency domain, component frequencies can be allocated bits according to how audible they are. Audibility of spectral components calculated using the absolute threshold of hearing and the principles of simultaneous masking—the phenomenon wherein a signal is masked by another signal separated by frequency—and, in some cases, temporal masking—where a signal is masked by another signal separated by time. Equal-loudness contours may also be used to weight the perceptual importance of components. Models of the human ear-brain combination incorporating such effects are often called psychoacoustic models.[17]

Other types of lossy compressors, such as the linear predictive coding (LPC) used with speech, are source-based coders. These coders use a model of the sound's generator (such as the human vocal tract with LPC) to whiten the audio signal (i.e., flatten its spectrum) before quantization. LPC may be thought of as a basic perceptual coding technique: reconstruction of an audio signal using a linear predictor shapes the coder's quantization noise into the spectrum of the target signal, partially masking it.[16]

Lossy formats are often used for the distribution of streaming audio or interactive applications (such as the coding of speech for digital transmission in cell phone networks). In such applications, the data must be decompressed as the data flows, rather than after the entire data stream has been transmitted. Not all audio codecs can be used for streaming applications, and for such applications a codec designed to stream data effectively will usually be chosen.[16]

Latency results from the methods used to encode and decode the data. Some codecs will analyze a longer segment of the data to optimize efficiency, and then code it in a manner that requires a larger segment of data at one time to decode. (Often codecs create segments called a "frame" to create discrete data segments for encoding and decoding.) The inherent latency of the coding algorithm can be critical; for example, when there is a two-way transmission of data, such as with a telephone conversation, significant delays may seriously degrade the perceived quality.

In contrast to the speed of compression, which is proportional to the number of operations required by the algorithm, here latency refers to the number of samples that must be analysed before a block of audio is processed. In the minimum case, latency is zero samples (e.g., if the coder/decoder simply reduces the number of bits used to quantize the signal). Time domain algorithms such as LPC also often have low latencies, hence their popularity in

cent of the original stream, rather than 50 percent to 60 percent), by discarding less-critical data.[16]

The innovation of lossy audio compression was to use psychoacoustics to recognize that not all data in an audio stream can be perceived by the human auditory system. Most lossy compression reduces perceptual redundancy by first identifying perceptually irrelevant sounds, that is, sounds that are very hard to hear. Typical examples include high frequencies or sounds that occur at the same time as louder sounds. Those sounds are coded with decreased accuracy or not at all.

Due to the nature of lossy algorithms, audio quality suffers when a file is decompressed and recompressed (digital generation loss). This makes lossy compression unsuitable for storing the intermediate results in professional audio engineering applications, such as sound editing and multitrack recording. However, they are very popular with end users (particularly MP3) as a megabyte can store about a minute's worth of music at adequate quality.

speech coding for telephony. In algorithms such as MP3, however, a large number of samples have to be analyzed to implement a psychoacoustic model in the frequency domain, and latency is on the order of 23 ms (46 ms for two-way communication)).

Speech encoding   Speech encoding is an important category of audio data compression. The perceptual models used to estimate what a human ear can hear are generally somewhat different from those used for music. The range of frequencies needed to convey the sounds of a human voice are normally far narrower than that needed for music, and the sound is normally less complex. As a result, speech can be encoded at high quality using a relatively low bit rate.

If the data to be compressed is analog (such as a voltage that varies with time), quantization is employed to digitize it into numbers (normally integers). This is referred to as analog-to-digital (A/D) conversion. If the integers generated by quantization are 8 bits each, then the entire range of the analog signal is divided into 256 intervals and all the signal values within an interval are quantized to the same number. If 16-bit integers are generated, then the range of the analog signal is divided into 65,536 intervals.

This relation illustrates the compromise between high resolution (a large number of analog intervals) and high compression (small integers generated). This application of quantization is used by several speech compression methods. This is accomplished, in general, by some combination of two approaches:

- Only encoding sounds that could be made by a single human voice.

- Throwing away more of the data in the signal— keeping just enough to reconstruct an "intelligible" voice rather than the full frequency range of human hearing.

Perhaps the earliest algorithms used in speech encoding (and audio data compression in general) were the A-law algorithm and the μ-law algorithm.

History   A literature compendium for a large variety of audio coding systems was published in the IEEE Journal on Selected Areas in Communications (JSAC), February 1988. While there were some papers from before that time, this collection documented an entire variety of finished, working audio coders, nearly all of them using perceptual (i.e. masking) techniques and some kind of frequency analysis and back-end noiseless coding.[18] Several of these papers remarked on the difficulty of obtaining good, clean dig-

Solidyne 922: The world's first commercial audio bit compression card for PC, 1990

ital audio for research purposes. Most, if not all, of the authors in the JSAC edition were also active in the MPEG-1 Audio committee.

The world's first commercial broadcast automation audio compression system was developed by Oscar Bonello, an engineering professor at the University of Buenos Aires.[19] In 1983, using the psychoacoustic principle of the masking of critical bands first published in 1967,[20] he started developing a practical application based on the recently developed IBM PC computer, and the broadcast automation system was launched in 1987 under the name Audicom. Twenty years later, almost all the radio stations in the world were using similar technology manufactured by a number of companies.

Video

See also: Video coding format and Video codec

Video compression uses modern coding techniques to reduce redundancy in video data. Most video compression algorithms and codecs combine spatial image compression and temporal motion compensation. Video compression is a practical implementation of source coding in information theory. In practice, most video codecs also use audio compression techniques in parallel to compress the separate, but combined data streams as one package.[21]

The majority of video compression algorithms use lossy compression. Uncompressed video requires a very high data rate. Although lossless video compression codecs perform an average compression factor of over 3, a typical MPEG-4 lossy compression video has a compression factor between 20 and 200.[22] As in all lossy compression, there is a trade-off between video quality, cost of processing the compression and decompression, and system requirements. Highly compressed video may present visible or distracting artifacts.

Some video compression schemes typically operate on square-shaped groups of neighboring pixels, often called macroblocks. These pixel groups or blocks of pixels are compared from one frame to the next, and the video compression codec sends only the differences within those blocks. In areas of video with more motion, the compression must encode more data to keep up with the larger number of pixels that are changing. Commonly during explosions, flames, flocks of animals, and in some panning shots, the high-frequency detail leads to quality decreases or to increases in the variable bitrate.

Encoding theory Video data may be represented as a series of still image frames. The sequence of frames contains spatial and temporal redundancy that video compression algorithms attempt to eliminate or code in a smaller size. Similarities can be encoded by only storing differences between frames, or by using perceptual features of human vision. For example, small differences in color are more difficult to perceive than are changes in brightness. Compression algorithms can average a color across these similar areas to reduce space, in a manner similar to those used in JPEG image compression.[23] Some of these methods are inherently lossy while others may preserve all relevant information from the original, uncompressed video.

One of the most powerful techniques for compressing video is interframe compression. Interframe compression uses one or more earlier or later frames in a sequence to compress the current frame, while intraframe compression uses only the current frame, effectively being image compression.[24]

The most powerful used method works by comparing each frame in the video with the previous one. If the frame contains areas where nothing has moved, the system simply issues a short command that copies that part of the previous frame, bit-for-bit, into the next one. If sections of the frame move in a simple manner, the compressor emits a (slightly longer) command that tells the decompressor to shift, rotate, lighten, or darken the copy. This longer command still remains much shorter than intraframe compression. Interframe compression works well for programs that will simply be played back by the viewer, but can cause problems if the video sequence needs to be edited.[25]

Because interframe compression copies data from one frame to another, if the original frame is simply cut out (or lost in transmission), the following frames cannot be reconstructed properly. Some video formats, such as DV, compress each frame independently using intraframe compression. Making 'cuts' in intraframe-compressed video is almost as easy as editing uncompressed video: one finds the beginning and ending of each frame, and simply copies bit-for-bit each frame that one wants to keep, and discards the frames one doesn't want. Another difference between intraframe and interframe compression is that, with intraframe systems, each frame uses a similar amount of data. In most interframe systems, certain frames (such as "I frames" in MPEG-2) aren't allowed to copy data from other frames, so they require much more data than other frames nearby.[16]

It is possible to build a computer-based video editor that spots problems caused when I frames are edited out while other frames need them. This has allowed newer formats like HDV to be used for editing. However, this process demands a lot more computing power than editing intraframe compressed video with the same picture quality.

Today, nearly all commonly used video compression methods (e.g., those in standards approved by the ITU-T or ISO) apply a discrete cosine transform (DCT) for spatial redundancy reduction. The DCT that is widely used in this regard was introduced by N. Ahmed, T. Natarajan and K. R. Rao in 1974.[26] Other methods, such as fractal compression, matching pursuit and the use of a discrete wavelet transform (DWT) have been the subject of some research, but are typically not used in practical products (except for the use of wavelet coding as still-image coders without motion compensation). Interest in fractal compression seems to be waning, due to recent theoretical analysis showing a comparative lack of effectiveness of such methods.[24]

Timeline The following table is a partial history of international video compression standards.

Genetics

See also: Compression of Genomic Re-Sequencing Data

Genetics compression algorithms are the latest generation of lossless algorithms that compress data (typically sequences of nucleotides) using both conventional compression algorithms and genetic algorithms adapted to the specific datatype. In 2012, a team of scientists from Johns Hopkins University published a genetic compression algorithm that does not use a reference genome for compression. HAPZIPPER was tailored for HapMap data and achieves over 20-fold compression (95% reduction in file size), providing 2- to 4-fold better compression and in much faster time than the leading general-purpose compression utilities. For this, Chanda, Elhaik, and Bader introduced MAF based encoding (MAFE), which reduces the heterogeneity of the dataset by sorting SNPs by their minor allele frequency, thus homogenizing the dataset.[27] Other algorithms in 2009 and

2013 (DNAZip and GenomeZip) have compression ratios of up to 1200-fold—allowing 6 billion basepair diploid human genomes to be stored in 2.5 megabytes (relative to a reference genome or averaged over many genomes).[28][29]

2.8.5 Outlook and currently unused potential

It is estimated that the total amount of data that is stored on the world's storage devices could be further compressed with existing compression algorithms by a remaining average factor of 4.5:1. It is estimated that the combined technological capacity of the world to store information provides 1,300 exabytes of hardware digits in 2007, but when the corresponding content is optimally compressed, this only represents 295 exabytes of Shannon information.[30]

2.8.6 See also

- Auditory masking
- Calgary corpus
- Canterbury corpus
- Context mixing
- Compression artifact
- Data compression ratio
- Data compression symmetry
- Dictionary coder
- Distributed source coding
- Dyadic distribution
- Dynamic Markov compression
- Elias gamma coding
- Entropy encoding
- Fibonacci coding
- Golomb coding
- HTTP compression
- Kolmogorov complexity
- Magic compression algorithm
- Minimum description length
- Modulo-N code
- Range encoding
- Sub-band coding
- Universal code (data compression)
- Vector quantization

2.8.7 References

[1] Wade, Graham (1994). *Signal coding and processing* (2 ed.). Cambridge University Press. p. 34. ISBN 978-0-521-42336-6. Retrieved 2011-12-22. The broad objective of source coding is to exploit or remove 'inefficient' redundancy in the PCM source and thereby achieve a reduction in the overall source rate R.

[2] Mahdi, O.A.; Mohammed, M.A.; Mohamed, A.J. (November 2012). "Implementing a Novel Approach an Convert Audio Compression to Text Coding via Hybrid Technique" (PDF). *International Journal of Computer Science Issues* **9** (6, No. 3): 53–59. Retrieved 6 March 2013.

[3] Pujar, J.H.; Kadlaskar, L.M. (May 2010). "A New Lossless Method of Image Compression and Decompression Using Huffman Coding Techniques" (PDF). *Journal of Theoretical and Applied Information Technology* **15** (1): 18–23.

[4] Salomon, David (2008). *A Concise Introduction to Data Compression*. Berlin: Springer. ISBN 9781848000728.

[5] S. Mittal and J. Vetter, "A Survey Of Architectural Approaches for Data Compression in Cache and Main Memory Systems", IEEE Transactions on Parallel and Distributed Systems, 2015.

[6] Tank, M.K. (2011). *Implementation of Limpel-Ziv algorithm for lossless compression using VHDL. Thinkquest 2010: Proceedings of the First International Conference on Contours of Computing Technology*. Berlin: Springer. pp. 275–283.

[7] Navqi, Saud; Naqvi, R.; Riaz, R.A.; Siddiqui, F. (April 2011). "Optimized RTL design and implementation of LZW algorithm for high bandwidth applications" (PDF). *Electrical Review* **2011** (4): 279–285.

[8] Mahmud, Salauddin (March 2012). "An Improved Data Compression Method for General Data" (PDF). *International Journal of Scientific & Engineering Research* **3** (3): 2. Retrieved 6 March 2013.

[9] Arcangel, Cory. "On Compression" (PDF). Retrieved 6 March 2013.

[10] Marak, Laszlo. "On image compression" (PDF). University of Marne la Vallee. Retrieved 6 March 2013.

[11] Mahoney, Matt. "Rationale for a Large Text Compression Benchmark". *http://cs.fit.edu/~{}mmahoney/*. Florida Institute of Technology. Retrieved 5 March 2013.

[12] Korn, D.; et al. "RFC 3284: The VCDIFF Generic Differencing and Compression Data Format". Internet Engineering Task Force. Retrieved 5 March 2013.

2.8. DATA COMPRESSION

[13] Korn, D.G.; Vo, K.P. (1995), B. Krishnamurthy, ed., *Vdelta: Differencing and Compression*, Practical Reusable Unix Software, New York: John Wiley & Sons, Inc.

[14] The Olympus WS-120 digital speech recorder, according to its manual, can store about 178 hours of speech-quality audio in .WMA format in 500MB of flash memory.

[15] Coalson, Josh. "FLAC Comparison". Retrieved 6 March 2013.

[16] Jaiswal, R.C. (2009). *Audio-Video Engineering*. Pune, Maharashtra: Nirali Prakashan. p. 3.41. ISBN 9788190639675.

[17] Faxin Yu, Hao Luo, Zheming Lu (2010). *Three-Dimensional Model Analysis and Processing*. Berlin: Springer. p. 47. ISBN 9783642126512.

[18] "File Compression Possibilities". *A Brief guide to compress a file in 6 different ways*.

[19] "Summary of some of Solidyne's contributions to Broadcast Engineering". *Brief History of Solidyne*. Buenos Aires: Solidyne. Retrieved 6 March 2013.

[20] Zwicker, Eberhard; et al. (Originally published in 1967; Translation published in 1999). *The Ear As A Communication Receiver*. Melville, NY: Acoustical Society of America. Check date values in: |date= (help)

[21] "Video Coding". *Center for Signal and Information Processing Research*. Georgia Institute of Technology. Retrieved 6 March 2013.

[22] Graphics & Media Lab Video Group (2007). *Lossless Video Codecs Comparison* (PDF). Moscow State University.

[23] Lane, Tom. "JPEG Image Compression FAQ, Part 1". *Internet FAQ Archives*. Independent JPEG Group. Retrieved 6 March 2013.

[24] Faxin Yu, Hao Luo, Zheming Lu (2010). *Three-Dimensional Model Analysis and Processing*. Berlin: Springer. p. 47. ISBN 9783642126512.

[25] Bhojani, D.R. "4.1 Video Compression" (PDF). *Hypothesis*. Retrieved 6 March 2013.

[26] Ahmed, N.; Natarajan, T.; Rao, K.R. (January 1974). "Discrete Cosine Transform". *IEEE Transactions on Computers* **C–23** (1): 90–93. doi:10.1109/T-C.1974.223784.

[27] Chanda P, Bader JS, Elhaik E; Elhaik; Bader (27 Jul 2012). "HapZipper: sharing HapMap populations just got easier" (PDF). *Nucleic Acids Research* **40** (20): e159. doi:10.1093/nar/gks709. PMC 3488212. PMID 22844100.

[28] Christley S, Lu Y, Li C, Xie X; Lu; Li; Xie (Jan 15, 2009). "Human genomes as email attachments". *Bioinformatics* **25** (2): 274–5. doi:10.1093/bioinformatics/btn582. PMID 18996942.

[29] Pavlichin DS, Weissman T, Yona G; Weissman; Yona (September 2013). "The human genome contracts again". *Bioinformatics* **29** (17): 2199–202. doi:10.1093/bioinformatics/btt362. PMID 23793748.

[30] Hilbert, Martin; López, Priscila (1 April 2011). "The World's Technological Capacity to Store, Communicate, and Compute Information". *Science* **332** (6025): 60–65. Bibcode:2011Sci...332...60H. doi:10.1126/science.1200970. PMID 21310967. Retrieved 6 March 2013.

2.8.8 External links

- Data Compression Basics (Video)
- Video compression 4:2:2 10-bit and its benefits
- Why does 10-bit save bandwidth (even when content is 8-bit)?
- Which compression technology should be used
- Wiley - Introduction to Compression Theory
- EBU subjective listening tests on low-bitrate audio codecs
- Audio Archiving Guide: Music Formats (Guide for helping a user pick out the right codec)
- MPEG 1&2 video compression intro (pdf format) at the Wayback Machine (archived September 28, 2007)
- hydrogenaudio wiki comparison
- Introduction to Data Compression by Guy E Blelloch from CMU
- HD Greetings - 1080p Uncompressed source material for compression testing and research
- Explanation of lossless signal compression method used by most codecs
- Interactive blind listening tests of audio codecs over the internet
- TestVid - 2,000+ HD and other uncompressed source video clips for compression testing
- Videsignline - Intro to Video Compression
- Data Footprint Reduction Technology
- What is Run length Coding in video compression.

2.9 Distortion

This article is about technology, especially electrical engineering. For other uses, see Distortion (disambiguation). "Distort" redirects here. For other uses, see Distort (disambiguation).

Distortion is the alteration of the original shape (or other characteristic) of something, such as an object, image, sound or waveform. Distortion is usually unwanted, and so engineers strive to eliminate distortion, or minimize it. In some situations, however, distortion may be desirable. The important signal processing operation of heterodyning is based on nonlinear mixing of signals to cause intermodulation. Distortion is also used as a musical effect, particularly with electric guitars.

The addition of noise or other outside signals (hum, interference) is not deemed distortion, though the effects of quantization distortion are sometimes deemed noise. A quality measure that explicitly reflects both the noise and the distortion is the Signal-to-noise-and-distortion (SINAD) ratio.

2.9.1 Electronic signals

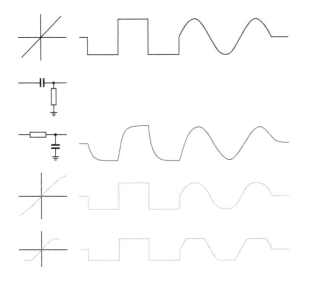

Graph of a waveform and some distorted versions of the same waveform

In telecommunication and signal processing, a noise-free system can be characterised by a transfer function, such that the output $y(t)$ can be written as a function of the input x as

$$y(t) = F(x(t))$$

When the transfer function comprises only a perfect gain constant A and perfect delay T

$$y(t) = A \cdot x(t - T)$$

the output is undistorted. Distortion occurs when the transfer function F is more complicated than this. If F is a linear function, for instance a filter whose gain and/or delay varies with frequency, the signal suffers linear distortion. Linear distortion does not introduce new frequency components to a signal but does alter the balance of existing ones.

This diagram shows the behaviour of a signal (made up of a square wave followed by a sine wave) as it is passed through various distorting functions.

1. The first trace (in black) shows the input. It also shows the output from a non-distorting transfer function (straight line).

2. A high-pass filter (green trace) distorts the shape of a square wave by reducing its low frequency components. This is the cause of the "droop" seen on the top of the pulses. This "pulse distortion" can be very significant when a train of pulses must pass through an AC-coupled (high-pass filtered) amplifier. As the sine wave contains only one frequency, its shape is unaltered.

3. A low-pass filter (blue trace) rounds the pulses by removing the high frequency components. All systems are low pass to some extent. Note that the phase of the sine wave is different for the lowpass and the highpass cases, due to the phase distortion of the filters.

4. A slightly non-linear transfer function (purple), this one gently compresses the peaks of the sine wave, as may be typical of a tube audio amplifier. This generates small amounts of low order harmonics.

5. A hard-clipping transfer function (red) generates high order harmonics. Parts of the transfer function are flat, which indicates that all information about the input signal has been lost in this region.

The transfer function of an ideal amplifier, with perfect gain and delay, is only an approximation. The true behavior of the system is usually different. Nonlinearities in the transfer function of an active device (such as vacuum tubes, transistors, and operational amplifiers) are a common source of non-linear distortion; in passive components (such as a coaxial cable or optical fiber), linear distortion can be caused by inhomogeneities, reflections, and so on in the propagation path.

2.9. DISTORTION

Amplitude distortion

Main article: Amplitude distortion
See also: Clipping (signal processing)

Amplitude distortion is distortion occurring in a system, subsystem, or device when the output amplitude is not a linear function of the input amplitude under specified conditions.

Harmonic distortion

Harmonic distortion adds overtones that are whole number multiples of a sound wave's frequencies.[1] Nonlinearities that give rise to amplitude distortion in audio systems are most often measured in terms of the harmonics (overtones) added to a pure sinewave fed to the system. Harmonic distortion may be expressed in terms of the relative strength of individual components, in decibels, or the root mean square of all harmonic components: Total harmonic distortion (THD), as a percentage. The level at which harmonic distortion becomes audible depends on the exact nature of the distortion. Different types of distortion (like crossover distortion) are more audible than others (like soft clipping) even if the THD measurements are identical. Harmonic distortion in radio frequency applications is rarely expressed as THD.

Frequency response distortion

See also: Frequency response

Non-flat frequency response is a form of distortion that occurs when different frequencies are amplified by different amounts in a filter. For example, the non-uniform frequency response curve of AC-coupled cascade amplifier is an example of frequency distortion. In the audio case, this is mainly caused by room acoustics, poor loudspeakers and microphones, long loudspeaker cables in combination with frequency dependent loudspeaker impedance, etc.

Phase distortion

Main article: Phase distortion

This form of distortion mostly occurs due to electrical reactance. Here, all the components of the input signal are not amplified with the same phase shift, hence making some parts of the output signal out of phase with the rest of the output.

Group delay distortion

Can be found only in dispersive media. In a waveguide, phase velocity varies with frequency. In a filter, group delay tends to peak near the cut-off frequency, resulting in pulse distortion. When analog long distance trunks were commonplace, for example in 12 channel carrier, group delay distortion had to be corrected in repeaters.

2.9.2 Correction of distortion

As the system output is given by y(t) = F(x(t)), then if the inverse function F^{-1} can be found, and used intentionally to distort either the input or the output of the system, then the distortion is corrected.

An example of a similar correction is where LP/vinyl recordings or FM audio transmissions are deliberately pre-emphasised by a linear filter, the reproducing system applies an inverse filter to make the overall system undistorted.

Correction is not possible if the inverse does not exist—for instance if the transfer function has flat spots (the inverse would map multiple input points to a single output point). This produces an uncorrectable loss of information. Such a situation can occur when an amplifier is overdriven—causing clipping or slew rate distortion when, for a moment, the amplifier characteristics alone and not the input signal determine the output.

Cancellation of even-order harmonic distortion

Many symmetrical electronic circuits reduce the magnitude of even harmonics generated by the non-linearities of the amplifier's components, by combining two signals from opposite halves of the circuit where distortion components that are roughly the same magnitude but out of phase. Examples include push-pull amplifiers and long-tailed pairs.

2.9.3 Teletypewriter or modem signaling

In binary signaling such as FSK, distortion is the shifting of the significant instants of the signal pulses from their proper positions relative to the beginning of the start pulse. The magnitude of the distortion is expressed in percent of an ideal unit pulse length. This is sometimes called 'bias' distortion.

Telegraphic distortion is a similar older problem, distorting the ratio between "mark" and "space" intervals.

2.9.4 Distortion in art

In the art world, a distortion is any change made by an artist to the size, shape or visual character of a form to express an idea, convey a feeling or enhance visual impact. Often referred to as "abstraction," examples of distortion include "The Weeping Woman" by Picasso and "The Adoration of the Shepherds" by El Greco.

2.9.5 Audio distortion

Main article: Distortion (music)

In this context, distortion refers to any kind of deforma-

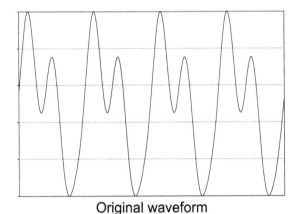

Original waveform

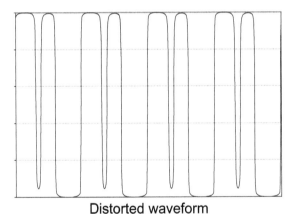

Distorted waveform

A graph of a waveform and the distorted version of the same waveform

tion of an output waveform compared to its input, usually clipping, harmonic distortion, or intermodulation distortion (mixing phenomena) caused by non-linear behavior of electronic components and power supply limitations.[2] Terms for specific types of nonlinear audio distortion include: crossover distortion, slew-Induced Distortion (SID) and transient intermodulation (TIM).

Distortion in music is sometimes intentionally used as an effect, see also overdrive and distortion synthesis. Other forms of audio distortion that may be referred to are non-flat frequency response, compression, modulation, aliasing, quantization noise, wow and flutter from analog media such as vinyl records and magnetic tape. The human ear cannot hear phase distortion, except that it may affect the stereo imaging. (See also: Audio system measurements.)

In most fields, distortion is characterized as unwanted change to a signal.

2.9.6 Optics

Main article: Distortion (optics)

In optics, image/optical distortion is a divergence from rectilinear projection caused by a change in magnification with increasing distance from the optical axis of an optical system.

2.9.7 Map projections

Main article: Map projection

In cartography, a distortion is the misrepresentation of the area or shape of a feature. The Mercator projection, for example, distorts by exaggerating the size of regions at high latitude.

2.9.8 See also

- Aliasing
- Amplitude distortion
- Attenuation distortion
- Bias distortion
- Crossover distortion
- Distortion (music)
- Distortion power factor
- Fading
- Image warping
- Intermodulation distortion
- Lossy compression
- Total harmonic distortion
- Tube sound

2.9.9 References

[1] Moscal, Tony (1994). *Sound Check: The Basics of Sound and Sound Systems*. Hal Leonard. p. 55.

[2] Audio Electronics by John Linsley Hood; page 162

This article incorporates public domain material from the General Services Administration document "Federal Standard 1037C" (in support of MIL-STD-188).

2.10 Electronica

This article is about the musical genre. For the major biennial international electronic trade fair in Munich, Germany, see Electronica (trade fair). For the Disney California Adventure attraction, see ElecTRONica.

Electronica is an umbrella term that encompasses a broad group of electronic-based styles such as techno, house, ambient, drum and bass, jungle, and industrial dance, among others.[1] It has been used to describe the rise of electronic music styles intended not just for dancing but also concentrated listening.[2]

2.10.1 Regional definitions

In North America, in the late 1990s, the mainstream music industry adopted and to some extent manufactured *electronica* as an umbrella term encompassing styles such as techno, big beat, drum and bass, trip hop, downtempo, and ambient, regardless of whether it was curated by indie labels catering to the "underground" nightclub and rave scenes,[3][4] or licensed by major labels and marketed to mainstream audiences as a commercially viable alternative to alternative rock music.[5] By the late 2000s, however, the industry abandoned *electronica* in favor of *EDM*, a term with roots in academia and an increasing association with outdoor music festivals and relatively mainstream, post-rave electro house and dubstep music. Nevertheless, the U.S.-based *AllMusic* still categorises electronica as a top-level genre, stating that it includes danceable grooves, as well as music for headphones and chillout areas.[6]

In other parts of the world, especially in the UK, *electronica* is also a broad term, but is associated with non-dance-oriented music, including relatively experimental styles of downtempo electronic music. It partly overlaps what is known chiefly outside the UK as *IDM*.

2.10.2 A wave of diverse acts

Electronica benefited from advancements in music technology, especially electronic musical instruments, synthesizers, music sequencers, drum machines, and digital audio workstations. As the technology developed, it became possible for individuals or smaller groups to produce electronic songs and recordings in smaller studios, even in project studios. At the same time, computers facilitated the use of music "samples" and "loops" as construction kits for sonic compositions.[7] This led to a period of creative experimentation and the development of new forms, some of which became known as *electronica*.[8][9]

Electronica currently includes a wide variety of musical acts and styles, linked by a penchant for overtly electronic production;[10] a range which includes more popular acts such as Björk, Madonna, Goldfrapp and IDM artists such as Autechre, and Aphex Twin to dub-oriented downtempo, downbeat, and trip hop. Madonna and Björk are said to be responsible for electronica's thrust into mainstream culture, with their albums *Ray of Light* (Madonna),[11] *Post* and *Homogenic* (Björk). Electronica artists that would later become commercially successful began to record in the late 1980s, before the term had come into common usage, including for example The Prodigy, Fatboy Slim, Daft Punk, The Chemical Brothers, The Crystal Method, Moby, Underworld and Faithless.[12] Electronica composers often create alternate versions of their compositions, known as "remixes"; this practice also occurs in related musical forms such as ambient, jungle, and electronic dance music.[13] Wide ranges of influences, both sonic and compositional, are combined in electronica recordings.[14]

2.10.3 New York City

New York City became one center of experimentation and growth for the electronica sound, with DJs and music producers from areas as diverse as Southeast Asia and Brazil bringing their creative work to the nightclubs of that city.[15][16]

2.10.4 Effect on mainstream popular music

Around the mid-1990s, with the success of the big beat sound exemplified by The Chemical Brothers and The Prodigy in the UK, and spurred by the attention from mainstream artists, including Madonna in her collaboration with William Orbit on her album *Ray of Light*[11] and Australian singer Dannii Minogue with her 1997 album *Girl*,[17] music of this period began to be produced with a higher budget, increased technical quality, and with more layers than most other forms of dance music, since it was backed by major record labels and MTV as the "next big thing".[18]

According to a 1997 *Billboard* article, "[t]he union of the club community and independent labels" provided the experimental and trend-setting environment in which electronica acts developed and eventually reached the mainstream. It cites American labels such as Astralwerks (The Future Sound of London, Fluke), Moonshine (DJ Keoki), Sims, and City of Angels (The Crystal Method) for playing a significant role in discovering and marketing artists who became popularized in the electronica scene.[3]

2.10.5 Included in contemporary media

In the late 1990s and early 2000s, electronica music was increasingly used as background scores for television advertisements, initially for automobiles. It was also used for various video games, including the *Wipeout* series, for which the soundtrack was composed of many popular electronica tracks that helped create more interest in this type of music[19]—and later for other technological and business products such as computers and financial services. Then in 2011, Hyundai Veloster, in association with The Grammys, produced a project that became known as Re: Generation.[20]

2.10.6 See also

- List of electronic music genres

2.10.7 References

[1] Campbell, Michael (2012). "Electronica and Rap". *Popular Music in America: The Beat Goes On* (4th ed.). Cengage Learning. ISBN 0840029764.

[2] Verderosa, Tony (2002). *The Techno Primer: The Essential Reference for Loop-Based Music Styles*. Hal Leonard Music/Songbooks. p. 28. ISBN 0-634-01788-8. Electronica is a broad term used to describe the emergence of electronic music that is geared for listening instead of strictly for dancing.

[3] Flick, Larry (May 24, 1997). "Dancing to the beat of an indie drum". *Billboard* **109** (21). pp. 70–71. ISSN 0006-2510.

[4] Kim Cascone (Winter 2002). "The Aesthetics of Failure: 'Post-Digital' Tendencies in Contemporary Computer Music". *Computer Music Journal* (MIT Press) **24** (4). The glitch genre arrived on the back of the electronica movement, an umbrella term for alternative, largely dance-based electronic music (including house, techno, electro, drum'n'bass, ambient) that has come into vogue in the past five years. Most of the work in this area is released on labels peripherally associated with the dance music market, and is therefore removed from the contexts of academic consideration and acceptability that it might otherwise earn. Still, in spite of this odd pairing of fashion and art music, the composers of glitch often draw their inspiration from the masters of 20th century music who they feel best describe its lineage.

[5] Norris, Chris (April 21, 1997). "Recycling the Future". *New York*: 64–65. With record sales slumping and alternative rock presumed over, the music industry is famously desperate for a new movement to replace its languishing grunge product. And so its gaze has fixed on a vital and international scene of knob-twiddling musicians and colorfully garbed clubgoers—a scene that, when it began in Detroit discos ten years ago, was called techno. If all goes according to marketing plan, 1997 will be the year "electronica" replaces "grunge" as linguistic plague, MTV buzz, ad soundtrack, and runway garb. The music has been freshly installed in Microsoft commercials, in the soundtrack to Hollywood's recycled action-hero pic *The Saint*, and in MTV's newest, hourlong all-electronica program, *Amp*.

[6] "'Reaching back to grab the grooves of '70s disco/funk and the gadgets of electronic composition, Electronica soon became a whole new entity in and of itself, spinning off new sounds and subgenres with no end in sight two decades down the pike. Its beginnings came in the post-disco environment of Chicago/New York and Detroit, the cities who spawned house and techno (respectively) during the 1980s. Later in that decade, club-goers in Britain latched onto the fusion of mechanical and sensual, and returned the favor to hungry Americans with new styles like jungle/drum'n'bass and trip hop. Though most all early electronica was danceable, by the beginning of the '90s, producers were also making music for the headphones and chill-out areas as well, resulting in dozens of stylistic fusions like ambient-house, experimental techno, tech-house, electro-techno, etc. Typical for the many styles gathered under the umbrella was a focus on danceable grooves, very loose song structure (if any), and, in many producers, a relentless desire to find a new sound no matter how tepid the results." Electronica Genre at AllMusic

[7] "This loop slicing technique is common to the electronica genre and allows a live drum feel with added flexibility and variation." Page 380, *DirectX Audio Exposed: Interactive Audio Development*, Todd Fay, Wordware Publishing, 2003, ISBN 1-55622-288-2

[8] "Electronically produced music is part of the mainstream of popular culture. Musical concepts that were once considered radical - the use of environmental sounds, ambient music, turntable music, digital sampling, computer music, the electronic modification of acoustic sounds, and music made from fragments of speech-have now been subsumed by many kinds of popular music. Record store genres including new age, rap, hip-hop, electronica, techno, jazz, and popular song all rely heavily on production values and techniques that originated with classic electronic music." Page 1, *Electronic*

and *Experimental Music: Pioneers in Technology and Composition*, Thomas B. Holmes, Routledge Music/Songbooks, 2002, ISBN 0-415-93643-8

[9] "Electronica and punk have a definite similarity: They both totally prescribe to a DIY aesthetic. We both tried to work within the constructs of the traditional music business, but the system didn't get us - so we found a way to do it for ourselves, before it became affordable.", quote from artist BT, page 45, *Wired: Musicians' Home Studios : Tools & Techniques of the Musical Mavericks*, Megan Perry, Backbeat Books Music/Songbooks 2004, ISBN 0-87930-794-3

[10] "Electronica lives and dies by its grooves, fat synthesizer patches, and fliter sweeps.". Page 376, *DirectX Audio Exposed: Interactive Audio Development*, Todd Fay, Wordware Publishing, 2003, ISBN 1-55622-288-2

[11] "Billboard: Madonna Hung Out on the Radio". *Billboard* (VNU Media). July 2006.

[12] "Crystal Method...grew from an obscure club-culture duo to one of the most recognizable acts in electronica, ...", page 90, *Wired: Musicians' Home Studios : Tools & Techniques of the Musical Mavericks*, Megan Perry, Backbeat Books Music/Songbooks 2004, ISBN 0-87930-794-3

[13] " For example, composers often render more than one version of their own compositions. This practice is not unique to the mod scene, of course, and occurs commonly in dance club music and related forms (such as ambient, jungle, etc.—all broadly designated 'electronica').". Page 48, *Music and Technoculture*, Rene T. A. Lysloff, Tandem Library Books, 2003, ISBN 0-613-91250-0

[14] Pages 233 & 242, *Popular Music in France from Chanson to Techno: Culture, Identity and Society* , By Steve Cannon, Hugh Dauncey, Ashgate Publishing, Ltd. 2003, ISBN 0-7546-0849-2

[15] "In 2000, [Brazilian vocalist Bebel] Gilberto capitalized on New York's growing fixation with cocktail lounge ambient music, an offshoot of the dance club scene that focused on drum and bass remixes with Brazilian sources. ...Collaborating with club music maestros like Suba and Thievery Corporation, Gilberto thrust herself into the leading edge of the emerging Brazilian electronica movement. On her immensely popular *Tanto Tempo* (2000)..." Page 234, *The Latin Beat: The Rhythms and Roots of Latin Music from Bossa Nova to Salsa and Beyond*, Ed Morales, Da Capo Press, 2003, ISBN 0-306-81018-2

[16] "founded in 1997,...under the slogan 'Musical Insurgency Across All Borders', for six years [Manhattan nightclub] Mutiny was an international hub of the south Asian electronica music scene. Bringing together artists from different parts of the south Asia diaspora, the club was host to a roster of British Asian musicians and DJs..." Page 165, *Youth Media* , Bill Osgerby, Routledge, 2004, ISBN 0-415-23807-2

[17] Girl (Dannii Minogue album)

[18] "Electronica reached new heights within the culture of rave and techno music in the 1990s." Page 185, *Music and Technoculture*, Rene T. A. Lysloff, Tandem Library Books, 2003, ISBN 0-613-91250-0

[19] *The Changing Shape of the Culture Industry; or, How Did Electronica Music Get into Television Commercials?*, Timothy D. Taylor, University of California, Los Angeles, Television & New Media, Vol. 8, No. 3, 235-258 (2007)

[20] Ed. The Grammys.Hyundai Veloster, The Recording Academy, GreenLight Media & Marketing, Art Takes Over (ATO), & RSA Films, n.d. Web. 24 May 2013. <http://regenerationmusicproject.com/>.

Literature

- Cummins, James. 2008. *Ambrosia: About a Culture - An Investigation of Electronica Music and Party Culture.* Toronto, ON: Clark-Nova Books. ISBN 978-0-9784892-1-2

2.11 FL Studio

FL Studio (formerly known as **FruityLoops**[2]) is a digital audio workstation developed by the Belgian company Image-Line. FL Studio features a graphical user interface based on a pattern-based music sequencer. The program is available in three different editions for Microsoft Windows, including **Fruity Edition**, **Producer Edition**, and the **Signature Bundle**.[3] Image-Line offers lifetime free updates to the program, which means customers receive all future updates of the software for free.[4] Image-Line also develops **FL Studio Mobile** for iPod Touch, iPhone, iPad and Android devices.[5]

FL Studio can be used as a VST instrument in other audio workstation programs and also functions as a ReWire client. Image-Line also offers other VST instruments and audio applications. FL Studio is used by electronic musicians and DJs such as Afrojack,[6] Avicii,[7] Boi-1da[8] and 9th Wonder,[9] as well as Deadmau5, Porter Robinson and Martin Garrix.

2.11.1 History

The first version of FruityLoops (1.0.0) was developed by Didier Dambrin for Image-Line and was partially released in December 1997. Its official launch was in early 1998, when it was still a four-channel[10] MIDI drum machine.[11] Dambrin became Chief Software Architect for the program,[12][13] and it quickly underwent a series of large upgrades that made it into a popular and complex digital audio workstation. FL Studio has undergone ten major updates since its inception, and FL Studio 11 was released in April 2013. Noted programmer Arguru contributed to various editions of FL Studio. [14]

2.11.2 Software overview

Editions

- **FL Studio Express** (discontinued after version 10[15])– This version allows for step sequencer-only editing and is chiefly suited for 64-step loop creation.[3] Each pattern can consist of an unlimited number of instruments—either samples, native, or VST instruments. Instruments in the pattern can be routed to the Mixer tool for effects processing, and effects as of version 10.0 include Delay, Delay Bank, Equo, Flangus, Love Philter, Vocoder, Parametric EQ & EQ2, Multiband Compressor, Spectroman, Stereo Enhancer, Wave Candy, Wave Shaper, and Soundgoodizer. There is no piano roll, playlist ability, automation, audio recording, or VST/ReWire client.[15]

- **Fruity Edition** – The Fruity Edition allows users to access the playlist, piano roll, and event automation features, which allow for complex and lengthy arranging and sequencing. There is also VST/ReWire support so that FL Studio can be used as an instrument in other hosts such as Cubase, Sonic Solutions, Logic, and other software. As of version 10.0 this edition includes the Simsynth Live synthesizer instrument, the DrumSynth live percussion synthesizer, the DX10FM synthesizer, and the Wasp/Wasp XT synthesizers. There is no audio recording feature.[15]

- **Producer Edition** – The Producer Edition includes all of the features of the Fruity Edition, as well as full recording for internal and external audio and post-production tools. It allows for hand-drawing point and curve based splines (referred to as "Automation Clips"). Plugins include Edison, Slicex (loop slicer and re-arranger), Sytrus, Maximus, Vocodex and Synthmaker. It also allows for waveform viewing of audio clips and the ability to add cue points.[15]

- **Signature Bundle** – This edition includes the Producer Edition as well as a series of plugins such as the Fruity Video player, DirectWave Sampler, Harmless, NewTone, Pitcher, Gross Beat and the Hardcore Guitar Effects Suite.[15]

- **Free Demo** – The free demo version includes all of the program's features and most plugins and allows users to render project audio to WAV, MIDI, MP3, and OGG.[3] However, there are several drawbacks to this limitation as projects saved in demo mode will only open fully once FL Studio and plugins have been registered. Also, instrument presets cannot be saved and the audio output of some instruments will cut out momentarily every few minutes until the programme and its plugins have been registered.[16]

- **Mobile** – On June 21, 2011, Image-Line released FL Studio Mobile for iOS and on April 2013 for Android. Both support the ability to create multi-track projects on mobile devices including iPod Touches, iPhones, iPads.,[5] Android 2.3.3 and higher Smart Phones and Tablets.

- **Groove** – On September 2, 2013, A new standalone app for Windows 8 was released. It is a Groovebox style application optimised for touch-based music creation.[17]

System requirements

FL Studio 12 works on Windows 2000/XP/Vista/7/8/10 (32-bit or 64-bit versions) or on Intel Macs with Boot Camp.[4] Image-Line is working on a native Mac version of the software which is currently in early testing stages. FL Studio requires a 2GHz AMD or Intel Pentium 3 CPU with full SSE1 support. It requires 1 GB of free disk space and at least 1 GB of RAM is recommended.[4]

FL Studio processes audio using an internal 32-bit floating point engine. It supports sampling rates up to 192 kHz using either WDM or ASIO enabled drivers.[12]

Program features

Version 12 is the newest version of FL Studio. It added a new UI design, updated plugins, multi-touch support, redesigned mixer, improved 32 & 64 bit plugin support and improved file management.[18] Version 11, Introduced in April 2013, it included multi-touch support, improved tempo automation, new plugins such as BassDrum, GMS, Effector, Patcher, and new piano roll features (VFX Key Mapper, VFX Color Mapper).[19][20]

Version 10, introduced on March 29, 2011, included a new project browser, fixed some bugs, and smoothed envelope points. It also introduced a patcher.[21]

Version 9 introduced support for multi-core effects processing and improved support for multi-core instrument processing.[11][12]

The mixer interface allows for any number of channel configurations. This allows mixing in 2.1, 5.1, or 7.1 surround sound, as long as the output hardware interface has an equivalent number of outputs. The mixer also supports audio-in, enabling FL Studio to record multitrack audio.[11]

FL Studio supports time stretching/pitch shifting, beat slicing, chopping, and editing of audio,[13] and as of version 8 it can record up to 64 simultaneous audio tracks.[13] Other key features include a digital piano roll.[13] Audio can be imported or exported as WAV, MP3, OGG, MIDI, ZIP, or the native project format with an .FLP filename extension.[12][13]

The demo is very functional, even allowing users to save their compositions for opening in the registered version, and mix their tracks to any of the popular formats.

2.11.3 Plug-ins

FL Studio comes with a variety of plugins and generators (software synthesizers) written in the program's own native plugin architecture. FL Studio also has support for third-party VST and DirectX plugins.[22] The API has a built in wrapper for full VST, VST2, VST3, DX, and ReWire compatibility. Many of the plugins also function independently as standalone programs.

- **Dashboard** – An included plugin which allows the creation of full automation-enabled interfaces for hardware MIDI devices. This allows FL Studio to control hardware from within the program. As of version 9.0 it also supports multiple controllers for different generators and effects.

- **Edison** – Edison is a wave-form editor and recording tool in VST format, though Image-Line also produces a stand-alone version that does not require FL Studio to run. It is included in the Producer Edition and allows spectral analysis, convolution reverb, loop-recording, and loop-construction, as well as support for cue points.[13][15]

- **Fruity Video Player** – Included in the Bundle Edition, it allows the composition and synchronization of audio and video.[15]

- **Deckadance** (often referred to as DD) – a standalone DJ console and mixing program which can also be used in conjunction with FL Studio as a VST plugin. Initially released in May 2007, it was made available starting with the release of FL Studio 7 as an optional part of the download package.

- **Maximus** – Maximus is a multi-band audio limiter and compressor for mastering projects or tracks. It also serves as a noise gate, expander, ducker, and de-esser, and is included in the Bundle edition.[15][23]

- **Riff Machine** – Self-generates melodies in the piano roll using a randomly selected instrument, with parameter controls for shaping melodies. Introduced in version 9.[11][22]

- **Fruity Stereo Shaper** – Stereo processor with a mixer for left and right channels and their inverted equivalents and controls for channel delay and phase offset. Introduced in version 9.[11]

Virtual effects

FL Studio is bundled with a variety of sound processing effects, including common audio effects such as chorus, compression, delay, flanger, phaser, reverb, equalization, vocoding, maximization, and limiting.[13]

- **Gross Beat** – A time, pitch, volume, and sidechain manipulation effect.[11]

- **Hardcore Guitar Effects Suite** – A multi-effects suite of plugins designed to resemble guitarists' stompboxes, which works for any instrument.[15]

- **Juice Pack** – A collection of proprietary plugins ported to VST format for use in other music hosts. The contents of this pack has changed since its release; at the time of this writing it includes the Delay, Delay Bank, EQUO, Flangus, LovePhilter, Multiband Compressor, Notebook, Parametric EQ, Parametric EQ 2, Spectroman, Stereo Enhancer, Vocoder, Wave Candy, and Wave Shaper plugins.[24]

- **Fruity Vocoder** – A real-time vocoder effect.[11]

- **Vocodex** – An advanced vocoder included in the Producer Edition of version 10.[11][15]

- **NewTone** – A pitch correction and time manipulation editor that allows for slicing, correcting, and editing vocals, instrumentals, and other recordings. Introduced as a demo with version 10.[25]

- **Pitcher** – Serves as a real-time pitch correction, manipulation, and harmonization tool for creating or correcting 4 voice harmonies under MIDI control from a keyboard or the piano roll. Introduced as a demo with version 10.[25]

- **Patcher** – Free plugin for chain effects that can then be quickly uploaded in new projects.[25]

- **ZGameEditor Visualizer** – Free visualization effect plugin based on the open source ZGameEditor, with movie rendering capability.[25]

Samplers

- **DirectWave Sampler** – A software sampler that provides sample recording, waveform editing, and DSP effects (works for both VST and live instruments).[15]

- **SliceX** – A beat-slicing sampler for processing and rearranging recorded drumloops, included in the Producer Edition.[15]

Synthesizers

FL Studio is bundled with 32 generator plugins (October 2011). Some are demos. The list includes;

- **3XOsc** – A generator with three programmable oscillators that subtractively produce bright sound with low memory use.[26]

- **Autogun** – A synthesizer with no controls and over 4 billion patches accessible by numbers only.[27] The free version of Ogun.[11][28]

- **Boo Bass** – A monophonic bass guitar emulator.[26]

- **Buzz Generator Adaptor** – A wrapper for a large number of generators from Buzzmachines.com[29]

- **Drumaxx** – A physical modeling synthesizer designed to emulate and create the sound of percussion instruments.

- **DrumSynth Live** – Allows for percussion synthesis. Included in all Editions.[11][15][28]

- **DX10FM** – Recreates a classic FM. Included in Fruity Edition and higher.[15][28]

- **FL Slayer** – FL Slayer is an electric guitar simulator originally developed by reFX which is equipped with a high quality amp and effects tools to allow for the realistic recreation of hundreds of guitar sounds and effects boxes. It is a VSTi plugin and is included in every version of FL Studio.[30]

- **Groove Machine** a virtual drum machine

- **Harmless** – Performs subtractive synthesis using an additive synthesis engine.[28] Demo

- **Harmor** – Additive / subtractive synth with ability to encode pictures into music and resynthesis.[31] Demo

- **Morphine** – An additive synthesizer that allows voices to be mixed and morphed under user control.[28] Demo

- **Ogun** – An advanced programmable additive synthesizer chiefly for creating metallic timbres from 32000 harmonic choices. Demo

- **PoiZone** – A subtractive synthesizer with non-essential control removed for easy navigation.[28]

- **Sakura** – Sakura is a physical modeling synthesizer which is designed to emulate string instruments.[24][28]

- **Sawer** – A vintage modeling synthesizer which attempts to emulate Soviet Union era subtractive synthesizers.[28]

- **SimSynth Live** – Modeled after the classic analog synthesizers of the 1980s with three oscillators, with a programmable LFO section. Created by David Billen, Frederic Vanmol, and Didier Dambrin.[11][28]

- **SynthMaker** – FL Studio 8 Producer Edition introduced a version of SynthMaker, a popular graphical programming environment for synthesizers. It allows for the creation and sharing of new instruments without the need to understand programming code.[13][15]

- **Sytrus** – A software synthesizer. The first version was released with FL Studio version 4.5.1. The second version of Sytrus (introduced with FL Studio 6) comes with an array of presets covering many types of sounds. Sytrus uses a combination of subtractive synthesis, additive synthesis, FM synthesis, and ring modulation, allowing the production of sounds ranging from drum sets to organs. Sytrus provides a large number of adjustments and controls, including shape shifting, harmonics editing, EQ, a modulator, filters, reverb, delay, unison, and detune.[28][32]

- **Toxic Biohazard** – A virtual FM synthesizer similar to Sytrus, using FM and subtractive synthesis.[24][28]

- **TS-404** - a 2-oscillator subtractive synthesizer designed to mimic the Roland TB-303 transistor bass module.

- **WASP/WASP XT** – A 3 oscillator synthesizer created by Richard Hoffman.[11][28]

- **FL Soundfont Player** - An FL Studio add-on that gives power to load, play and render soundfonts (.sf2 files) in FL Studio.

2.11.4 Version history

2.11.5 Support

Support for the software is provided through extensive HTML help documents. Users may also register for the official Image-Line forums, which are commonly recognized as a focal point for the FL Studio community. After initially buying the software, all future updates are free for life.[4][12]

2.11.6 Notable users

- 808 Mafia[37]
- 9th Wonder[9]
- Afrojack[6]
- Aleksander Vinter (Savant)[38]
- Alex da Kid[39]
- Aone Beats[40]
- Avicii[7]
- Basshunter[41]
- Beat Bully[42]
- Benga[43]
- Boi-1da[39]
- Cardiak[44]
- Cazzette[45][46]
- DJ Mustard[47][48]
- Doughboy Beatz[49]
- Hit-Boy[39][50]
- Hopsin[51]
- Jahlil Beats[52][53]
- Kane Beatz[54]
- Kouhei Matsunaga[55]
- Lee On the Beats[56]
- Lex Luger[11]
- Madeon[57]
- Martin Garrix[58]
- Max Tannone[59]
- Metro Boomin[60]
- Mike Will Made It[47][61]
- Nic Nac[62]
- Pogo[63]
- Oliver Heldens
- SAP[64]
- Skream[65]
- Sonny Digital[66]
- Soulja Boy[67]
- Southside[37][68]
- Tom Ellard[69]
- Vinylz[70]
- Young Chop[71]
- Yung Carter[72]
- Zircon[73]

2.11.7 See also

- Comparison of multitrack recording software

2.11.8 References

[1] "FL Studio 12.01 Update".

[2] Accessed October 27, 2011.

[3] "What is FL Studio?". Image-Line. Retrieved 2011-05-28.

[4] "FL Studio Overview". Image-Line. Retrieved 2011-05-28.

[5] "FL Studio Mobile". Image-Line. Retrieved 2011-05-28.

[6] "Interview: Afrojack". *The Fresh Beat*. Retrieved 2011-05-28. I use and always used for almost 10 years now Fruity Loops, started with Fruity Loops 3, and now its FL Studio 8, its been a while. I use almost only standard Fruity compressors for effects, my main synths come out of the Arturia Juno and NI Massive / Pro 53, but also Fruity's old 3xosc, for the mastering.

[7] "Interview: Future Music with Avicii".

[8] "BOI-1DA". Tara Muldoon.

[9] "In the Studio: 9th Wonder". XLR8R. 2008-05-29. Retrieved 2010-05-12.

[10] Silva, Joe. "Review: Image-Line FL Studio 8". *Music Tech Magazine*. Retrieved 2011-05-28.

[11] "Review: Producer Lex Luger Talks About Working With Rick Ross & Waka Flocka". 2010-06-12.

[12] Template:Cite news also risky on the beat is

[13] "FL Studio 8 XXL". Quick Selling Software. March 2, 2011. Retrieved 2011-05-28.

[14] "FL Studio Creator Died in Car Accident". Future Producers forums. Retrieved 2011-05-28.

[15] "Editions". Image-Line. Retrieved 2015-04-26.

[16] "Limitations in demo version". Retrieved 2014-02-12.

[17] "FL Studio Groove App". Image-Line. Retrieved 2013-09-02.

[18] http://www.image-line.com/documents/news.php?entry_id=1429029712&title=announcing-fl-studio-12

[19] http://www.image-line.com/documents/flstudio.html

[20] http://www.image-line.com/support/FLHelp/html/basics_new.htm

[21] "History".

[22] Kirn, Peter (March 2011). "Image-Line FL Studio 9: Creative Jump-Starter Like No Other". *Keyboard Magazine*. Retrieved 2011-05-28.

[23] "Maximus". Image-Line. Retrieved 2011-05-28.

[24] "FL Studio Features". Image-Line. Retrieved 2011-05-28.

[25] "FL Studio 10: New Features". Image-Line. Retrieved 2011-05-28.

[26] http://flstudio.image-line.com/documents/generatorsandfx.html?id=3xOSC

[27] http://www.image-line.com/documents/autogun.html

[28] "Plugins". Deckadance. Retrieved 2011-05-28.

[29]

[30] "Fruity Slayer". Image-Line. Retrieved 2011-05-28.

[31] http://www.image-line.com/documents/harmor.html

[32] "Sytrus". Image-Line. Retrieved 2011-05-28.

[33] "FruityLoops Versions". *Sonic Spot*. Retrieved 2011-05-28.

[34] "Version History". Image-Line. Retrieved 2011-05-28.

[35] "FL Studio vs Fruity Loops vs a Stick?". Retrieved 17 August 2013.

[36] "FL Studio 12 beta". Retrieved 2015-03-14.

[37] David Drake (Feb 28, 2014). "What's Young Thug Like In the Studio? We Interviewed "Danny Glover" Producers 808 Mafia". Complex. Retrieved 26 July 2014.

[38] Ferry, Matt (2013-02-22). "Interview: The secrets behind enigmatic Norwegian electro producer Savant". Retrieved 2013-03-17.

[39] "9 Popular Music Producers Who Use FL Studio". Hiphopmakers. Retrieved 26 July 2014.

[40] "The Resource Magazine Vol. 4". Resource Magazine. 2013-01-27.

[41] "Basshunter Turns FruityLoops Into Gold". *http://www.seattleweekly.com/*.

[42] "Brothers Jahlil and Tone Beats Are Making Beats for the Biggest Names in the Game". Philadelphia Weekly. Retrieved 12 January 2015.

[43] "Benga in the studio with Future Music 2008". Future Music Magazine.

[44] Slava Pastuk. "Behind the Boards... With Cardiak". Noisey by Vice.

[45] Chris Barker (December 12, 2012). "Me in my studio: Cazzette". Future Music. Retrieved October 28, 2014.

[46] "Cazzette In The Studio explaining the making of One Cry". Future Music. February 7, 2014. Retrieved October 28, 2014.

[47] Matthew Schnipper, Naomi Zeichner, JORDAN SARGENT, Olivia Graham (12 December 2012). "Drum Majors: Four Producers to Watch". The Fader. Retrieved 10 March 2015.

[48] "PRODUCER WEEK: DJ Mustard, "I'll Make A Beat With My Eyes Closed" [EXCLUSIVE]". Urban Daily. Jun 11, 2014. Retrieved 10 March 2015.

[49] K Benoit (2011). *Doughboy Beatz*. Dict. ISBN 9786139881086.

[50] "Fruity Loops- From kids toy to Producer Choice". Concrete. Retrieved 26 July 2014.

[51] Justin Hunte (October 31, 2013). "Hopsin Makes a Beat in FL Studio". Hiphopmakers. Retrieved 3 May 2014.

[52] "Pardon The Introduction: Jahlil Beats Talks Getting Into Music, Working With Chris Brown, Meek Mill And Mixtape". Vibe. March 7, 2011. Retrieved 26 July 2014.

[53] Rose Lilah (March 20, 2012). "Exclusive Interview: Jahlil Beats Talks On Working With No I.D & More". Hotnewhiphop. Retrieved 26 July 2014.

[54] "Producer's Corner: Kane Beatz". HiphopDX. Retrieved 3 November 2014.

[55] "AAA: Ask Autechre Anything : Sean and Rob on WATMM". We Are the Music Makers. Retrieved 20 February 2015.

[56] "Interview: Anthony "Lee" Norris: The Man Behind The Summer Jam "Pop That" !". Bestofbothoffices.com. Retrieved 2013-11-07.

[57] Ben Rogerson (May 23, 2013). "Interview with Madeon for Computer Music Magazine". Computer Music. Retrieved October 28, 2014.

[58] "Interview: Future Music with Martin Garrix". Future Music. January 10, 2014.

[59] Beastie Mania (2009). Interview with Taco Zip, Max Tannone and DJAK47." *Beastie Mania'.'* Retrieved 2010-08-27.

[60] Agnew, Thomas (February 5, 2014). "Metro Boomin: Elevated Movements". Jenesis Magazine.

[61] ""Producers Week" Day 2: Mike Will Made It And M-Sixteen!". V-103. January 31, 2012. Retrieved 10 March 2015.

[62] "Beat Construction: "Loyal" Producer Nic Nac Talks Chris Brown, DJ Mustard, and the West Coast's Hottest Summer". The Fader. September 3, 2014. Retrieved 5 June 2015.

[63] Mar Belle (15 August 2012). "Pogo Shares His Sampling Techniques for Creating Movie Mashups". No Film School. Retrieved 17 November 2014.

[64] "Sap Da Beatman Interview". The Nerd At The Cool Table. Retrieved 2013-09-02.

[65] O'Connell, Sharon (4 October 2006). "Dubstep". *Time Out London*. Retrieved 13 June 2007.

[66] "Sonny Digital". Musicislife. April 2012. Retrieved 26 July 2014.

[67] Jake Paine (December 10, 2007). "Soulja Boy Comments On Fruity Loops Production". HiphopDX. Retrieved 18 June 2014.

[68] "Brick Squad Producer Southside Interview". Arkatechbeatz. 15 November 2010. Retrieved 26 July 2014.

[69] "Interview: Tom Keeps Severed Head Under Gail Succubus". Dec 2006. Retrieved Aug 6, 2012.

[70] "13 Things All Fruity Loops Producers Know To Be True". October 30, 2014. Retrieved February 7, 2015.

[71] Cho, Jaeki (February 7, 2013). "Interview: Young Chop Talks Lex Luger, Chief Keef, and Studio Habits". Retrieved January 6, 2015. My cousin showed me how to use the program, then I just been learning how Fruity Loops and FL Studio.

[72] "Skylatics.com interviews Carter X formerly know as Yung Carter". *Skylatics*.

[73] Andrew Aversa. "Carving Your Own Path". Retrieved 4 March 2015.

2.11.9 External links

- Official website
- Official Power Users List

2.12 Generative music

Generative music is a term popularized by Brian Eno to describe music that is ever-different and changing, and that is created by a system.

2.12.1 Theory

There are four primary perspectives on generative music (Wooller, R. et al., 2005) (reproduced with permission):

Linguistic/structural

Music composed from analytic theories that are so explicit as to be able to generate structurally coherent material (Loy and Abbott 1985; Cope 1991). This perspective has its roots in the generative grammars of language (Chomsky 1956) and music (Lerdahl and Jackendoff 1983), which generate material with a recursive tree structure.

Interactive/behavioural

Music generated by a system component that has no discernible musical inputs. That is, "not transformational" (Rowe 1991; Lippe 1997:34; Winkler 1998). The Koan software by SSEYO – used by Brian Eno to create *Generative Music 1* – is an example of this.

Creative/procedural

Music generated by processes that are designed and/or initiated by the composer. Steve Reich's *It's Gonna Rain* and Terry Riley's *In C* are examples of this (Eno 1996).

Biological/emergent

Non-deterministic music (Biles 2002), or music that cannot be repeated, for example, ordinary wind chimes (Dorin 2001). This perspective comes from the broader generative art movement. This revolves around the idea that music, or sounds may be "generated" by a musician "farming" parameters within an ecology, such that the ecology will perpetually produce different variation based on the parameters and algorithms used. An example of this technique is Joseph Nechvatal's Viral symphOny: a collaborative electronic noise music symphony[1] created between the years 2006 and 2008 using custom artificial life software based on a viral model.[2]

2.12.2 Software

Many software programs have been written to create generative music, including:

- SSEYO Koan Pro (1994–2007), used by Brian Eno to create his hybrid album *Generative Music 1*. The SSEYO Koan software was created by Pete Cole and

Tim Cole of Intermorphic, who re-acquired the Koan technology in 2008. The software was displayed in the London Science Museum's Oramics exhibition (2011-2012)

- Intermorphic's Noatikl (2007–present). Noatikl is described by Intermorphic as "The Evolution of Koan", and was launched in 2007 as a replacement for the no-longer-available Koan. Noatikl is a generative music engine that generates MIDI events in accordance with a rule set that can be manipulated in real-time through a graphical user interface. Noatikl can operate as a Hyperinstrument by responding to incoming MIDI event data, with optional extension through user-supplied Lua scripts. Noatikl is available as a standalone tool for both Mac OS X and Windows, and there are VST and AU plug-ins for desktop music sequencers. Noatikl 2 was released in May 2012. Noatikl 2 for iPhone, iPod, iPad is scheduled for release in 2013.

- Intermorphic's Mixtikl (2004–present), a portable generative music lab and loop mixing system with variants for the iPhone, iPod, iPad, Android, Mac OS X and Microsoft Windows, as well as VST and Audio Unit plug-ins for desktop music sequencers. Mixtikl includes an embedded Noatikl generative music engine and Noatikl editor, and the Partikl modular synthesizer system.

- IMPROVISOR for AudioCubes IMPROVISOR for Audiocubes, used by Mark Mosher and other electronic music composers. IMPROVISOR and Audiocubes were created by Bert Schiettecatte of Percussa.

- FractMus, developed by Gustavo Díaz-Jerez is a real-time algorithmic music generator.

- Bronze a new format for recorded music that reinterprets the piece on each listening. created by Gwilym Gold and Lexx and released on [Mac OS X] [Mac iOS]

- Tune Smithy, developed by Robert Walker, for Windows generates music real time using a musical construction similar to the Koch snowflake fractal.

- Nodal (2007–present), a graph-based generative composition system for real-time MIDI sequence generation (for Mac OS X and Windows)

- Bubble Harp developed 1997-2011 by Scott Snibbe for the iPad, iPhone, and iPod Touch.

- Bloom developed 2008 by Peter Chilvers together with Brian Eno for the iPhone and iPod Touch.

- Karlheinz Essl's sound environments fLOW (1998–2004) and SEELEWASCHEN (2004)

- Metascore (Sorensen, Brown and Hedemann 2008) supports the generative composition of music to video timing cues.

- MusiGenesis (2005), a generative music program for Windows.

- Lauri Gröhn has developed Synestesia software that generates music (midi file) from any photos in a few seconds.

- Many algorithmic music projects are also considered to be generative (see algorithmic.net for some of them).

- Modern generative music games such as *Rez* have been considered generative in character.

- Sergio Maltagliati generative music software .

- Kepler's Orrery, an interactive gravity simulator that generates music, developed in 2007 as an open-source Java project and ported to the iPhone in 2009.

- Dub Cadet, is the generative arduino based software and hardware interface for creating music through rotational motion developed by Noah Hornberger in 2012.

- 'Scape' (software) app developed by Brian Eno and Peter Chilvers for the iPod in 2012.

- Capture is a generative rock band [3] based on emergent and procedural software. Capture generate pop music, lyrics, images and videos 24/7 on the web. (see chatonsky.net for more infos).

- Loligo image-based development environment for generative music, developed 2014 by Vanja Cuk

- Generative a MaxMSP based application designed to create continually evolving soundscapes and drones, second version released in 2015 by Michael Sweeton.

- StyleMachineLite a MAX for Live application by Canadian company Metacreative, released in 2015.

2.12.3 Other notes

- Brian Eno, who coined the term *generative music*, has used generative techniques on many of his works, starting with *Discreet Music* (1975) up to and including (according to Sound on Sound Oct 2005) *Another Day on Earth*. His works, lectures, and interviews on the subject[4] have done much to promote generative music in the avant-garde music community. Eno used SSEYO's Koan generative music system (created by Pete Cole and Tim Cole of Intermorphic), to create his hybrid album *Generative Music 1* (published by SSEYO and Opal Arts in April 1996), which is probably his first public use of the term generative music.

- Lerdahl and Jackendoff's publication described a generative grammar for homophonic tonal music, based partially on a Schenkerian model. While originally intended for analysis, significant research into automation of this process in software is being carried out by Keiji Hirata and others.

- In *It's Gonna Rain*, an early work by contemporary composer Steve Reich, overlapping tape loops of the spoken phrase "it's gonna rain" are played at slightly different speeds, generating different patterns through phasing.

- A limited form of generative music was attempted successfully by members of the UK electronic music act Unit Delta Plus; Delia Derbyshire, Brian Hodgson and Peter Zinovieff, in 1968. However, its use would only be popularized later on.

2.12.4 See also

- Generative art
- Algorithmic composition
- Cellular automaton
- Change ringing
- Computer-generated music
- Interactive music
- Live coding
- List of music software
- *Musikalisches Würfelspiel*

2.12.5 Footnotes

[1] *Observatori 2008: After The Future*, p. 80

[2] Joseph Nechvatal Interview: see end for mention of *viral symphOny*

[3] Grégory Chatonsky's "Capture": generative art pushed to its limits

[4] Artscape - Brian Eno In Conversation 2009(video)

2.12.6 References

- *Artística de Valencia, After The Net*, 5 – 29 June 2008, Valencia, Spain: catalogue: *Observatori 2008: After The Future*, p. 80

- Biles, A. 2002a. GenJam in Transition: from Genetic Jammer to Generative Jammer. In International Conference on Generative Art, Milan, Italy.

- Chomsky, N. 1956. Three models for the description of language. IRE Transcripts on Information Theory, 2: 113-124.

- Collins, N. 2008. The analysis of generative music programs. Organised Sound, 13(3): 237–248.

- Cope, D. 1991. Computers and musical style. Madison, Wis.: A-R Editions.

- Dorin, A. 2001. Generative processes and the electronic arts. Organised Sound, 6 (1): 47-53.

- Eno, B. 1996. Generative Music. http://www.inmotionmagazine.com/eno1.html (accessed 26 February 2009).

- Essl, K. 2002. Generative Music. http://www.essl.at/bibliogr/generative-music.html (accessed 22 Mar 2010).

- García, A. et al. 2010. Music Composition Based on Linguistic Approach. 9th Mexican International Conference on Artificial Intelligence, MICAI 2010, Pachuca, Mexico. pp. 117–128.

- Intermorphic Limited History of Noatikl, Koan and SSEYO (accessed 26 February 2009).

- Lerdahl, F. and R. Jackendoff. 1982. A generative theory of tonal music. Cambridge, Mass: MIT Press.

- Lippe, C. 1997. Music for piano and computer: A description. Information Processing Society of Japa SIG Notes, 97 (122): 33-38.

- Loy, G. and C. Abbott. 1985. Programming languages for computer music synthesis, performance and composition. ACM Computing Surveys, 17 (2): 235-265.

- Nierhaus, G. Algorithmic Composition - Paradigms of Automated Music Generation. Springer 2009.

- Rowe, R. 1991. Machine Learning and Composing: Making Sense of Music with Cooperating Real-Time Agents. Thesis from Media Lab. Mass.: MIT.

- Viral symphOny is downloadable for free at www.archive.org

- Winkler, T. 1998. Composing Interactive Music. Cambridge, Massachusetts: MIT Press.

- Wooller, R., Brown, A. R, et al. A framework for comparing algorithmic music systems. In: Symposium on Generative Arts Practice (GAP). 2005. University of Technology Sydney.

2.13 Jeskola Buzz

Jeskola Buzz is a freeware modular software music studio environment designed to run on Microsoft Windows via Microsoft .NET. It is centered on a modular plugin-based machine view and a multiple pattern sequencer tracker.[1]

Buzz consists of a plugin architecture that allows the audio to be routed from one plugin to another in many ways, similar to how cables carry an audio signal between physical pieces of hardware. All aspects of signal synthesis and manipulation are handled entirely by the plugin system. Signal synthesis is performed by "generators" such as synthesizers, noise generator functions, samplers, and trackers. The signal can then be manipulated further by "effects" such as distortions, filters, delays, and mastering plugins. Buzz also provides support through adapters to use VST/VSTi, DirectX/DXi, and DirectX Media Objects as generators and effects.

A few new classes of plugins do not fall under the normal generator and effect types. These include peer machines (signal and event automated controllers), recorders, wavetable editors, scripting engines, etc. Buzz signal output also uses a plugin system; the most practical drivers include ASIO, DirectSound, and MME. Buzz supports MIDI both internally and through several enhancements. Some midi features are limited or hacked together such as MIDI clock sync.

2.13.1 Development

Buzz was created by Oskari Tammelin who named the software after his demogroup, Jeskola.

In 1997-98 Buzz was a "3rd Generation Tracker" and has since evolved beyond the traditional tracker model.

The development of the core program, buzz.exe, was halted on October 5, 2000, when the developer lost the source code to the program. It was announced in June 2008 that development would begin again, eventually regaining much of the functionality.[2]

2.13.2 Plugin system

Buzz's plugin system is intended to operate according to a free software model. The header files used to compile new plugins (known as the Buzzlib) contain a small notice that they are only to be used for making freeware plugins and Buzz file music players. The restriction requires that developers who wish to use the Buzz plugin system in their own sequencers pay a fee to the author.[3]

2.13.3 Notable users

Some notable electronic musicians who use Jeskola Buzz include:

- Andrew Sega[4]
- Hunz
- Andreas Tilliander[5]
- James Holden, whose early work was produced entirely within Buzz.[6][7]
- Lackluster
- Oliver Lieb
- The Field[8]

2.13.4 See also

- Buzztrax is an effort to recreate a Buzz-like environment under a free software license which runs under Linux.
- Visual programming language

2.13.5 References

[1] Future Music magazine, June 2000, p100. http://aijai.net/~{}apo/buzz/Buzz-FM.jpg

[2] http://www.buzzchurch.com/viewtopic.php?t=2280

[3] http://www.activemusician.com/Fruityloops-3-3-Adds-ASIO-and-BUZZ-Support--t101i5545

[4] Andrew Sega (2007-04-27). "Taking Tracking Mainstream Part 5" (video). notacon.org. Retrieved 2012-10-21.

[5] "BUZZ/SAW : Mokira in Miami". 2002-07-18. Archived from the original on 2009-03-26. Retrieved 2011-01-21.

[6] Napora, Lukasz (2003-08-22). "James Holden Interview". Archived from the original on 2009-04-04. Retrieved 2012-01-21.

[7] "James Holden". beatfactor.net. Archived from the original on 2011-07-23. Retrieved 2012-05-05. *The stuff everyone is really interested in begins aged 19, with a track called "Horizons". Written during his summer holidays from his maths degree at Oxford University on a £500 PC and a piece of revolutionary music software called Buzz (a freeware internet download), this crossover anthem of the summer of 1999 propelled young James and his bedroom set-up into the top flight of dance music production.*

[8] Day, David (2007-04-16). "The Field". pitchfork.com. Retrieved 2012-10-21.

2.13.6 External links

- BuzzMachines.com - The central buzz website for the last couple of years, since Oskari's own web site ceased to host Buzz distributions anymore. Several distributions of Buzz which include the core and selected plugins are distributed through this website.

- Jeskola Buzz Latest beta versions of Buzz

- Andrew Sega: Taking Tracking Mainstream Part 1, Part 2, Part 3, Part 4, Part 5 Tracking history with Buzz presentation, Notacon conference, April 27, 2007

2.14 Max (software)

Max is a visual programming language for music and multimedia developed and maintained by San Francisco-based software company Cycling '74. During its 20-year history, it has been used by composers, performers, software designers, researchers, and artists to create recordings, performances, and installations.

The Max program is modular. Most routines exist as shared libraries. An application programming interface (API) allows third-party development of new routines (named *external objects*). Thus, Max has a large user base of programmers unaffiliated with Cycling '74 who enhance the software with commercial and non-commercial extensions to the program. Because of its extensible design and graphical user interface (GUI), which represents the program structure and the user interface as presented to the user simultaneously, Max has been described as the lingua franca for developing interactive music performance software.[1]

2.14.1 History

Miller Puckette originally wrote Max at IRCAM in the mid-1980s, as the *Patcher* editor for the Macintosh to provide composers with an authoring system for interactive computer music. It was first used by Philippe Manoury in 1988 to write a piano and computer piece named *Pluton*, which synchronized a computer to a piano and controlled a Sogitec 4X for audio processing.[2]

In 1989, IRCAM developed and maintained a concurrent version of Max ported to the IRCAM Signal Processing Workstation (ISPW) for the NeXT, and later Silicon Graphics (SGI) and Linux, named Max *Faster Than Sound* (Max/FTS), and being analogous to a forerunner to MSP enhanced by a hardware digital signal processor (DSP) board on the computer.[3][4]

In 1989, IRCAM licensed it to Opcode Systems, which sold a commercial version in 1990 named Max (developed and extended by David Zicarelli). As the software was never a perfect fit for Opcode Systems, the firm ceased actively developing it in the mid-90s. The current commercial version of Max has since been distributed by Zicarelli's company, Cycling '74 (founded in 1997[5]), since 1999.[6]

Various synthesizers and instruments connected to Max.

Puckette released a fully redesigned free software computer program in 1996 named *Pure Data* (Pd), which, despite several fundamental differences from the IRCAM original, is superficially very similar and remains an open-source alternative to Max/MSP.

Max has several extensions and incarnations; most notably, a set of audio extensions to the software appeared in 1997, derived partly from Puckette's subsequent work in Pure Data. Named *Max Signal Processing* (MSP), or for the initials of Miller S. Puckette, this add-on package for Max allowed manipulatingng digital audio signals in real-time, allowing users to create their own synthesizers and effects processors (Max had formerly been designed to interface with hardware synthesizers, samplers, etc. as a control language using Musical Instrument Device Interface (MIDI) or some other protocol).

In 1998, a direct descendant of Max/FTS was developed in

Java (jMax) and released as open-source.

In 1999, Netochka Nezvanova released nato.0+55, a suite of externals that added extensive real time video control to Max. Though nato became increasingly popular among multimedia artists, its development stopped in 2001. Canadian media artist David Rokeby developed SoftVNS, a third-party package for visual processing in Max, and released it in 2002.

In the meantime, Cycling '74 developed their own set of video extensions. They released a major package for Max/MSP named *Jitter* in 2003, which provides real-time video, 3-D, and matrix processing ability.

In addition, several Max-like programs share the same concept of visual programming in real time, such as Quartz Composer (by Apple) and vvvv, which both focus on realtime video synthesis and processing. Pure Data also remains widely used.

A major update to Max/MSP/Jitter, Max 5, was released in 2008. It included a revamped user interface and new objects.

In November 2011, Cycling '74 released Max 6, a major overhaul with further improvements to the user interface and a new audio engine compatible with 64-bit operating systems. Gen, an add-on for patching and code compiling [7] was also released.

In November 2014, Cycling '74 released Max 7, an update that featured an optimized interface, higher performance, and new tools for organizing files and tutorials.[8]

2.14.2 Language

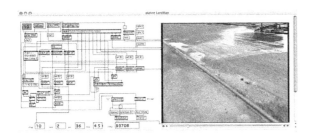

Screenshot of an older Max/Msp interface.

Max is named after the late Max Mathews, and can be considered a descendant of MUSIC, though its graphical nature disguises that fact. As with most MUSIC-N languages, Max/MSP/Jitter distinguishes between two levels of time: that of an *event* scheduler, and that of the DSP (this corresponds to the distinction between k-rate and a-rate processes in Csound, and control rate vs. audio rate in SuperCollider).

The basic language of Max and its sibling programs is that of a data-flow system: Max programs (named *patches*) are made by arranging and connecting building-blocks of *objects* within a *patcher*, or visual canvas. These objects act as self-contained programs (in reality, they are dynamically-linked libraries), each of which may receive input (through one or more visual *inlets*), generate output (through visual *outlets*), or both. Objects pass messages from their outlets to the inlets of connected objects.

Max supports six basic atomic data types that can be transmitted as messages from object to object: int, float, list, symbol, bang, and signal (for MSP audio connections). Several more complex data structures exist within the program for handling numeric arrays (*table* data), hash tables (*coll* data), and XML information (*pattr* data). An MSP data structure (*buffer~*) can hold digital audio information within program memory. In addition, the Jitter package adds a scalable, multi-dimensional data structure for handling large sets of numbers for storing video and other datasets (*matrix* data).

Max is typically learned through acquiring a vocabulary of objects and how they function within a patcher; for example, the *metro* object functions as a simple metronome, and the *random* object generates random integers. Most objects are non-graphical, consisting only of an object's name and several arguments-attributes (in essence class properties) typed into an *object box*. Other objects are graphical, including sliders, number boxes, dials, table editors, pull-down menus, buttons, and other objects for running the program interactively. Max/MSP/Jitter comes with about 600 of these objects as the standard package; extensions to the program can be written by third-party developers as Max patchers (e.g. by encapsulating some of the functionality of a patcher into a sub-program that is itself a Max patch), or as objects written in C, C++, Java, or JavaScript.

The order of execution for messages traversing through the graph of objects is defined by the visual organization of the objects in the patcher itself. As a result of this organizing principle, Max is unusual in that the program logic and the interface as presented to the user are typically related, though newer versions of Max provide several technologies for more standard GUI design.

Max documents (named patchers) can be bundled into stand-alone applications and distributed free or sold commercially. In addition, Max can be used to author audio plugin software for major audio production systems.

With the increased integration of laptop computers into live music performance (in electronic music and elsewhere), Max/MSP and Max/Jitter have received attention as a development environment available to those serious about laptop music/video performance.

2.14.3 See also

- Pure Data
- Comparison of audio synthesis environments
- List of music software

2.14.4 References

[1] Place, T. and Lossius, T.: Jamoma: A modular standard for structuring patches in Max. In Proc. of the International Computer Music Conference 2006, pages 143–146, New Orleans, US, 2006.

[2] Miller S. Puckette. "Pd Repertory Project - History of *Pluton*". CRCA. Archived from the original on 2004-07-07. Retrieved March 3, 2012.

[3] "A brief history of MAX". IRCAM. Archived from the original on 2009-06-03.

[4] "Max/MSP History - Where did Max/MSP come from?". Cycling74. Archived from the original on 2009-06-09. Retrieved March 3, 2012.

[5] About Us. Cycling74.com. Retrieved March 3, 2012.

[6] "FAQ Max4". Cycling74.com. Retrieved March 3, 2012.

[7] "GEN - Extend the power of Max". Cycling74.com.

[8] Cycling '74 (2014). "Max 7 is Patching Reimagined." https://cycling74.com/max7/

2.14.5 External links

Official website

- lloopp a ready to use modular and experimental software built in Max/MSP/Jitter
- Lobjects, a set of external objects developed by Peter Elsea
- RTC-lib Software library for algorithmic composition in Max/MSP/Jitter
- List of powerful librairies References & links of a bunch of libraries & externals
- Max Javascript Reference – complete Javascript Reference for Max/MSP/Jitter
- Klankwereld Software, tutorials and resources to learn Max/MSP/Jitter.
- Percussa AudioCubes is an electronic musical instrument that allows you to create your own Max/Msp patches using an OSC server and flext external

- Ligeti's Artikulate was created fully with Max/MSP/Jitter.

2.15 Microsound

Microsound includes all sounds on the time scale shorter than musical notes, the sound object time scale, and longer than the sample time scale. Specifically this is shorter than one tenth of a second and longer than 10 milliseconds, including the audio frequency range (20 Hz to 20 kHz) and the infrasonic frequency range (below 20 Hz, rhythm).[1]

These sounds include transient audio phenomena and are known in acoustics and signal processing by various names including sound particles, quantum acoustics, sonal atom, grain, glisson, grainlet, trainlet, microarc, wavelet, chirplet, FOF, time-frequency atom, pulsar, impulse, toneburst, tone pip, acoustic pixel, and others. In the frequency domain they may be named kernel, logon, and frame, among others.[1]

Physicist Dennis Gabor was an important pioneer in microsound.[1] Micromontage is musical montage with microsound.

Microtime is the level of "sonic" or aural "syntax" or the "time-varying distribution of...spectral energy.".[2]

2.15.1 See also

- Glitch (music)
- Granular synthesis
- Lowercase (music)
- Microtonality
- Microsound.org (mailing list focused on the Microsound aesthetic)

2.15.2 References

[1] Roads, Curtis (2001). *Microsound*, p.vii and 20-28. Cambridge: MIT Press. ISBN 0-262-18215-7.

[2] Horacio Vaggione, "Articulating Microtime", *Computer Music Journal*, Vol. 20, No. 2. (Summer, 1996), pp. 33–38.

2.15.3 Sources

- Horacio Vaggione. "Articulating Microtime", *Computer Music Journal* (MIT Press), Vol. 20, No. 2. (Summer, 1996), pp. 33–38. Stable URL: http:

//links.jstor.org/sici?sici=0148-9267%28199622%
2920%3A2%3C33%3AAM%3E2.0.CO%3B2-0
(Subscription necessary for full access)

2.16 Music software

Music software is the internal programming of computers that supports musical production. Music software has been around for nearly 40 years.[1] It has been seen to have profound impacts on education involving music and creative expression. Musical software has become an outlet for people who do not bond with traditional musical instruments, giving people new and creative ways to compose and perform music in ways that has never been seen before.[2]

2.16.1 History

Music software development dates back to the 1960s and 70s.[1] While this software was at best primitive, it nonetheless helped lay the foundation for the future development of the software and synthetic musical production. The early music software was run on large computers at several universities such as Stanford and Penn State.[1] Much of what development came to music software came as a result of the continuous improvement to computers over time.[1] Chain of development is seen clearly in 1978 when nearly 50 music programs came out as a result of MIDI technology, a form of computer communication still used today.[1] MIDI technology provided the key link in hardware for musical software, giving a person a tactile control of an instrument and playing directly into the software in the computer and allowing for maximum control of the production.[1] Fourth generation music software came out in the early 1990s. The largest improvement with this software was the addition of more detailed displays allowing the music software to show more on the screen making the program much easier to use and understand.[1] An important recent development is to automatically transcribe performed music directly to sheet music as developed by ScoreCloud.[3]

2.16.2 Effects

The effects of music software are seen in almost every song heard today in one way or another.[1] More than ever before, songs are being recorded into DAWs (digital audio workstations) because of their ease of use and their ability to easily manipulate audio files. Much of what used to take a team of professionals to do in a recording studio can now be done on a single computer.[1]

2.16.3 Humans/education

Music software has led to new ways of education in relation to music.[2] New and emerging science and studies are proving that music software is an effective way in making students more creative at a younger age by providing them with all of the instruments they could ever want within one, streamlined music program.[2] With live loop and sample playing DAWS that can play multiple samples of audio or midi files live with a controller triggering these samples, a new breed of instruments are available to students, allowing them to express themselves in ways never before seen.[2]

Various schools and colleges have emerged with courses in Music Production and more so in electronic music production. Every Continent has at-least one such notable institute with The North American and European continents leading the way forward. Among the most popular among the youth are, in no specific order:

- Berklee -USA
- dBs Music - UK
- Full Sail University - USA
- Point Blank Music College - UK
- Dubspot - USA
- London School of Sound - UK
- Garnish Music Production Courses -UK
- DBS Music - Germany
- ILM Academy - India
- Alchemea College - UK
- SAE -Australia

2.16.4 The future

Computers have now been made that can improvise music scores on their own, using complex algorithms.[4] While functioning on a mathematical algorithm, it is nevertheless producing notes of its own without human instruction. Educators are beginning to recognize that computers hold the future of music.[2] The software being developed for these machines will take music to new and startling heights with the help of computer-based production.[1]

2.16.5 See Also

- List of music software

2.16.6 References

[1] Peters, David (November 1992). "Music Software and Emerging Technology.". *Music Educators Journal*. No. 3 79: 22–63.

[2] Nikolaidou, Georgia (22 Feb 2010). "A New Insight In Pupils' Collaborative Talk, Actions and Balance During a Computer-Mediated Music Task.". *Computers and Education*: 720–740.

[3] Glass, Nick. "Is this Google Translate for Music". *CNN.com*.

[4] Brown, Oliver (29 Aug 2009). "Experiments in Modular Design for the Creative Composition of Live Algorithms.". *Centre for Electronic Media Art*.

2.16.7 External links

- Example of music composing software
- Glass, Nick. "Is this Google Translate for Music". *CNN International*.

2.17 Noise music

"Noise (music)" redirects here. For the general occurrence of noise in music, see noise in music.

Noise music is a category of music that is characterised by the expressive use of noise within a musical context. This type of music tends to challenge the distinction that is made in conventional musical practices between musical and non-musical sound.[1] Noise music includes a wide range of musical styles and sound-based creative practices that feature noise as a primary aspect. It can feature acoustically or electronically generated noise, and both traditional and unconventional musical instruments. It may incorporate live machine sounds, non-musical vocal techniques, physically manipulated audio media, processed sound recordings, field recording, computer-generated noise, stochastic process, and other randomly produced electronic signals such as distortion, feedback, static, hiss and hum. There may also be emphasis on high volume levels and lengthy, continuous pieces. More generally noise music may contain aspects such as improvisation, extended technique, cacophony and indeterminacy, and in many instances conventional use of melody, harmony, rhythm and pulse is dispensed with.[2][3][4][5]

The Futurist art movement was important for the development of the noise aesthetic, as was the Dada art movement (a prime example being the *Antisymphony* concert performed on April 30, 1919 in Berlin),[6][7] and later the Surrealist and Fluxus art movements, specifically the Fluxus artists Joe Jones, Yasunao Tone, George Brecht, Robert Watts, Wolf Vostell, Dieter Roth, Yoko Ono, Nam June Paik, Walter De Maria's *Ocean Music*, Milan Knížák's *Broken Music Composition*, early LaMonte Young and Takehisa Kosugi.[8]

Contemporary noise music is often associated with extreme volume and distortion.[9] In the domain of experimental rock, examples include Jimi Hendrix's use of feedback,[10] Lou Reed's *Metal Machine Music*, and Sonic Youth.[11] Other examples of music that contain noise-based features include works by Iannis Xenakis, Karlheinz Stockhausen, Helmut Lachenmann, Cornelius Cardew, Theatre of Eternal Music, Glenn Branca, Rhys Chatham, Ryoji Ikeda, Survival Research Laboratories, Whitehouse, Brighter Death Now, Merzbow, Cabaret Voltaire, Psychic TV, Blackhouse, Jean Tinguely's recordings of his sound sculpture (specifically *Bascule VII*), the music of Hermann Nitsch's *Orgien Mysterien Theater*, and La Monte Young's bowed gong works from the late 1960s.[12] Genres such as industrial, industrial techno, lo-fi music, black metal, sludge metal, and glitch music employ noise-based materials.[13][14]

2.17.1 Development

The Art of Noises

Luigi Russolo, a Futurist artist of the very early 20th century, was perhaps the first noise artist.[15][16] His 1913 manifesto, *L'Arte dei Rumori*, translated as *The Art of Noises*, stated that the industrial revolution had given modern men a greater capacity to appreciate more complex sounds. Russolo found traditional melodic music confining and envisioned noise music as its future replacement. He designed and constructed a number of noise-generating devices called *intonarumori* and assembled a noise orchestra to perform with them. Works entitled *Risveglio di una città* (Awakening of a City) and *Convegno d'aeroplani e d'automobili* (The Meeting of Aeroplanes and Automobiles) were both performed for the first time in 1914.[17]

A performance of his *Gran Concerto Futuristico* (1917) was met with strong disapproval and violence from the audience, as Russolo himself had predicted. None of his intoning devices have survived, though recently some have been reconstructed and used in performances. Although Russolo's works bear little resemblance to contemporary noise music such as Japanoise his efforts helped to introduce noise as a musical aesthetic and broaden the perception of sound as an artistic medium.[18][19]

> At first the art of music sought purity, limpidity and sweetness of sound. Then different

Luigi Russolo ca. 1916

sounds were amalgamated, care being taken, however, to caress the ear with gentle harmonies. Today music, as it becomes continually more complicated, strives to amalgamate the most dissonant, strange and harsh sounds. In this way we come ever closer to *noise-sound*.
— Luigi Russolo *The Art of Noises* (1913)[20]

Antonio Russolo, Luigi's brother and fellow Italian Futurist composer, produced a recording of two works featuring the original *intonarumori*. The 1921 made phonograph with works entitled *Corale* and *Serenata*, combined conventional orchestral music set against the famous noise machines and is the only surviving sound recording.[21]

An early Dada-related work from 1916 by Marcel Duchamp also worked with noise, but in an almost silent way. One of the found object Readymades of Marcel Duchamp, *A Bruit Secret* (With Hidden Noise), was a collaborative work that created a noise instrument that Duchamp accomplished with Walter Arensberg.[22] What rattles inside when *A Bruit Secret* is shaken remains a mystery.[23]

Found sound

In the same period the utilisation of found sound as a musical resource was starting to be explored. An early example is *Parade*, a performance produced at the Chatelet Theatre, Paris, on May 18, 1917, that was conceived by Jean Cocteau, with design by Pablo Picasso, choreography by Leonid Massine, and music by Eric Satie. The extra-musical materials used in the production were referred to as *trompe l'oreille* sounds by Cocteau and included a dynamo, Morse code machine, sirens, steam engine, airplane motor, and typewriters.[24] Arseny Avraamov's composition *Symphony of Factory Sirens* involved navy ship sirens and whistles, bus and car horns, factory sirens, cannons, foghorns, artillery guns, machine guns, hydro-airplanes, a specially designed steam-whistle machine creating noisy renderings of *Internationale* and *Marseillaise* for a piece conducted by a team using flags and pistols when performed in the city of Baku in 1922.[25] In 1923, Arthur Honegger created *Pacific 231*, a modernist musical composition that imitates the sound of a steam locomotive.[26] Another example is Ottorino Respighi's 1924 orchestral piece *Pines of Rome*, which included the phonographic playback of a nightingale recording.[24] Also in 1924, George Antheil created a work titled Ballet Mécanique with instrumentation that included 16 pianos, 3 airplane propellers, and 7 electric bells. The work was originally conceived as music for the Dada film of the same name, by Dudley Murphy and Fernand Léger, but in 1926 it premiered independently as a concert piece.[27][28]

In 1930 Paul Hindemith and Ernst Toch recycled records to create sound montages and in 1936 Edgard Varèse experimented with records, playing them backwards, and at varying speeds.[29] Varese had earlier used sirens to create what he called a "continuous flowing curve" of sound that he could not achieve with acoustic instruments. In 1931, Varese's *Ionisation* for 13 players featured 2 sirens, a lion's roar, and used 37 percussion instruments to create a repertoire of unpitched sounds making it the first musical work to be organized solely on the basis of noise.[30][31] In remarking on Varese's contributions the American composer John Cage stated that Varese had "established the present nature of music" and that he had "moved into the field of sound itself while others were still discriminating 'musical tones' from noises".[32]

In an essay written in 1937, Cage expressed an interest in using extra-musical materials[33] and came to distinguish between found sounds, which he called noise, and musical sounds, examples of which included: rain, static between radio channels, and "a truck at fifty miles per hour". Essentially, Cage made no distinction, in his view all sounds have the potential to be used creatively. His aim was to capture and control elements of the sonic environment and employ a method of sound organisation, a term borrowed from Varese, to bring meaning to the sound materials.[34] Cage began in 1939 to create a series of works that explored his stated aims, the first being *Imaginary Landscape #1* for instruments including two variable speed turntables with frequency recordings.[35]

In 1961, James Tenney composed *Analogue #1: Noise Study* (for tape) using computer synthesized noise and *Collage No.1 (Blue Suede)* (for tape) by sampling and manipulating a famous Elvis Presley recording.[36]

Experimental music

George Maciunas performing George Brecht's Drip Music *at the Amsterdam Fluxfest, 1963*

> I believe that the use of noise to make music will continue and increase until we reach a music produced through the aid of electrical instruments which will make available for musical purposes any and all sounds that can be heard.
> — John Cage *The Future of Music: Credo* (1937)

In 1932, Bauhaus artists László Moholy-Nagy, Oskar Fischinger and Paul Arma experimented with modifying the physical contents of record grooves.[36]

Under the influence of Henry Cowell in San Francisco in the late 1940s,[37] Lou Harrison and John Cage began composing music for *junk* (waste) percussion ensembles, scouring junkyards and Chinatown antique shops for appropriately tuned brake drums, flower pots, gongs, and more.

In Europe, during the late 1940s, Pierre Schaeffer coined the term *musique concrète* to refer to the peculiar nature of sounds on tape, separated from the source that generated them initially.[38] Pierre Schaeffer helped form Studio d'Essai de la Radiodiffusion-Télévision Française in France during World War II. Initially serving the French Resistance, Studio d'Essai became a hub for musical development centered around implementing electronic devices in compositions. It was from this group that musique concrète was developed. A type of electroacoustic music, musique concrète is characterized by its use of recorded sound, electronics, tape, animate and inanimate sound sources, and various manipulation techniques. The first of Schaeffer's *Cinq études de bruits*, or *Five Noise Etudes*, consisted of transformed locomotive sounds.[39] The last étude, *Étude pathétique*, makes use of sounds recorded from sauce pans and canal boats.

Following musique concrète, other modernist art music composers such as Richard Maxfield, Karlheinz Stockhausen, Gottfried Michael Koenig, Pierre Henry, Iannis Xenakis, La Monte Young, and David Tudor, composed significant electronic, vocal, and instrumental works, sometimes using found sounds.[36] In late 1947, Antonin Artaud recorded *Pour en Finir avec le Jugement de dieu* (*To Have Done with the Judgment of God*), an audio piece full of the seemingly random cacophony of xylophonic sounds mixed with various percussive elements, mixed with the noise of alarming human cries, screams, grunts, onomatopoeia, and glossolalia.[40][41] In 1949, Nouveau Réalisme artist Yves Klein wrote *The Monotone Symphony* (formally *The Monotone-Silence Symphony*, conceived 1947–1948), a 40-minute orchestral piece that consisted of a single 20-minute sustained chord (followed by a 20-minute silence)[42] — showing how the sound of one drone could make music. Also in 1949, Pierre Boulez befriended John Cage, who was visiting Paris to do research on the music of Erik Satie. John Cage had been pushing music in even more startling directions during the war years, writing for prepared piano, junkyard percussion, and electronic gadgetry.[43]

In 1951, Cage's *Imaginary Landscape #4*, a work for twelve radio receivers, was premiered in New York. Performance of the composition necessitated the use of a score that contained indications for various wavelengths, durations, and dynamic levels, all of which had been determined using chance operations.[44][45] A year later in 1952, Cage applied his aleatoric methods to tape-based composition. Also in 1952, Karlheinz Stockhausen completed a modest musique concrète student piece entitled *Etude*. Cage's work resulted in his famous work *Williams Mix*, which was made up of some six hundred tape fragments arranged according to the demands of the *I Ching*. Cage's early radical phase reached its height that summer of 1952, when he unveiled the first art "happening" at Black Mountain College, and *4'33"*, the so-called controversial "silent piece". The premiere of *4'33"* was performed by David Tudor. The audience saw him sit at the piano, and close the lid of the piano. Some time later, without having played any notes, he opened the lid. A while after that, again having played nothing, he closed the lid. And after a period of time, he opened the lid once more and rose from the piano. The piece had passed without a note being played, in fact without Tudor or anyone else on stage having made any deliberate sound, although he timed the lengths on a stopwatch while turning the pages of the score. Only then could the audience recognize what Cage insisted upon: that there is no such thing as silence. Noise is always happening that makes musical sound.[46] In 1957, Edgard Varèse created on tape an extended piece of electronic music using noises created by scraping, thumping and blowing titled *Poème électronique*.[47][48]

In 1960, John Cage completed his noise composition *Cartridge Music* for phono cartridges with foreign objects replacing the 'stylus' and small sounds amplified contact microphones. Also in 1960, Nam June Paik composed *Fluxusobjekt* for fixed tape and hand-controlled tape playback head.[36] On May 8, 1960, six young Japanese musicians, including Takehisa Kosugi and Yasunao Tone, formed the Group Ongaku with two tape recordings of noise music: *Automatism* and *Object*. These recordings made use of a mixture of traditional musical instruments along with a vacuum cleaner, a radio, an oil drum, a doll, and a set of dishes. Moreover, the speed of the tape recording was manipulated, further distorting the sounds being recorded.[49] Canada's Nihilist Spasm Band, the world's longest-running noise act, was formed in 1965 in London, Ontario and continues to perform and record to this day, having survived to work with many of the newer generation which they themselves had influenced, such as Thurston Moore of Sonic Youth and Jojo Hiroshige of Hijokaidan. In 1967, Musica Elettronica Viva, a live acoustic/electronic improvisational group formed in Rome, made a recording titled *SpaceCraft*[50] using contact microphones on such "non-musical" objects as panes of glass and motor oil cans that was recorded at the Akademie der Kunste in Berlin.[51] At the end of the sixties, they took part in the collective noise action called *Lo Zoo* initiated by the artist Michelangelo Pistoletto.

The art critic Rosalind Krauss argued that by 1968 artists such as Robert Morris, Robert Smithson, and Richard Serra had "entered a situation the logical conditions of which can no longer be described as modernist."[52] Sound art found itself in the same condition, but with an added emphasis on distribution.[53] Antiform process art became the terms used to describe this postmodern post-industrial culture and the process by which it is made.[54] Serious art music responded to this conjuncture in terms of intense noise, for example the La Monte Young Fluxus composition *89 VI 8 C. 1:42–1:52 AM Paris Encore* from *Poem For Chairs, Tables, Benches, Etc.* Young's composition *Two Sounds* (1960) was composed for amplified percussion and window panes and his *Poem for Tables, Chairs and Benches* (1960) used the sounds of furniture scraping across the floor.

Popular music

Recorded noise in popular music can be heard as early as in the work of Spike Jones, who in the 1930s performed and released recordings that used buckets, cans, train whistles, neighing, croaking, and chirping sounds.[55] Later in rock music, the 1964 song "Walking in the Rain", performed by The Ronettes and produced by Phil Spector contained sound effects of thunder and lightning, which earned engineer Larry Levine a Grammy nomination.[56] In 1966, *Pet Sounds* by the American rock band The Beach Boys featured arrangements that included unconventional instruments such as bicycle bells, dog whistles, Coca-Cola cans and barking dogs, along with the more usual keyboards and guitars. The album closes with a sampled recording of passing trains.[57][58][59] *Freak Out!*, the debut album by The Mothers of Invention made use of avant-garde sound collage—sparticularly the 1966 track *The Return of the Son of Monster Magnet*. The same year, art rock group The Velvet Underground made their first recording while produced by Andy Warhol, a track entitled "Noise".[60]

"Tomorrow Never Knows" is the final track of The Beatles' 1966 studio album *Revolver*; credited as a Lennon–McCartney song, it was written primarily by John Lennon with major contributions to the arrangement by Paul McCartney. The track included looped tape effects. For the track, McCartney supplied a bag of $\frac{1}{4}$-inch audio tape loops he had made at home after listening to Stockhausen's *Gesang der Jünglinge*. By disabling the erase head of a tape recorder and then spooling a continuous loop of tape through the machine while recording, the tape would constantly overdub itself, creating a saturation effect, a technique also used in musique concrète. The tape could also be induced to go faster and slower. McCartney encouraged the other Beatles to use the same effects and create their own loops.[61] After experimentation on their own, the various Beatles supplied a total of "30 or so" tape loops to George Martin, who selected 16 for use on the song.[62] Each loop was about six seconds long.[62] The tape loops were played on BTR3 tape machines located in various studios of the Abbey Road building[63] and controlled by EMI technicians in studio two at Abbey Road.[64][65] Each machine was monitored by one technician, who had to keep a pencil within each loop to maintain tension.[62] The four Beatles controlled the faders of the mixing console while Martin varied the stereo panning and Geoff Emerick watched the meters.[66][67] Eight of the tapes were used at one time, changed halfway through the song.[66] The tapes were made (like most of the other loops) by superimposition and acceleration (0:07).[68][69] According to Martin, the finished mix of the tape loops cannot be repeated because of the complex and random way in which they were laid over the music.[70]

The Beatles would continue these efforts with "Revolution

9", a track produced in 1968 for *The White Album*. It made sole use of sound collage, credited to Lennon–McCartney, but created primarily by John Lennon with assistance from George Harrison and Yoko Ono. As Lennon described it, "Revolution 9" was made with the cut-up technique, cutting classical music tapes into about thirty loops (some played backwards). These loops were fed onto one master track.[71] The composition style is similar to the avant-garde Fluxus style of Ono as well as the musique concrète works of composers such as Pierre Schaeffer and Pierre Henry. Lennon followed up this experiment with even more explicit noise music recordings, the first being *Unfinished Music No.1: Two Virgins*, an avant-garde recording by John Lennon and Yoko Ono from 1968 consisting of repeating tape loops as Lennon plays different instruments such as piano, organ, and drums with sound effects (including reverb, delay and distortion), changes tapes and plays other recordings, and converses with Ono, who vocalises ad-lib in response to the sounds.[72] They followed this recording with another noise recording in 1969 entitled *Unfinished Music No.2: Life with the Lions*. Beatles member George Harrison also released a noise/musique concrète recording in 1969, titled *Electronic Sound*.

In 1975, Ned Lagin released an album of electronic noise music full of spacey rumblings and atmospherics filled with burps and bleeps entitled *Seastones* on Round Records.[73] The album was recorded in stereo quadraphonic sound and featured guest performances by members of the Grateful Dead, including Jerry Garcia playing treated guitar and Phil Lesh playing electronic Alembic bass.[74] David Crosby, Grace Slick and other members of the Jefferson Airplane also appear on the album.[75]

2.17.2 Postmodern developments: Noise as genre

Noise rock and No Wave music

Main articles: Noise rock and No Wave
Lou Reed's double LP *Metal Machine Music* (1975) is cited as containing the primary characteristics of what would in time become a genre known as noise music.[76] The album is an early, well-known example of commercial studio noise music[77] that the music critic Lester Bangs has sarcastically called the "greatest album ever made in the history of the human eardrum".[78] It has also been cited as one of the "worst albums of all time".[79] Reed was well aware of the drone music of La Monte Young.[80][81] Young's Theatre of Eternal Music was a minimal music noise group in the mid-60s with John Cale, Marian Zazeela, Henry Flynt, Angus Maclise, Tony Conrad, and others.[82] The Theatre of Eternal Music's discordant sustained notes and loud amplification had influenced Cale's subsequent contribution to The

Lou Reed's double LP record, Metal Machine Music

Velvet Underground in his use of both discordance and feedback.[83] Cale and Conrad have released noise music recordings they made during the mid-sixties, such as Cale's *Inside the Dream Syndicate* series (*The Dream Syndicate* being the alternative name given by Cale and Conrad to their collective work with Young).[84]

Kim Gordon of Sonic Youth walking over her bass to create sound during a concert

The aptly named noise rock fuses rock to noise, usually with recognizable "rock" instrumentation, but with greater use of distortion and electronic effects, varying degrees of atonality, improvisation, and white noise. One notable band of this genre is Sonic Youth who took inspiration from the No Wave composers Glenn Branca and Rhys Chatham (himself a student of LaMonte Young).[85] Marc Masters, in his book on the No Wave, points out that aggressively innovative early dark noise groups like Mars and DNA drew on punk rock, avant-garde minimalism and performance art.[86] Important in this noise trajectory are the nine nights of noise music called *Noise Fest* that was organized by Thurston Moore of Sonic Youth in the NYC art space White Columns in June 1981[87][88] followed by the *Speed Trials* noise rock series organized by Live Skull members in May 1983.

Industrial music

Main article: Industrial music
See also: Post-industrial music
In the 1970s, the concept of art itself expanded and groups

Cover of Tellus Audio Cassette Magazine #13 Power Electronics *(1986)*

Cover of Pagan Muzak *7" vinyl released by NON*

like Survival Research Laboratories, Borbetomagus and Elliott Sharp embraced and extended the most dissonant and least approachable aspects of these musical/spatial concepts. Around the same time, the first postmodern wave of industrial noise music appeared with Throbbing Gristle, Cabaret Voltaire, and NON (aka Boyd Rice).[89] These cassette culture releases often featured zany tape editing, stark percussion and repetitive loops distorted to the point where they may degrade into harsh noise.[90] In the 1970s and 1980s, industrial noise groups like Current 93, Hafler Trio, Throbbing Gristle, Coil, Laibach, Steven Stapleton, Thee Temple ov Psychick Youth, Smegma, Nurse with Wound, Einstürzende Neubauten, The Haters, and The New Blockaders performed industrial noise music mixing loud metal percussion, guitars, and unconventional "instruments" (such as jackhammers and bones) in elaborate stage performances. These industrial artists experimented with varying degrees of noise production techniques.[91] Interest in the use of shortwave radio also developed at this time, particularly evident in the recordings and live performances of John Duncan. Other postmodern art movements influential to post-industrial noise art are Conceptual Art and the Neo-Dada use of techniques such as assemblage, montage, bricolage, and appropriation. Bands like Test Dept, Clock DVA, Factrix, Autopsia, Nocturnal Emissions, Whitehouse, Severed Heads, Sutcliffe Jügend, and SPK soon followed. The sudden post-industrial affordability of home cassette recording technology in the 1970s, combined with the simultaneous influence of punk rock, established the No Wave aesthetic, and instigated what is commonly referred to as noise music today.[91]

Japanese noise music

Main article: Japanoise
Since the early 1980s,[92] Japan has produced a significant output of characteristically harsh bands, sometimes referred to under the portmanteau *Japanoise*, with perhaps the best known being Merzbow (pseudonym for the Japanese noise artist Masami Akita who himself was inspired by the Dada artist Kurt Schwitters's *Merz* art project of psychological collage).[93][94] In the late 1970s and early 1980s, Akita took *Metal Machine Music* as a point of departure and further abstracted the noise aesthetic by freeing the sound from guitar based feedback alone, a development that is thought to have heralded *noise music* as a genre.[95] According to Hegarty (2007), "in many ways it only makes sense to talk of noise music since the advent

Merzbow, prominent Japanoise musician, in 2007

of various types of noise produced in Japanese music, and in terms of quantity this is really to do with the 1990s onwards ... with the vast growth of Japanese noise, finally, noise music becomes a genre".[96] Other key Japanese noise artists that contributed to this upsurge of activity include Hijokaidan, Boredoms, C.C.C.C., Incapacitants, KK Null, Yamazaki Maso's Masonna, Solmania, K2, The Gerogerigegege and Hanatarash.[94][97] Nick Cain of *The Wire* identifies the "primacy of Japanese Noise artists like Merzbow, Hijokaidan and Incapacitants" as one of the major developments in noise music since 1990.[98]

Post-digital music

Main article: Glitch (music)

Following the wake of industrial noise, noise rock, no wave, and harsh noise, there has been a flood of noise musicians whose ambient, microsound, or glitch-based work is often subtler to the ear.[99] Kim Cascone refers to this development as a postdigital movement and describes it as an "aesthetic of failure."[100] Some of this music has seen wide distribution thanks to peer-to-peer file sharing services and netlabels offering free releases. Goodman characterizes this widespread outpouring of free noise based media as a "noise virus."[101][102]

2.17.3 Definitions

According to Danish noise and music theorist Torben Sangild, one single definition of noise in music is not possible. Sangild instead provides three basic definitions of noise: a musical acoustics definition, a second communicative definition based on distortion or disturbance of a communicative signal, and a third definition based in subjectivity (what is noise to one person can be meaningful to another; what was considered unpleasant sound yesterday is not today).[103]

According to Murray Schafer there are four types of noise: unwanted noise, unmusical sound, any loud sound, and a disturbance in any signaling system (such as static on a telephone).[104] Definitions regarding what is considered noise, relative to music, have changed over time.[105] Ben Watson, in his article *Noise as Permanent Revolution*, points out that Ludwig van Beethoven's *Grosse Fuge* (1825) "sounded like noise" to his audience at the time. Indeed, Beethoven's publishers persuaded him to remove it from its original setting as the last movement of a string quartet. He did so, replacing it with a sparkling *Allegro*. They subsequently published it separately.[106]

In attempting to define noise music and its value, Paul Hegarty (2007) cites the work of noted cultural critics Jean Baudrillard, Georges Bataille and Theodor Adorno and through their work traces the history of "noise". He defines noise at different times as "intrusive, unwanted", "lacking skill, not being appropriate" and "a threatening emptiness". He traces these trends starting with 18th-century concert hall music. Hegarty contends that it is John Cage's composition *4'33"*, in which an audience sits through four and a half minutes of "silence" (Cage 1973), that represents the beginning of noise music proper. For Hegarty, "noise music", as with *4'33"*, is that music made up of incidental sounds that represent perfectly the tension between "desirable" sound (properly played musical notes) and undesirable "noise" that make up all noise music from Erik Satie to NON to Glenn Branca. Writing about Japanese noise music, Hegarty suggests that "it is not a genre, but it is also a genre that is multiple, and characterized by this very multiplicity ... Japanese noise music can come in all styles, referring to all other genres ... but crucially asks the question of genre—what does it mean to be categorized, categorizable, definable?" (Hegarty 2007:133).

Writer Douglas Kahn, in his work *Noise, Water, Meat: A History of Sound in the Arts* (1999), discusses the use of noise as a medium and explores the ideas of Antonin Artaud, George Brecht, William Burroughs, Sergei Eisenstein, Fluxus, Allan Kaprow, Michael McClure, Yoko Ono, Jackson Pollock, Luigi Russolo, and Dziga Vertov.

In *Noise: The Political Economy of Music* (1985), Jacques Attali explores the relationship between noise music and the future of society. He indicates that noise in music is a predictor of social change and demonstrates how noise acts as the subconscious of society—validating and testing new social and political realities.[107]

2.17.4 Characteristics

Like much of modern and contemporary art, noise music takes characteristics of the perceived negative traits of noise mentioned below and uses them in aesthetic and imaginative ways.[108]

In common use, the word noise means unwanted sound or noise pollution.[109] In electronics noise can refer to the electronic signal corresponding to acoustic noise (in an audio system) or the electronic signal corresponding to the (visual) noise commonly seen as 'snow' on a degraded television or video image.[110] In signal processing or computing it can be considered data without meaning; that is, data that is not being used to transmit a signal, but is simply produced as an unwanted by-product of other activities. Noise can block, distort, or change the meaning of a message in both human and electronic communication. White noise is a random signal (or process) with a flat power spectral density.[111] In other words, the signal contains equal power within a fixed bandwidth at any center frequency. White noise is considered analogous to white light which contains all frequencies.[112]

In much the same way the early modernists were inspired by naïve art, some contemporary digital art noise musicians are excited by the archaic audio technologies such as wire-recorders, the 8-track cartridge, and vinyl records.[113] Many artists not only build their own noise-generating devices, but even their own specialized recording equipment and custom software (for example, the C++ software used in creating the *viral symphOny* by Joseph Nechvatal).[114][115]

2.17.5 Compilations

- *An Anthology of Noise & Electronic Music, Volumes 1–6* Sub Rosa, Various Artists (1920–2010)

- *Bip-Hop Generation* (2001–2008) Volumes 1–9, various artists, Paris

- *Independent Dark Electronics Volume #1* (2008) IDE

- *Japanese Independent Music* (2000) various artists, Paris *Sonore*

- *Just Another Asshole* #5 (1981) compilation LP (CD reissue 1995 on Atavistic #ALP39CD), producers: Barbara Ess & Glenn Branca

- *New York Noise, Vol. 1–3* (2003, 2006, 2006) Soul Jazz B00009OYSE, B000CHYHOG, B000HEZ5CC

- *Noise May-Day 2003*, various artists, *Coquette* Japan CD Catalog#: NMD-2003

- *No New York* (1978) Antilles, (2006) Lilith, B000B63ISE

- *Women take back the Noise Compilation* (2006) ubuibi

- "The Allegheny White Fish Tapes" (2009), Tobacco, Rad Cult

- *The Japanese-American Noise Treaty* (1995) CD, Relapse

2.17.6 See also

- Noise in music
- Chip music
- Circuit bending
- Colors of noise
- Dark ambient
- Death growl
- Digital hardcore
- List of Japanoise artists
- List of noise musicians
- No-Fi
- Post-punk
- Phonation
- Screaming (music)
- Sonic artifact

2.17.7 Footnotes

[1] Priest, Eldritch. "Music Noise" in *Boring Formless Nonsense: Experimental Music and The Aesthetics of Failure*, p. 132. London: Bloomsbury Publishing; New York: Bloomsbury Academic, 2013.

[2] Chris Atton, "Fan Discourse and the Construction of Noise Music as a Genre", *Journal of Popular Music Studies* 23, no. 3 (September 2011): 324–42. Citation on 326.

[3] Torben Sangild, *The Aesthetics of Noise* (Copenhagen: Datanom, 2002):. ISBN 87-988955-0-8. Reprinted at UbuWeb.

[4] Paul Hegarty, *Noise/Music: A History* (London: Continuum International Publishing Group, 2007): 3–19.

[5] Caleb Kelly, *Cracked Media: The Sound of Malfunction* (Cambridge, Ma.: MIT Press, 2009): 60–76.

[6] Matthew Biro, *The Dada Cyborg: Visions of the New Human in Weimar Berlin*, 2009, p. 50.

[7] Documents at The International Dada archive at The University of Iowa show that *Antisymphonie* was held at the Graphisches Kabinett, Kurfürstendamm 232, at 7:45 PM. The printed program lists 5 numbers: "Proclamation dada 1919" by Huelsenbeck, "Simultan-Gedicht" performed by 7 people, "Bruitistisches Gedicht" performed by Huelsenbeck (these latter 2 pieces grouped together under the category "DADA-machine"), "Seelenautomobil" by Hausmann, and finally, Golyscheff's Antisymphonie in 3 movements, subtitled "Musikalische Kriegsguillotine". The 3 movements of Golyscheff's piece are titled "provokatorische Spritze", "chaotische Mundhöhle oder das submarine Flugzeug", and "zusammenklappbares Hyper-fis-chendur".

[8] Owen Smith, *Fluxus: The History of an Attitude* (San Diego: San Diego State University Press, 1998), pp. 7 & 82.

[9] Piekut, Benjamin. *Experimentalism Otherwise: The New York Avant-Garde and Its Limits*. 2012. p. 193

[10] Jimi Hendrix Biography at Rolling Stone Magazine

[11] Lou Reed and Amanda Petrusich "Interview: Lou Reed", Pitchfork Media (2007-09-17). (Archive from 23 November 2011, accessed 9 December 2013).

[12] Such as *23 VIII 64 2:50:45 – 3:11 am The Volga Delta From Studies In The Bowed Disc* from *The Black Record (1969)*

[13] Paul Hegarty, *Noise/Music: A History* (London: Continuum International Publishing Group, 2007), pp. 189–92.

[14] Caleb Kelly, *Cracked Media: The Sound of Malfunction* (Cambridge, Massachusetts: MIT Press, 2009), pp. 6–10.

[15] In "Futurism and Musical Notes", Daniele Lombardi discusses the mysterious case of the French composer Carol-Bérard; a pupil of Isaac Albéniz. Carol-Bérard is said to have composed a *Symphony of Mechanical Force*s in 1910, but little evidence has emerged thus far to establish this assertion.

[16] Unknown.nu Luigi Russolo, "The Art of Noises".

[17] Benjamin Thorn,"Luigi Russolo (1885–1947)", in *Music of the Twentieth-Century Avant-Garde: A Biocritical Sourcebook*, edited by Larry Sitsky, foreword by Jonathan Kramer, 415–19 (Westport and London: Greenwood Publishing Group, 2002). ISBN 0-313-29689-8. Citation on page 419.

[18] Paul Hegarty, *Noise/Music: A History* (London: Continuum International Publishing Group, 2007), pp. 13–14.

[19] László Moholy-Nagy in 1923 recognized the unprecedented efforts of the Italian Futurists to broaden our perception of sound using noise. In an article in *Der Storm #7*, he outlined the fundamentals of his own experimentation: "I have suggested to change the gramophone from a reproductive instrument to a productive one, so that on a record without prior acoustic information, the acoustic information, the acoustic phenomenon itself originates by engraving the necessary Ritchriftreihen (etched grooves)." He presents detailed descriptions for manipulating discs, creating "real sound forms" to train people to be "true music receivers and creators" (Rice 1994,).

[20] Russolo, Luigi from *The Art of Noises*, March 1913.

[21] Albright, Daniel (ed.) *Modernism and Music: An Anthology of Source*. Chicago: University Of Chicago Press, 2004. p. 174

[22] Chilvers, Ian & Glaves-Smith, John eds., *Dictionary of Modern and Contemporary Art*, Oxford: Oxford University Press, 2009. pp. 587–588

[23] Michel Sanouillet & Elmer Peterson (Eds.), *The Writings of Marcel Duchamp*, Da Capo Press, p. 135.

[24] Chadabe 1996, p. 23

[25] Sonification.eu, Martin John Callanan (artist), *Sonification of You.*

[26] Albright, Daniel (ed.) *Modernism and Music: An Anthology of Source*. Chicago: University Of Chicago Press, 2004. p. 386

[27] , The *Ballet Mécanique.*

[28] Chadabe 1996, pp. 23–24

[29] UbuWeb Papers *A Brief history of Anti-Records and Conceptual Records* by Ron Rice.

[30] Chadabe 1996, p. 59

[31] Nyman 1974, p. 44

[32] Chadabe 1996, p. 58

[33] Griffiths 1995, p. 27

[34] Chadabe 1996, p. 26

[35] Griffiths 1995, p. 20

[36] Paul Doornbusch, *A Chronology / History of Electronic and Computer Music and Related Events 1906–2011*

[37] Henry Cowell, "The Joys of Noise", in *Audio Culture: Readings in Modern Music* (New York: Continuum, 2004), pp. 22–24.

[38] D. Teruggi, "Technology and Musique Concrete: The Technical Developments of the Groupe de Recherches Musicales and Their Implication in Musical Composition", *Organised Sound* 12, no. 3 (2007): 213–31.

[39] Alex Ross, *The Rest Is Noise: Listening to the Twentieth Century* (New York: Farrar, Straus and Giroux, 2007), p. 369.

[40] Antonin Artaud *Pour en finir avec le jugement de dieu*, original recording, edited with an introduction by Marc Dachy. Compact Disc (Sub Rosa/aural documents, 1995).

[41] Paul Hegarty, *Noise/Music: A History*, pp. 25–26.

[42] An account and sound recording of *The Monotone Symphony* performed March 9, 1960 (Archive.org copy of 2001).

[43] Alex Ross, *The Rest Is Noise: Listening to the Twentieth Century*(New York: Farrar, Straus and Giroux, 2007), p. 365.

[44] Griffiths 1995, p. 25

[45] John Cage, *Silence: Lectures and Writings* (Middletown, Connecticut: Wesleyan University Press, 1961), p. 59.

[46] Alex Ross, *The Rest Is Noise: Listening to the Twentieth Century* (New York: Farrar, Straus and Giroux, 2007), p. 401.

[47] "OHM- The Early Gurus of Electronic Music: Edgard Varese's "Poem Electronique"", *Perfect Sound Forever* website (accessed 20 October 2009).

[48] Albright, Daniel (ed.) *Modernism and Music: An Anthology of Source*. Chicago: University Of Chicago Press, 2004. p. 185.

[49] Charles Mereweather (ed.), *Art Anti-Art Non-Art* (Los Angeles: Getty Research Institute, 2007), pp. 13 & 16.

[50] *Spacecraft* was recorded in Cologne in 1967 by Bryant, Curran, Rzewski, Teitelbaum and Vandor

[51] *Liner Notes* for Musica Elettronica Viva recording set *MEV 40 (1967–2007)* 80675-2 (4CDs)

[52] Rosalind E. Krauss, *The Originality of the Avant Garde and Other Modernist Myths: Sculpture in the Expanded Field* (Cambridge, Massachusetts: MIT Press, 1986), pp. 30–44.

[53] Joseph Nechvatal & Carlo McCormick essays in *TellusTools* liner notes (New York: Harvestworks ed., 2001).

[54] Rosalind Krauss, "Sculpture in the Expanded Field", *October* 8 (Spring 1979), pp. 30–44.

[55] Hayward, Philip (1999). *Widening the Horizon: Exoticism in Post-war Popular Music*. J. Libbey. pp. 79–80. ISBN 978-1-86462-047-4.

[56] Walking in the Rain song review

[57] Cobley, Mike (September 9, 2007). "Brighton Beach Boys: 'Getting Better' All The Time!". *The Brighton Magazine*. Archived from the original on October 6, 2007. Retrieved March 3, 2009.

[58] "Richie Unterberger review of Pet Sounds". AllMusic.

[59] Laura Tunbridge, *The Song Cycle* (Cambridge and New York: Cambridge University Press, 2011), ISBN 0-521-72107-5, p.173.

[60] Warhol Live: Music and Dance in Andy Warhol's Workat the Frist Center for the Visual Arts by Robert Stalker

[61] Spitz 2005, p. 601.

[62] Martin 1994, p. 80.

[63] Martin 1994, pp. 80–81.

[64] McCartney 1995.

[65] Miles 1997, p. 291.

[66] Martin 1994, p. 81.

[67] MacDonald 1995.

[68] Miles 1997, p. 292.

[69] MacDonald 1995, p. 190.

[70] Martin 1995b.

[71] from *Rolling Stone* issues # 74 & 75 (21 Jan & 4 Feb, 1971). "John Lennon: The Rolling Stone Interview" by editor Jann Wenner

[72] Mark Kemp, "She Who Laughs Last: Yoko Ono Reconsidered", *Option Magazine* (July–August 1992), pp. 74–81.

[73] *Seastones*

[74] "Grateful Dead Biography", *Rolling Stone*. Retrieved June 23, 2012.

[75] *Seastones* was re-released in stereo on CD by Rykodisc in 1991. The CD version includes the original nine-section "Sea Stones" (42:34) from February 1975, and a live, previously unreleased, six-section version (31:05) from December 1975.

[76] Atton (2011:326)

[77] *Metal Machine Music* 8-Track Hall of Fame.

[78] Lester Bangs, *Psychotic Reactions and Carburetor Dung: The Work of a Legendary Critic*, Greil Marcus, ed. (1988) Anchor Press, p. 200.

[79] Charlie Gere, *Art, Time and Technology: Histories of the Disappearing Body*, (2005) Berg, p. 110.

[80] Reed mentions (and misspells) Young's name on the cover of *Metal Machine Music*: "Drone cognizance and harmonic possibilities vis a vis Lamont Young's Dream Music".

[81] Asphodel.com Zeitkratzer Lou Reed*Metal Machine Music*.

[82] "Minimalism (music)", *Encarta* (Accessed 20 October 2009). Archived 2009-11-01.

[83] Steven Watson, *Factory Made: Warhol and the Sixties* (2003) Pantheon, New York, p. 157.

[84] Watson, *Factory Made*, p. 103.

[85] "Rhys Chatham", *Kalvos-Damien* website. (Accessed 20 October 2009).

[86] Marc Masters, *No Wave* (London: Black Dog Publishing, 2007), pp. 42–44.

[87] Rob Young (ed.), *The Wire Primers: A Guide To Modern Music* (London: Verso, 2009), p. 43.

[88] Marc Masters, *No Wave* (London: Black Dog Publishing, 2007), pp. 170–71.

[89] Media.hyperreal.org, *Prehistory of Industrial Music* 1995 Brian Duguid, esp. chapter "Access to Information".

[90] Rob Young (ed.), *The Wire Primers: A Guide To Modern Music* (London: Verso, 2009), p. 29.

[91] Media.hyperreal.org, *Prehistory of Industrial Music* 1995 Brian Duguid, esp. chapter "Organisational Autonomy / Extra-Musical Elements".

[92] Hegarty 2007, p. 133

[93] Paul Hegarty, "Full With Noise: Theory and Japanese Noise Music", Ctheory.net.

[94] Young, Rob (ed.), *The Wire Primers: A Guide To Modern Music* (London: Verso, 2009), p. 30.

[95] Van Nort (2006:177)

[96] Hegarty (2007:133)

[97] Japanoise.net, japanoise noisicians profiled at japnoise.net.

[98] Nick Cain, "Noise" *The Wire Primers: A Guide to Modern Music*, Rob Young, ed., London: Verso, 2009, p. 29.

[99] Caleb Kelly, *Cracked Media: The Sound of Malfunction* (Cambridge, Massachusetts: MIT Press, 2009), pp. 6–24.

[100] Cascone, Kim. "The Aesthetics of Failure: 'Post-Digital' Tendencies in Contemporary Computer Music". *Computer Music Journal* 24, no. 4 (Winter 2002): pp. 12–18.

[101] Goodman, Steve. "Contagious Noise: From Digital Glitches to Audio Viruses", in Parikka, Jussi and Sampson, Tony D. (eds.) *The Spam Book: On Viruses, Porn and Other Anomalies From the Dark Side of Digital Culture*. Cresskill, New Jersey: Hampton Press. 2009. pp. 128.

[102] Goodman, Steve. "Contagious Noise: From Digital Glitches to Audio Viruses", in Parikka and Sampson (eds.) *The Spam Book: On Viruses, Porn and Other Anomalies From the Dark Side of Digital Culture*. Cresskill, New Jersey: Hampton Press. 2009. pp. 129–130.

[103] Sangild, Torben, *The Aesthetics of Noise*. Copenhagen: Datanom. 2002. pp. 12–13

[104] Schafer 1994:182

[105] Joseph Nechvatal, *Immersion Into Noise* (Ann Arbor: Open Humanities Press, 2012), p. 19.

[106] Watson 2009, 109–10.

[107] Allen S. Weiss, *Phantasmic Radio* (Durham, North Carolina: Duke University Press, 1995), p. 90.

[108] Ctheory.net Paul Hegarty, "Full With Noise: Theory and Japanese Noise Music", in *Life in the Wires*, edited by Arthur Kroker and Marilouise Kroker, 86–98 (Victoria, Canada: NWP Ctheory Books, 2004).

[109] Nonoise.org *About Noise, Noise Pollution, and the Clearinghouse.*

[110] Noise generator to explore different types of noise.

[111] white noise in wave(.wav) format.

[112] Eugene Hecht, *Optics*, 4th edition (Boston: Pearson Education, 2001), p.

[113] UBU.com, Torben Sangild, "The Aesthetics of Noise", Datanom, 2002.

[114] UBU.com, Steven Mygind Pedersen, Joseph Nechvatal: *viral symphOny* (Alfred, New York: Institute for Electronic Arts, School of Art & Design, Alfred University, 2007).

[115] Observatori A.C. (ed.), *Observatori 2008: After The Future* (Valencia, Spain: Museo de Bellas Artes de Valencia, 2008), p. 80.

2.17.8 References

- Albright, Daniel (ed.) *Modernism and Music: An Anthology of Source.* Chicago: University Of Chicago Press, 2004.

- Attali, Jacques. *Noise: The Political Economy of Music*, translated by Brian Massumi, foreword by Fredric Jameson, afterword by Susan McClary. Minneapolis: University of Minnesota Press, 1985.

- Atton, Chris (2011). "Fan Discourse and the Construction of Noise Music as a Genre". *Journal of Popular Music Studies*, Volume 23, Issue 3, pages 324–42, September 2011.

- Bangs, Lester. *Psychotic Reactions and Carburetor Dung: The Work of a Legendary Critic*, collected writings,edited by Greil Marcus. Anchor Press, 1988.

- Biro, Matthew. *The Dada Cyborg: Visions of the New Human in Weimar Berlin*. Minneapolis: University of Minnesota Press, 2009.

- Cage, John. *Silence: Lectures and Writings*. Wesleyan University Press, 1961. Reprinted 1973.

- Cage, John. "The Future of Music: Credo (1937)". In John Cage, *Documentary Monographs in Modern Art*, edited by Richard Kostelanetz, Praeger Publishers, 1970

- Cahoone, Lawrence. *From Modernism to Postmodernism: An Anthology*. Cambridge, Mass: Blackwell, 1996.

- Cain, Nick "Noise" in *The Wire Primers: A Guide to Modern Music*, Rob Young, ed., London: Verso, 2009.

- Cascone, Kim. "The Aesthetics of Failure: 'Post-Digital' Tendencies in Contemporary Computer Music".*Computer Music Journal* 24, no. 4 (Winter 2002): 12–18.

- Chadabe, Joel (1996). *Electronic Sound: The Past and Promise of Electronic Music*. New Jersey: Prentice Hall. p. 370. ISBN 0-13-303231-0.

- Cowell, Henry. *The Joys of Noise* in *Audio Culture. Readings in Modern Music*, edited by Christoph Cox and Dan Warner, pp. 22–24. New York: Continuum, 2004. ISBN 0-8264-1614-4 (hardcover) ISBN 0-8264-1615-2 (pbk)

- De Maria, Walter *Ocean Music* (1968)

- Gere, Charles. *Art, Time and Technology: Histories of the Disappearing Body*. Oxford: Berg Publishers, 2005.

- Griffiths, Paul (1995). *Modern Music and After: Directions Since 1945*. Oxford: Oxford University Press. p. 373. ISBN 0-19-816511-0.

- Goodman, Steve. 2009. "Contagious Noise: From Digital Glitches to Audio Viruses". In *The Spam Book: On Viruses, Porn and Other Anomalies From the Dark Side of Digital Culture*, edited by Jussi Parikka and Tony D. Sampson, 125–40.. Cresskill, New Jersey: Hampton Press.

- Hecht, Eugene. *Optics*, 4th edition. Boston: Pearson Education, 2001.

- Hegarty, Paul. 2004. "Full with Noise: Theory and Japanese Noise Music". In *Life in the Wires*, edited by Arthur Kroker and Marilouise Kroker, 86–98. Victoria, Canada: NWPCtheory Books.

- Hegarty, Paul. *Noise/Music: A History*. London: Continuum International Publishing Group, 2007.

- Piekut, Benjamin. *Experimentalism Otherwise: The New York Avant-Garde and Its Limits*. Berkeley: University of California Press, 2012.

- Kahn, Douglas. *Noise, Water, Meat: A History of Sound in the Arts*. Cambridge: MIT Press, 1999.

- Kelly, Caleb. *Cracked Media: The Sound of Malfunction* Cambridge, Ma.: MIT Press, 2009.

- Kemp, Mark. 1992. "She Who Laughs Last: Yoko Ono Reconsidered". *Option Magazine* (July–August): 74–81.

- Krauss, Rosalind E.. 1979. *The Originality of the Avant Garde and Other Modernist Myths*. Cambridge: MIT Press. Reprinted as *Sculpture in the Expanded Field*. Cambridge: MIT Press, 1986.

- LaBelle, Brandon. 2006. *Background Noise: Perspectives on Sound Art*. New York and London: Continuum International Publishing.

- Landy, Leigh (2007),*Understanding the Art of Sound Organization*, Cambridge, Massachusetts: MIT Press, xiv, 303p.

- Lewisohn, Mark. 1988. *The Beatles Recording Sessions*. New York: Harmony Books.

- Lombardi, Daniele. 1981. "Futurism and Musical Notes". *Artforum*.

- McCartney, Paul (1995). *The Beatles Anthology* (DVD). Event occurs at Special Features, Back at Abbey Road May 1995, 0:12:17.

- MacDonald, Ian (2005). *Revolution in the Head: The Beatles' Records and the Sixties* (Second Revised ed.). London: Pimlico (Rand). ISBN 1-84413-828-3.

- Martin, George (1994). *Summer of Love: The Making of Sgt Pepper*. MacMillan London Ltd. ISBN 0-333-60398-2.

- Masters, Marc. 2007. *No Wave* London: Black Dog Publishing.

- Mereweather, Charles (ed.). 2007. *Art Anti-Art Non-Art*. Los Angeles: Getty Research Institute.

- Miles, Barry (1997). *Many Years From Now*. Vintage – Random House. ISBN 0-7493-8658-4.

- Nechvatal, Joseph. 2012. *Immersion Into Noise*. Ann Arbor: Open Humanities Press. ISBN 978-1-60785-241-4.

- Nechvatal, Joseph. 2000. *Towards a Sound Ecstatic Electronica*. New York: The Thing. Post.thing.net

- Nyman, Michael (1974). *Experimental Music: Cage and Beyond*. London: Studio Vista. p. 196. ISBN 0-19-816511-0.

- Pedersen, Steven Mygind. 2007. *Notes on Joseph Nechvatal: Viral SymphOny*. Alfred, New York: Institute for Electronic Arts, School of Art & Design, Alfred University.

- Petrusich, Amanda. "Interview: Lou Reed Pitchfork net. (Accessed 13 September 2009)

2.17. NOISE MUSIC

- Priest, Eldritch. "Music Noise". In his *Boring Formless Nonsense: Experimental Music and The Aesthetics of Failure*, 128–39. London: Bloomsbury Publishing; New York: Bloomsbury Academic, 2013. ISBN 978-1-4411-2475-3; ISBN 978-1-4411-2213-1 (pbk).

- Rice, Ron. 1994. *A Brief History of Anti-Records and Conceptual Records. Unfiled: Music under New Technology* 0402 [i.e., vol. 1, no. 2]: Republished online, Ubuweb Papers (Accessed 4 December 2009).

- Ross, Alex. 2007. *The Rest Is Noise: Listening to the Twentieth Century*. New York: Farrar, Straus and Giroux.

- Sangild, Torben. 2002. *The Aesthetics of Noise*. Copenhagen: Datanom. ISBN 87-988955-0-8. Reprinted at UbuWeb

- Sanouillet, Michel, and Elmer Peterson (eds.). 1989. *The Writings of Marcel Duchamp*. New York: Da Capo Press.

- Smith, Owen. 1998. *Fluxus: The History of an Attitude*. San Diego: San Diego State University Press.

- Spitz, Bob (2005). *The Beatles: The Biography*. New York: Little, Brown and Company. ISBN 1-84513-160-6.

- Tunbridge, Laura. 2011. *The Song Cycle*. Cambridge and New York: Cambridge University Press. ISBN 0-521-72107-5.

- Watson, Ben. "Noise as Permanent Revolution: or, Why Culture Is a Sow Which Devours Its Own Farrow". In *Noise & Capitalism*, edited by Anthony and Mattin Iles, 104–20. Kritika Series. Donostia-San Sebastián: Arteleku Audiolab, 2009.

- Watson, Steven. 2003. *Factory Made: Warhol and the Sixties*. New York: Pantheon.

- Weiss, Allen S. 1995. *Phantasmic Radio*. Durham NC: Duke University Press.

- Young, Rob (ed.). 2009. *The Wire Primers: A Guide To Modern Music*. London: Verso.

- Van Nort, Doug. (2006), Noise/music and representation systems, *Organised Sound*, 11(2), Cambridge University Press, pp 173–178.

2.17.9 Further reading

- Álvarez-Fernández, Miguel. "Dissonance, Sex and Noise: (Re)Building (Hi)Stories of Electroacoustic Music". In *ICMC 2005: Free Sound Conference Proceedings*. Barcelona: International Computer Music Conference; International Computer Music Association; SuviSoft Oy Ltd., 2005.

- Thomas Bey William Bailey, *Unofficial Release: Self-Released And Handmade Audio In Post-Industrial Society*, Belsona Books Ltd., 2012

- Barthes, Roland. "Listening". In his *The Responsibility of Forms: Critical Essays on Music, Art, and Representation*, translated from the French by Richard Howard. New York: Hill and Wang, 1985. ISBN 0-8090-8075-3 Reprinted Berkeley: University of California Press, 1991. ISBN 0-520-07238-3 (pbk.)

- Brassier, Ray. "Genre is Obsolete". *Multitudes*, no. 28 (Spring 2007) Multitudes.samizdat.net.

- Cobussen, Marcel. "Noise and Ethics: On Evan Parker and Alain Badiou". *Culture, Theory & Critique*, 46(1) pp. 29–42. 2005.

- Collins, Nicolas (ed.) "Leonardo Music Journal" Vol 13: "Groove, Pit and Wave: Recording, Transmission and Music" 2003.

- Court, Paula. *New York Noise: Art and Music from the New York Underground 1978–88*. London: Soul Jazz Publishing, in association with Soul Jazz Records, 2007. ISBN 0-9554817-0-8

- DeLone, Leon (ed.), *Aspects of Twentieth-Century Music*. Englewood Cliffs, New Jersey: Prentice-Hall, 1975.

- Demers, Joanna. *Listening Through The Noise*. New York: Oxford University Press. 2010.

- Dempsey, Amy. *Art in the Modern Era: A Guide to Schools and Movements*. New York: Harry A. Abrams, 2002.

- Doss, Erika. *Twentieth-Century American Art*. Oxford and New York: Oxford University Press, 2002

- Foege, Alec. *Confusion Is Next: The Sonic Youth Story*. New York: St. Martin's Press, 1994.

- Gere, Charlie. *Digital Culture*, second edition. London: Reaktion, 2000. ISBN 1-86189-388-4

- Goldberg, RoseLee. *Performance: Live Art Since 1960*. New York: Harry N. Abrams, 1998.

- Goodman, Steve a.k.a. kode9. *Sonic Warfare: Sound, Affect, and the Ecology of Fear*. Cambridge, Ma.: MIT Press, 2010.

- Hainge, Greg (ed.). *Culture, Theory and Critique* 46, no. 1 (Issue on Noise, 2005)

- Harrison, Charles, and Paul Wood. *Art in Theory, 1900-2000: An Anthology of Changing Ideas*. Oxford: Blackwell Publishing, 1992.

- Harrison, Thomas J. *1910: The Emancipation of Dissonance*. Berkeley: University of California Press, 1996.

- Hegarty, Paul *The Art of Noise*. Talk given to Visual Arts Society at University College Cork, 2005.

- Hegarty, Paul. *Noise/Music: A History*. New York, London: Continuum, 2007. ISBN 978-0-8264-1726-8 (cloth); ISBN 978-0-8264-1727-5 (pbk).

- Hensley, Chad. "The Beauty of Noise: An Interview with Masami Akita of Merzbow". In *Audio Culture: Readings in Modern Music*, edited by C. Cox and Dan Warner, pp. 59–61. New York: Continuum, 2004.

- Helmholtz, Hermann von. *On the Sensations of Tone as a Physiological Basis for the Theory of Music*, 2nd English edition, translated by Alexander J. Ellis. New York: Longmans & Co. 1885. Reprinted New York: Dover Publications, 1954.

- Hinant, Guy-Marc. "TOHU BOHU: Considerations on the nature of noise, in 78 fragments". In *Leonardo Music Journal* Vol 13: *Groove, Pit and Wave: Recording, Transmission and Music*. 2003. pp. 43–47

- Huyssen, Andreas. *Twilight Memories: Marking Time in a Culture of Amnesia*. New York: Routledge, 1995.

- Iles, Anthony & Mattin (eds) *Noise & Capitalism*. Donostia-San Sebastián: Arteleku Audiolab (Kritika series). 2009.

- Juno, Andrea, and Vivian Vale (eds.). *Industrial Culture Handbook*. RE/Search 6/7. San Francisco: RE/Search Publications, 1983. ISBN 0-940642-07-7

- Kahn, Douglas, and Gregory Whitehead (eds.). *Wireless Imagination: Sound, Radio and the Avant-Garde*. Cambridge, Ma.: MIT Press, 1992.

- Kocur, Zoya, and Simon Leung. *Theory in Contemporary Art Since 1985*. Boston: Blackwell Publishing, 2005.

- LaBelle, Brandon. *Noise Aesthetics* in *Background Noise: Perspectives on Sound Art*, New York and London: Continuum International Publishing, pp 222–225. 2006.

- Lander, Dan. *Sound by Artists*. Toronto: Art Metropole, 1990.

- Licht, Alan. *Sound Art: Beyond Music, between Categories*. New York: Rizzoli, 2007.

- Lombardi, Daniele. *Futurism and Musical Notes*, translated by Meg Shore. *Artforum*Danielelombardi.it

- Malpas, Simon. *The Postmodern*. New York: Routledge, 2005.

- McGowan, John P. *Postmodernism and Its Critics*. Ithaca: Cornell University Press, 1991.

- Miller, Paul D. [a.k.a. DJ Spooky] (ed.). *Sound Unbound: Sampling Digital Music and Culture*. Cambridge, Ma.: MIT Press, 2008.

- Morgan, Robert P. "A New Musical Reality: Futurism, Modernism, and 'The Art of Noises'", *Modernism/Modernity* 1, no. 3 (September 1994): 129–51. Reprinted at *UbuWeb*.

- Moore, Thurston. *Mix Tape: The Art of Cassette Culture*. Seattle: Universe, 2004.

- Nechvatal, Joseph. *Immersion Into Noise*. Open Humanities Press in conjunction with the University of Michigan Library's Scholarly Publishing Office. Ann Arbor. 2011.

- David Novak, *Japanoise: Music at the Edge of Circulation*, Duke University Press. 2013

- Nyman, Michael. *Experimental Music: Cage and Beyond*, 2nd edition. Music in the Twentieth Century. Cambridge and New York: Cambridge University Press, 1999.ISBN 0-521-65297-9 (cloth) ISBN 0-521-65383-5 (pbk)

- Pratella, Francesco Balilla. "Manifesto of Futurist Musicians" from Apollonio, Umbro, ed. *Documents of 20th-century Art: Futurist Manifestos*. Brain, Robert, R.W. Flint, J.C. Higgitt, and Caroline Tisdall, trans. New York: Viking Press, pp. 31–38. 1973.

- Popper, Frank. *From Technological to Virtual Art*. Cambridge: MIT Press/Leonardo Books, 2007.

- Popper, Frank. *Art of the Electronic Age*. New York: Harry N. Abrams; London: Thames & Hudson, 1993. ISBN 0-8109-1928-1 (New York); ISBN 0-8109-1930-3 (New York); ISBN 0-500-23650-X (London); Paperback reprint, New York: Thames & Hudson, 1997. ISBN 0-500-27918-7.

- Ruhrberg, Karl, Manfred Schneckenburger, Christiane Fricke, and Ingo F. Walther. *Art of the 20th Century*. Cologne and London: Taschen, 2000. ISBN 3-8228-5907-9

- Russolo, Luigi. *The Art of Noises*. New York: Pendragon, 1986.

- Samson, Jim. *Music in Transition: A Study of Tonal Expansion and Atonality, 1900–1920*. New York: W. W. Norton & Company, 1977.

- Schaeffer, Pierre. "Solfege de l'objet sonore". *Le Solfège de l'Objet Sonore* (*Music Theory of the Sound Object*), a sound recording that accompanied *Traité des Objets Musicaux* (*Treatise on Musical Objects*) by Pierre Schaeffer, was issued by ORTF (French Broadcasting Authority) as a long-playing record in 1967.

- Schafer, R. Murray. *The Soundscape* Rochester, Vt: Destiny Books, 1993. ISBN 978-0-89281-455-8

- Sheppard, Richard. *Modernism-Dada-Postmodernism*. Chicago: Northwestern University Press, 2000.

- Steiner, Wendy. *Venus in Exile: The Rejection of Beauty in 20th-Century Art*. New York: The Free Press, 2001.

- Stuart, Caleb. "Damaged Sound: Glitching and Skipping Compact Discs in the Audio of Yasunao Tone, Nicolas Collins and Oval" In *Leonardo Music Journal* Vol 13: *Groove, Pit and Wave: Recording, Transmission and Music*. 2003. pp. 47–52

- Tenney, James. *A History of "Consonance" and "Dissonance"*. White Plains, New York: Excelsior; New York: Gordon and Breach, 1988.

- Thompson, Emily. *The Soundscape of Modernity: Architectural Acoustics and the Culture of Listening in America, 1900–1933*. Cambridge, Ma.: MIT Press, 2002.

- Voegelin, Salome. *Listening to Noise and Silence: Towards a Philosophy of Sound Art*. London: Continuum. 2010. Chapter 2 *Noise*, pp. 41–76.

- Woods, Michael. *Art of the Western World*. Mandaluyong City: Summit Books, 1989.

- Woodward, Brett (ed.). *Merzbook: The Pleasuredome of Noise*. Melbourne and Cologne: Extreme, 1999.

- Young, Rob (ed.) *Undercurrents: The Hidden Wiring of Modern Music*. London: Continuum Books. 2002.

2.17.10 External links

- *Noise* A short noise music documentary film by N.O. Smith

- Freshwidow.com, Marcel Duchamp playing and discussing his noise ready-made *With Hidden Noise*

- Paul Hegarty, *Full With Noise: Theory and Japanese Noise Music* on Ctheory.net

- *The Future of Music: Credo*, John Cage (1937) from *Silence*, John Cage, Wesleyan University Press

- Alphamanbeast's noise directory Information base with links to noise artists and labels

- White noise in wave(.wav) format (1 minute)

- UBU.armob.ca La Monte Young's *89 VI 8 c. 1:42–1:52 AM Paris Encore* (10:33) on Tellus Audio Cassette Magazinearchive hosted at UbuWeb

- Noise generator to explore different types of noise

- PNF-library.org, *Free Noise Manifesto*

- Torben Sangild: "The Aesthetics of Noise"

- UBU.com, mp3 audio files of the noise music of Luigi Russolo on UbuWeb

- Noiseweb

- List of noise bands in the Noise Wiki created by noise artists for noise artists

- #13 Power Electronics at Tellus Audio Cassette Magazine housed at UbuWeb

- MP3 files by harsh noise artists

- UBU.com, Wolf Vostell's De/Collage LP Fluxus Multipla, Italy (1980) at UbuWeb

- UBU.wfmu.org, noise music of Antonio Russolo from Tellus Audio Cassette Magazine

- Noise.as, Noise: NZ/Japan

- UBU.artmob.ca Walter De Maria *Ocean Music* (1968)

- Torben Sangild: "The Aesthetics of Noise"

- Weirdmusic.net WeirdMusic.net, an e-zine dedicated to *weird experimental music*

- Japanoise.net

- Dotdotmusic.com, Paul Hegarty, *General Ecology of Sound: Japanese Noise Music as Low Form* (2005)

- UBU.artmob.ca, audio excerpt from *The Monotone Symphony* by Yves Klein

- UBU.com, Genesis P-Orridge on the origins of Throbbing Gristle: interview by Tony Oursler on UbuWeb

- UBU.com, Group Ongaku (1960–61) at Ubuweb Recorded in 1960 & 1961 at Sogetsu Art Center, Tokyo

- RWM.macba.cat, mp3 radio lecture on Fluxus noise music

- Continuo.wordpress.com, Sound recordings from Nicolas Schöffer's spatiodynamic sculptures sourced from the DVD of an exhibition at Espace Gantner, France, 2004, titled *Précurseur de l'art cybernétique*.

- Marc Weidenbaum, "Classic Tellus Noise MP3s (Controlled Bleeding, Merzbow, etc.)", *Classic Tellus Audio Cassette Magazine Noise*

- Nam June Paik in UbuWeb Sound

2.18 Pure Data

Pure Data (**Pd**) is a visual programming language developed by Miller Puckette in the 1990s for creating interactive computer music and multimedia works. While Puckette is the main author of the program, Pd is an open source project with a large developer base working on new extensions. It is released under a license similar to the BSD license. It runs on GNU/Linux, Mac OS X, iOS, Android and Windows. Older ports exist for FreeBSD and IRIX.

Pd is very similar in scope and design to Puckette's original Max program, developed while he was at IRCAM, and is to some degree interoperable with Max/MSP, the commercial successor to the Max language. They may be collectively discussed as members of the Patcher[2] family of languages.

With the addition of the Graphics Environment for Multimedia (GEM) external, and externals designed to work with it (like Pure Data Packet / PiDiP for Linux, Mac OS X), framestein for Windows, GridFlow (as n-dimensional matrix processing, for Linux, Mac OS X, Windows), it is possible to create and manipulate video, OpenGL graphics, images, etc., in realtime with extensive possibilities for interactivity with audio, external sensors, etc.

Pd is natively designed to enable live collaboration across networks or the Internet, allowing musicians connected via LAN or even in disparate parts of the globe to create music together in real time. Pd uses FUDI as a networking protocol.

2.18.1 Similarities to Max

Pure Data and Max are both examples of dataflow programming languages. In such languages, functions or "objects" are linked or "patched" together in a graphical environment which models the flow of the control and audio. Unlike the original version of Max, however, Pd was always designed to do control-rate and audio processing on the host central processing unit (CPU), rather than offloading the sound synthesis and signal processing to a digital signal processor (DSP) board (such as the Ariel ISPW which was used for Max/FTS). Pd code forms the basis of David Zicarelli's MSP extensions to the Max language to do software audio processing.[3]

Like Max, Pd has a modular code base of *externals* or objects which are used as building blocks for programs written in the software. This makes the program arbitrarily extensible through a public API, and encourages developers to add their own control and audio routines, in the programming languages C, or with the help of other externals, in Python, Scheme, Lua, Tcl, and many others. However, Pd is also a programming language. Modular, reusable units of code written natively in Pd, called "patches" or "abstractions", are used as standalone programs and freely shared among the Pd user community, and no other programming skill is required to use Pd effectively.

2.18.2 Language features

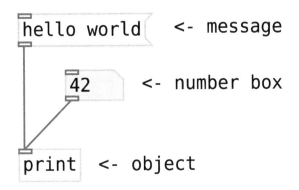

Pure Data objects. The text strings to the right of the boxes are comments.

Like Max, Pd is a data flow programming language. As with most DSP software, there are two primary rates at which data is passed: sample (audio) rate, usually at 44,100 samples per second, and control rate, at 1 block per 64 samples. Control messages and audio signals generally flow from the top of the screen to the bottom between "objects" connected via inlets and outlets.

Pd supports 4 basic types of text entities: messages, objects,

2.18. PURE DATA

atoms, and comments. Atoms are the most basic unit of data in Pd, and they consist of either a float, a symbol, or a pointer to a data structure (in Pd, all numbers are stored as 32-bit floats). Messages are composed of one or more atoms and provide instructions to objects. A special type of message with null content called a *bang* is used to initiate events and push data into flow, much like pushing a button.

Pd's native objects range from the basic mathematical, logical, and bitwise operators found in every programming language to general and specialized audio-rate DSP functions (designated by a tilde (~) symbol), such as wavetable oscillators, the Fast Fourier transform (fft~), and a range of standard filters. Data can be loaded from file, read in from an audio board, MIDI, via Open Sound Control (OSC) through a Firewire, USB, or network connection, or generated on the fly, and stored in tables, which can then be read back and used as audio signals or control data.

Data structures

One of the key innovations in Pd over its predecessors has been the introduction of graphical data structures, which can be used in a large variety of ways, from composing musical scores, sequencing events, to creating visuals to accompany Pd patches or even extending Pd's GUI.

Living up to Pd's name, data structures enable Pd users to create arbitrarily complex static as well as dynamic or animated graphical representations of musical data. Much like C structs, Pd's structs are composed of any combination of floats, symbols, and array data, which can be used as parameters to describe the visual appearance of the data structure or, conversely, to control messages and audio signals in a Pd patch. In Puckette's words:

> Pd is designed to offer an extremely unstructured environment for describing data structures and their graphical appearance. The underlying idea is to allow the user to display any kind of data he or she wants to, associating it in any way with the display. To accomplish this Pd introduces a graphical data structure, somewhat like a data structure out of the C programming language, but with a facility for attaching shapes and colors to the data, so that the user can visualize and/or edit it. The data itself can be edited from scratch or can be imported from files, generated algorithmically, or derived from analyses of incoming sounds or other data streams.
> — Miller Puckette, Pd Documentation Chapter 2 — 2.9. Data structures

Score for Hans-Christoph Steiner's Solitude, *created using Pd's data structures.*

2.18.3 Language limitations

Though Pd is a powerful language it has certain limitations in its implementation of Object Oriented concepts.[4] For example it is very difficult to create massively parallel processes because instantiating and manipulating large lists of objects (spawning..etc..) is impossible due to a lack of a constructor function. Further, Pd arrays and other entities are susceptible to name space collisions because passing the patch instance ID is an extra step and is sometimes difficult to accomplish.

2.18.4 Projects using Pure Data

Pure Data has been used as the basis of a number of projects, as a prototyping language and a sound engine. The table interface called the Reactable[5] and the iPhone app RjDj both embed Pd as a sound engine.

Pd has been used for prototyping audio for video games by a number of audio designers. For example, EAPd is the internal version of Pd that is used at Electronic Arts (EA). It has also been embedded into EA Spore[6]

Pd has also been used for networked performance, in the Networked Resources for Collaborative Improvisation (NRCI) Library.[7]

2.18.5 Code examples

1. The first patch prints "Hello world" to the display.

2. The second patch applies reverberation to the incoming signal from channel 1, then emits it on channels 1 and 2.

3. The last, more complex patch filters white noise at 9000 hertz (with a Q of 20), then fades it in and out each second over the course of a half second. As in all of Pd, time is measured in milliseconds, thus the '1000' is one second and the '500' is a half second.

2.18.6 See also

- Graphics Environment for Multimedia
- Max/Msp

- reacTable
- Puredyne
- Comparison of audio synthesis environments
- List of music software

2.18.7 Notes

[1] SourceForge file page

[2] Puckette, M. (1988). The patcher. In Proceedings of International Computer Music Conference.

[3] Where did Max/MSP come from?

[4] http://pedrolopesresearch.wordpress.com/2010/03/02/possibilities2-audio-layer/

[5] Jorda, Sergi; Kaltenbrunner, Martin; Geiger, Gunter; Bencina, Ross (2005). "ICMC2005: The ReacTable" (PDF). Music Technology Group/IUA, Universitat Pompeu Fabra.

[6] Kosak, Dave (20 February 2008). "Gamespy: The Beat Goes on: Dynamic Music in Spore". *GameSpy*. IGN Entertainment, Inc.

[7] "Networked Resources for Collaborative Improvisation (NRCI)". *Center for Computer Research in Music and Acoustics*. Department of Music, Stanford University.

2.18.8 References

- Danks, M. (1996). The graphics environment for max. In: Proceedings of the International Computer Music Conference, pp. 67–70. International Computer Music Association.

- Danks, M. (1997). Real-time image and video processing in Gem. In: Proceedings of the International Computer Music Conference, pp. 220–223. International Computer Music Association.

- Puckette, M. S. (1996) Pure Data. Proceedings, International Computer Music Conference. San Francisco: International Computer Music Association, pp. 269–272.

- Puckette, M. S. (1997). Pure data. In: Proceedings of the International Computer Music Conference, pp. 224–227. International Computer Music Association.

2.18.9 Further reading

- Puckette, Miller Smith (2007). *The Theory and Technique of Electronic Music*. World Scientific, Singapore. ISBN 978-981-270-541-9.

- Kreidler, Johannes (2009). *Loadbang: Programming Electronic Music in Pure Data*. Wolke Verlag, Hofheim. ISBN 978-3-936000-57-3.

- FLOSS, Manuals (2012). *Pure Data*. FLOSS Manuals, Amsterdam, Netherlands.

- Pd~graz (ed.), ed. (2006). *bang Pure Data* (PDF). Wolke Verlag, Hofheim. ISBN 978-3-936000-37-5.

- Farnell, Andy J (2010). *Designing Sound*. The MIT Press. ISBN 978-0-262-01441-0.

- Brinkmann, Peter (2012). *Making Musical Apps – Real-time audio synthesis on Android and iOS*. O'Reilly Media. ISBN 978-1-4493-1490-3.

- Barkl, Michael (2012). *Composition: Pure Data as a Meta-Compositional Instrument*. ISBN 3-8383-1647-9.

- Matsumura, Sei (2012). *Pd Recipe Book —Pure Data▯▯▯▯▯▯▯▯▯▯▯▯▯▯▯▯*. ISBN 978-4-86100-780-4.

- Habibdoost, Mansoor (2013). *Pd Elementary Method (in Farsi) - pdf and patches (▯▯▯ ▯▯▯▯▯▯▯ ▯▯▯▯▯ ▯▯▯▯ ▯▯▯▯ ▯▯▯▯▯ ▯▯▯▯▯ ▯▯ ▯▯ ▯▯▯▯▯)*.

2.18.10 External links

- Software by Miller Puckette — the latest Pd releases, documentation, and source code

- Pure Data Portal - hosted by Institute of Electronic Music and Acoustics (IEM)

- Forum - Pd user's forum

2.19 Raster-Noton

Raster-Noton is a German electronic music record label established in 1999. Based in Chemnitz, Germany, it emerged from the fusion of Rastermusik, founded by Olaf Bender and Frank Bretschneider in 1996, and Noton (*Archiv für Ton und Nichtton*), a sublabel which was run by Carsten Nicolai.

"raster-noton. archiv für ton und nichtton" is meant to be a platform — a network covering the overlapping border

2.19. RASTER-NOTON

Carsten Nicolai as Noto, *playing live at MUTEK 2004*

Olaf Bender as Byetone, *playing live at MUTEK 2004*

areas of pop, art and science. It realizes music projects, publications and installation works. A common idea behind all releases is an experimental approach — an amalgamation of sound, art and design, which is not only apparent in the music, but also visible from the artwork and cover design.[1]

The collective label's aesthetic focus is on rhythmic, minimal electronic music alternating between playful pop and introspection.

2.19.1 Artists

- Alva Noto
- Blixa Bargeld
- Anne-James Chaton
- AOKI Takamasa
- Atom™
- Blir
- Byetone
- Carl Michael von Hausswolff
- Ivan Pavlov (CoH)
- Cosey Fanni Tutti
- Cyclo
- Elph
- Emptyset
- Frank Bretschneider (Komet)
- Frans de Waard, Roel Meelkop and Peter Duimelinks (Goem)
- Grischa Lichtenberger
- Herve Boghossian
- Ilpo Väisänen
- Kangding Ray
- Kim Cascone
- Komet
- Kyborg
- Kyoka
- Marc Behrens
- Mark Fell
- Mika Vainio
- Mitchell Akiyama
- Modul
- Mokira
- NHK
- Nibo
- Noto
- Opiate
- Mika Vainio (Ø)

- Ø
- Pixel
- Franz Pomassl
- Produkt
- Richard Chartier
- Robert Lippok
- Ryoji Ikeda
- Ryuichi Sakamoto
- Robin Rimbaud (Scanner)
- Jens Massel (Senking)
- Signal
- SND
- Taylor Deupree
- Vladislav Delay
- William Basinski
- Wolfgang Voigt

[2]

2.19.2 Catalogue

20' to 2000

20' to 2000 is a monthly series of twelve CDs released over the course of 1999, with each month's artist contributing a 20-minute project expressing "possibly a manifest of the millennium". Each disc was packaged in a thin plastic slipcase with a hollow core. A separate kit containing twelve magnets fit into the core and allowed the individual discs to be joined into one set (pictured). This series received the "Golden Nica" award from Ars Electronica in 2000.

2.19.3 References

[1] http://www.raster-noton.net. |first1= missing |last1= in Authors list (help); Missing or empty |title= (help)

[2] http://www.raster-noton.net

2.19.4 External links

- Official Site
- Music guide to Raster-Noton by pontone.pl

2.20 Reaktor

This article is about the audio software program. For the personal computer game, see Reaktor (computer game).

Reaktor is a graphical modular software music studio developed by Native Instruments (NI). It lets musicians and sound specialists design and build their own instruments, samplers, effects and sound design tools. It is supplied with many ready-to-use instruments and effects, from emulations of classic synthesizers to futuristic sound design tools. In addition, more than 3000 free instruments can be downloaded from the growing User Library. One of Reaktor's unique selling points is that all of its instruments can be freely examined, customized or taken apart; Reaktor is a tool that effectively encourages reverse engineering. Reaktor Player is a free limited version of the software that allows musicians to play NI-released Reaktor instruments, but not edit or reverse-engineer them.

2.20.1 Development History

Early development

In 1996, Native Instruments released Generator version 0.96 - a modular synthesizer for PC, requiring a proprietary audio card for low-latency operation. By 1998, Native Instruments had redesigned the program to include new hierarchy, and integrated third-party drivers for use with any standard Windows sound card. By 1999, Reaktor 2.0 (a.k.a. Generator/Transformator) is released for Windows and Macintosh. Integrated real-time display of filters and envelopes and granular synthesis are among most notable features. Plug-in support for VST, VSTi, DirectConnect, MOTU, and DirectX formats is integrated by 2000 (software version 2.3).

With version 3.0 (released in 2001), Native Instruments introduced a redesigned audio engine and new graphic design. Further expansion of synthesis and sampling modules, addition of new control-based modules (XY control) and data management (event tables) greatly expands the abilities of the program. The earliest version to really resemble the modern incarnation of the software is version 3.5, which improved greatly in VST performance and sample handling. Reaktor 3.5 is the first release that features full cross-platform compatibility.[1]

Reaktor 4 was a major enhancement in terms of stability, instrument library, GUI, and VSTi ease-of-use in external sequencers. It shipped almost six months behind schedule.

Version 5

In 2003 Native Instruments hired Vadim Zavalishin, developer of the Sync Modular software package. Zavalishin ceased the development of his software,[2] yet integrated a deeper DSP-level operation within Reaktor, known as Reaktor Core Technology.[3] His contributions, along with those of Reaktor Core developer Martijn Zwartjes, were released within Reaktor 5 in April 2005. Core Technology initially confused a lot of instrument designers because of its complexity, but is now steadily making its way into new instruments and ensembles.

Reaktor 5.1, released on 22 December 2005, and presented as a Christmas present, features new Core Cell modules, and a new series of FX and ensembles. Also a number of bug fixes were implemented.

The release of Reaktor 5.5 was announced for 1 September 2010. It features a revised interface as well as other changes.

Version 6

Reaktor 6.0 was released on September 9th 2015. It features many new improvements for advanced programmers. A new "Blocks" feature allowed for the development of rackmount style modular "patches" for creating synthesizers and effects.[4]

2.20.2 Functionality

From the end-user standpoint, Reaktor is a sound creation/manipulation tool with a modular interface.[5] Its patches consist of modules, connected by lines to provide a visual interpretation of signal flow. The building blocks used give Reaktor users freedom of choice to help shape their sound design. The modules are categorized into particular hierarchy to aid clarity in patching.

The patcher window allows one to navigate the inner structure of user's models. Many factory-shipped objects within Reaktor can be accessed and edited, and new objects can be generated on the fly. Each of the Reaktor modules is defined by its inner workings, and expansion thereof to the users' specification comes with relative ease.[6]

The objects that are available within Reaktor range from simple math operators to large sound modules. Implementation of Core Technology with version 5 enables user to view and edit the structure of any "Core Module" building block. Although such editing can be an exceptionally powerful tool,[7] successful manipulation of Core Cells with predictable results requires in-depth knowledge of algorithmic implementation of signal generation and processing. Native Instruments promote this functionality with online side-by-side comparison of Core implementation of simple DSP algorithm against C++ pseudocode.[8][9]

Reaktor enables a user to implement variables (static or dynamic) which are used as defining properties of the patch. Users have an ability to generate a GUI of their own to provide dynamic control to their systems. Starting with version 4, Reaktor supports user-generated graphical content, enabling many users to generate original look and feel of their instruments.

A finished Reaktor ensemble may be loaded into a host sequencer (such as Steinberg Cubase or Ableton Live), and used as a stand-alone software plug-in for audio generation or processing (a multi-format proprietary loader is included with the software). Each panel control in the ensemble is capable of MIDI automation in the host sequencer.

2.20.3 Reaktor Ensembles

The Reaktor Library is one of the prominent features of the software, featuring a large variety of sound generators and effects that can be used as stand-alone instruments, or as an educational resource for backwards engineering. Reaktor 4 featured a library of 31 Reaktor ensembles. The fifth generation of software came with 32 new modules (though some were upgrades of Reaktor 4 Library tools). The libraries provide a mixture of conventional implementation of software synthesizers, samplers, and effects, along with a few ensembles of experimental nature, with emphasis on parametric algorithmic composition and extensive sound processing. Due to complete backwards-compatibility between later versions of the software, Reaktor 5 users have access to all 63 proprietary ensembles in Reaktor Library.

Furthermore, home-brew Reaktor ensembles can be shared by its users. Such exchange is encouraged by Native Instruments, characterized by the company's dedication for providing web-based tools and webspace for individual and third-party Reaktor extensions (this includes user Ensembles and presets for Reaktor Instruments and Effects).

Reaktor 4 Library

[10]

Reaktor 5 Library

2.20.4 See also

- Comparison of audio synthesis environments
- List of music software

2.20.5 References

[1] "REAKTOR TIPS". SoundOnSound. May 2002. Retrieved 2007-03-07.

[2] "SynC Modular Discontinued". The Sonic Spot. 2000-11-29. Retrieved 2007-03-08.

[3] "NI Reaktor 5". Sound On Sound. 2005-09-01. Retrieved 2007-03-08.

[4] https://www.native-instruments.com/en/products/komplete/synths/reaktor-6/

[5] "Native Instruments' Reaktor 5 Review". FutureMusic. 2006-05-08. Retrieved 2007-03-09.

[6] "NI Reaktor 5 Review". Sound On Sound. 2005-09-01. Retrieved 2007-03-09.

[7] "Reaktor 5: Core Technology". Native Instruments. 2005. Archived from the original on 2006-11-25. Retrieved 2007-03-09.

[8] http://co.native-instruments.com/index.php?id=r5core1

[9] http://co.native-instruments.com/index.php?id=r5core2

[10] "Native Instruments Reaktor 4 Library". Native Instruments. 1999. Retrieved 2007-03-08.

[11] "Native Instruments Reaktor 5 Library (page 1)". Native Instruments. 2004. Retrieved 2007-03-08.

[12] "Native Instruments Reaktor 5 Library (page 2)". Native Instruments. 2004. Archived from the original on 2007-09-27. Retrieved 2007-03-08.

[13] "Native Instruments Reaktor 5 Library (page 3)". Native Instruments. 2004. Archived from the original on 2007-09-27. Retrieved 2007-03-08.

2.20.6 External links

- Reaktor 5 homepage
- Reaktor Tips, the Reaktor tutorial project tutorials and downloads
- Kore, Komplete, Reaktor at CDM tutorials, screencasts and downloads of Reaktor ensembles and other Native Instruments related material
- Wikibooks Reaktor pages
- Reaktor Resources - links to anyone and anything Reaktor related
- Swiftkick - downloadable Reaktor 3 Wizoo book - out of date but still useful for new builders
- Reaktor Diary no longer updated but has some great info
- matsc:s Reaktor tutorial some tutorials here
- Reaktor For You Community archived resources, no longer actively maintained

2.21 Reason (software)

Reason is a digital audio workstation for creating and editing music and audio developed by Swedish software developers Propellerhead Software. It emulates a rack of hardware synthesizers, samplers, signal processors, sequencers, and mixers, all of which can be freely interconnected in an arbitrary manner. Reason can be used either as a complete virtual music studio or as a set of virtual instruments to be used with other sequencing software in a fashion that mimics live performance.

2.21.1 Overview

Reason 1.0 was released in December 2000. The program's design mimics a studio rack into which users can insert virtual devices such as instruments, effects processors, and mixers. These modules can be controlled from Reason's built-in MIDI sequencer or from other sequencing applications such as Pro Tools, Logic, FL Studio, REAPER, Digital Performer, Cubase, Sonar, and GarageBand via Propellerhead's ReWire protocol in the 32-bit versions of these programs. Since the release of version 6 Reason supports ReWire with 64-bit hosts.

As of version 7.0.1, devices available include:

- Subtractor: a subtractive synthesizer

- Malström: a graintable synthesizer (granular synthesis + wavetable synthesis)[1]

- NN-19: a simple sampler, which loads pre-recorded instrumental and vocal sounds

- NN-XT: an advanced sampler, which features the option of tweaking the various modulation, oscillation, and filter parameters of a preloaded sample or patch

- Dr Octo Rex: a loop playback device, which slices pre-recorded samples

- Redrum: a sample based drum machine with a step sequencer

- Thor: a semi-modular synthesizer which features, among others, wavetable synthesis,[2] frequency modulation synthesis (FM), and phase distortion synthesis

- Kong Drum Designer: a 16-pad drum synthesizer with analog synthesizers emulating the classic generators of drums like the Roland TR series, physical modelling drum synthesizers and sampler akin to the Akai MPC series.

- Neptune: A voice synthesizer and pitch correction tool, capable of Vocoder-like polyphonic voice synthesis as well as robotic, AutoTune-like pitch adjustment and more subtle pitch corrections.[3]

- Alligator: A triple filtered gate, sometimes known as a "trance gate". Alligator splits an incoming signal into three signals, which are then gated and filtered using lowpass, bandpass and highpass filters on each respective channel. Alligator also is capable of adding delay, distortion, phasing and stereo panning effects to each channel, and each of the filters can be modulated with a filter envelope embedded in the unit.[4]

- Pulveriser: A multi-purpose piece of virtual hardware that combines compression, distortion, filters, tremolo, parallel signal processing and an envelope follower.[5]

- The Echo: An echo unit based on tape echo and delay.[6]

- External MIDI Instrument: A device which allows for MIDI output from Reason to an external MIDI instrument

Sounds from these devices can be routed via either of two mixing devices or simple merging and splitting utilities. Effects include distortion, reverb, chorus, a vocoder, and mastering effects. The Combinator device, introduced in Reason 3.0, allows users to combine multiple modules into one. Another device connects Reason to Propellerhead's (now discontinued) ReBirth RB-338.

Reason's interface includes a Toggle Rack command, which turns the "rack" around to display the devices from the rear. Here the user can route virtual audio and CV cables from one piece of equipment to another. This cable layout enables the creation of complex effects chains and allows devices to modulate one another. This offers flexibility in the way that is familiar to users of physical electronic music hardware. For example, Redrum's main outputs could be connected to a single channel of the mixing desk, or instead each of its drum sounds could be routed to a separate EQ before sending them to separate channels in the mixer, or rather than audio output the channels of the ReDrum could be used to trigger the gates of an Alligator via CV. The user can always choose where to draw the line between simplicity and precision, allowing the software to remain useful at various levels of knowledge on the user's part.

Reason 6 introduced audio recording (by incorporating Record), turning it into a digital audio workstation. It does not support third-party plug-ins, being one of the few software sequencers to lack VST support. This has been a frequent cause of criticism, although it also contributes to the product's stability. However, Reason 6.5 introduces rack extensions, which are rack instruments and signal processors that may be developed by third parties.

A stripped-down version of Reason known as Reason Adapted, which restricts the user to a limited number of devices, is packaged as bonus software with other audio software such as Pro Tools LE and ReCycle.

Reason 5

Reason 5 was released on 25 August 2010. For the first time, Reason can directly sample audio[7] with any of its sample-playing instruments such as the Redrum, the NN-19, the NN-XT, and the Kong Drum Designer.

- *Dr. Octo Rex* - The Dr. Rex loop player was given an overhaul and is now called "Dr. Octo Rex"[8] and can play up to eight sample loops (one at a time), and includes many new features for editing the loops and individual clips.

- *Kong Drum Designer* - This is new to the program[9] a 16-pad device that can create drum and percussion sounds using various sound production techniques, including physical modeling, sample playback (the "NN-Nano" module), and virtual analog synthesis.

Signature Patches created by well known Reason users have been added, including patches made by Two Lone Swordsmen, Vengeance, and Richard Barbieri.

Finally, a new pattern editing tool called "Blocks"[10] has been created for easier song arrangement and mixing.

Reason 6

On July 12, 2011, Propellerhead announced the release of the next generation of the Reason line, Reason 6, which was released on September 30, 2011.[11] It integrates all of the features found in Record 1.5 – such as the ability to record live sound, the mixing desk modeled on the SSL 9000k, and the Neptune pitch corrector – into its setup. The Record name has been phased out altogether.

As well as bringing all of Record's features into the Reason rack, Reason 6 is 64-bit and features three new effects units, as also audio transposing direct on the sequencer, and improved tuning and stretching algorithms:

- *Pulveriser* - a combined compression, distortion, and filtering unit.[5]

- *The Echo* - an advanced stereo echo unit modeled on analog tape echo machines like the Roland RE-201.[6]

- *Alligator* - a pattern-based gate effect which splits sound signals into three channels, allowing for differing multiple effects on each separate channel.[4]

- *ID-8 Instrument Device* - a sound module with a built-in palette of 36 preset sound banks, such as a piano, organ, guitar and drum kits. The ID-8 also functions as a default MIDI device that will play sounds when a MIDI file is loaded into Reason 6.

Reason 6 also requires a USB software protection dongle called the "Ignition Key" to prevent unauthorized use of the software. Without the dongle, Reason 6 will not open saved files, nor will it dump audio to a sound file, but is otherwise fully functional. If the key is lost, or chosen not to be used, a user must log onto Propellerhead's server for internet verification, requiring the host computer to have an internet connection.

Reason 6.5

On March 20, 2012, Propellerhead announced the planned release for Reason 6.5 in 2012 Q2 to coincide with the release of Rack Extensions (which allow the use of 3rd party designed instruments and effect modules inside of Reason).[12]

Along with Rack Extensions developed by various third parties, Propellerhead offered three optional devices at launch:

- *Polar* - a harmonizing and pitch-shifter effect unit.

- *Pulsar* - a dual-channel low frequency oscillator unit.

- *Radical Piano* - a piano synthesizer based on sampling technology and physical modeling algorithms that is capable of creating new and unique piano sounds based on audio samples from two types of grand pianos and an upright piano.

Reason 6 and 6.5 include the features of Record and are now able to record external audio. Reason project file sizes that include audio record takes tend to be larger than for previous versions since there is currently no way to save Reason projects with the record takes as external (non-embedded) audio.

Reason 7

On March 12, 2013, Propellerhead announced the planned release of Reason 7 in Q2 of 2013, which was released on April 30, 2013.[13] New features include a MIDI Output Rack Device, audio quantize, loop slicing with export to Dr. Octo REX, native mix bus routing, and a spectrum EQ.

New Rack Extensions by Propellerhead include:

- *A-List Acoustic Guitarist* - A sample-based acoustic guitar emulator that produces realistic strumming guitar sounds which can be modified by selecting various playing styles and chord characteristics.

- *Audiomatic* - This is a sound effects unit that adds vintage audio quirks to music, making it sound as if it were being played back from past devices such as analog tape, a vinyl record, a crackling radio, an old television set, etc.

- *Parsec* - This is described as a spectral synthesizer using additive synthesis to sculpt various sounds.

- *Pop Chords A-List Electric Guitarist* - Similar to the A-List Acoustic Guitarist, this emulates realistic sounding electric rhythm guitar chords in a wide variety of strum methods commonly performed in pop rock, alternative and funk styles of music.

- *Power Chords A-List Electric Guitarist* - Similar to the A-List Acoustic Guitarist, this emulates realistic sounding electric guitar power chords in various strumming styles popular in rock and metal styles of music.

- *PX7* - This rack device emulates the 80's sounds of the classic Yamaha DX series of synthesizers that used frequency modulation synthesis. The PX7 can even use patches converted from DX synths.

- *Radical Keys* - Similar to Radical Piano, this emulates various electric pianos and organs such as the Rhodes Mk1, the Wurlitzer and the Hohner Pianet-T.

- *Rotor* - This is a rotating speaker emulator modeled after the Leslie 122 rotary speaker of the 1940s to add realistic vintage flavors to music, especially organ and guitar tracks.

- *Synchronous* - Described as a timed effect modulator, this adds various effects to a music device it is linked to such as distortion, filtering and delay which can be controlled by drawing various waveforms in the device's main display. For example, it can be used to add characteristic synthesizer wobbles and beat glitches that are popular in dubstep and drum and bass.

Reason 7 no longer requires the use of the Ignition Key USB dongle to fully function, instead, one computer can be licensed to use the software on installation. If a license holder wishes to use the software on other computers, they can purchase an Ignition Key separately for that purpose, or verify their license over the internet.

Reason 8

Reason 8 was released September 30, 2014. This version's newest feature is the improved file browser that accompanies, or optionally fully replaces the rack window. Users can easily audition sound files, loops and instruments patches in the browser then drag the files from the browser right to the rack window or the sequencer allowing improved and faster workflow. This version also comes with two free rack extensions; the *Softube Amp*, a guitar amplifier emulator and *Softube Bass Amp*, a bass guitar amplifier emulator designed by the veteran Rack Extension developer Softube. Both rack extensions are also available separately for Reason 6.5 and 7 and do not require the version 8 upgrade.

2.21.2 Devices

Basic devices

- *Hardware Interface* – This handles the connection between software and hardware and supports up to sixty-four separate outputs. As it is integral to Reason's functionality, it cannot be removed.

- *Mixer 14:2* – Reason's mixer is used to group numerous device outputs into a stereo output. It has fourteen stereo channels with level meters, fixed bass and treble EQ and four stereo auxiliary sends. It is possible to mute or solo any given channel, as well as alter its level, pan and auxiliary output level. The console has chaining master inputs to allow several line mixers to be daisy chained together, effectively allowing for an unlimited number of channels.

- *Line Mixer 6:2* – Similar to the Mixer 14:2, and also known as the *Micromix*, it is a smaller, six channel mixer, with only one auxiliary send and return, no EQ, smaller level controls and limited metering.

Synthesizers

- *Subtractor Analogue Synthesizer* – This is a polyphonic synthesizer device based on subtractive synthesis, which is the method used in classic, analog synthesizers. Its two oscillators can produce basic waveforms such as square, sawtooth, triangle, and sine. Additional waveforms based on samples can also be generated. The Subtractor device can be fully automated from a controlling device, such as Reason's sequencer.[14]

- *Thor Polysonic Synthesizer* – This device simulates a semi-modular synthesizer. Six filter and oscillator slots allow loading up to three different filter modules and three different oscillator modules simultaneously, allowing dialing in novel sounds. A modulation matrix gives full control over signal flow, to modulate anything within Thor. Thor also has a simulation of an analog style step sequencer with more than one twist. This step sequencer can be used as a modulation tool, trigger phrases from specific keys and create arpeggios and percussion lines.[2][15]

- *Malström Graintable Synthesizer* – This device creates its sounds using Graintable technology. This technology is a cross between granular synthesis and wavetable synthesis.[1] Malström features many filtering and modulation options. It is capable of real-time waveform stretching, spectral modulation, and wavetable sweeping. Malström comes with a wide range of Graintables.[1][16]

Samplers

- *NN-19 Digital Sampler* – This is Reason's original sampler, introduced in the first version. All of its controls can be fully automated from a controlling device. There are two ways to get sound out of NN19: load a single wav/aiff sample or load a sampler patch. Loading a single wav/aiff file will instantly transpose the audio across the keyboard by speeding up or slowing down the playback of the sample. The NN19 can import and play mono or stereo files.[17]

- *NN-XT Advanced Sampler* – This is an advanced sampler with many features. It is designed for working with multiple samples which can be assigned to different keys on the keyboard. It can be used for both sound design and instrument emulation. Useful features include alternate sample playback, auto-pitch detection, keyboard zones with individual parameters, and tempo syncable LFOs.[18]

Rhythm sequencers

- *Dr. Octo REX Loop Player* – This update of the Dr.Rex device, it plays back samples created by the ReCycle (program) in the .rex and .rx2 formats. These formats allow manipulating a sample's tempo without affecting its pitch. Imagine a sample of a drum loop. The loop is 140 bpm and a track is 120 bpm. Instead of stretching the sample, which would change the sample's timbre and pitch, ReCycle slices the loop into little pieces so that each beat gets its own sample. ReCycle also creates a MIDI file with the samples played the way the loop was originally played. The 'octo' in the device's name refers to the fact that up to eight of these samples can be loaded in the device at once.[19]

- *Redrum Drum Computer* – This device is a sample-playback drum module with a built in pattern sequencer. It has ten channels that plays samples loaded individually or from a preset kit. In addition to the pattern sequencer, Redrum can also be played from Reason's main sequencer or via MIDI. By combining the pattern sequencer and the main sequencer, one can easily create fills and variations to the patterns without having to create new patterns for every variation.[20]

Mastering

- *MClass Equalizer* – This is a 4-band, professional level mastering EQ with low and high shelving bands, two peak filters and a low cut switch. It allows making subtle or drastic frequency adjustments to the audio.[21]

- *MClass Stereo Imager* – This splits the incoming audio into low and high frequency bands, and allows adjusting each independently. Increasing the width for the high band while making the low band slightly more mono gives wide, open sounding mixes with a tight low end.[21]

- *MClass Compressor* – This is a single-band compressor with a sidechain input for advanced compression such as ducking or de-essing, and CV out for dynamically controlling other devices.[21]

- *MClass Maximizer* – This is a tool designed to maximize the volume of Reason tracks, without crushing them or introducing other unwanted artifacts. The Maximizer features a Limiter section - with switchable look-ahead, for distortion-free brickwall limiting - and a Soft Clip section which gently rounds off the edges.[21]

Effects

- *RV7000 Advanced Reverb* – This contains basic reverb controls located on the main panel, and eight separate knobs for algorithms and their parameters, which can be accessed from a fold-out remote when pressed.[22]

- *Scream 4 Distortion* – With Scream 4's cut and body filters, two parameters for its ten modes including overdrive, distortion, feedback and tape damage, it can be used for digital bit crushing, or regular crushing, or for simulating adding analog warmth to audio.[23]

- *BV512 Digital Vocoder* – The BV-512 is a 4 to 512-band vocoder that can modulate sound in several ways, and can also be used as an automated equalizer.[24]

Other effects

Reason also features numerous simple effect devices.

- *RV-7 Digital Reverb*
- *DDL-1 Digital Delay Line*
- *D-11 Foldback Distortion*
- *ECF-42 Envelope Controlled Filter*
- *CF-101 Chorus/Flanger*
- *PH-90 Phaser*
- *UN-16 Unison*
- *COMP-01 Compressor/Limiter*
- *PEQ-2 Two Band Parametric EQ*

Other devices

- *Combinator* – This is a device that allows creating chains of Reason units - instruments, effects, pattern sequencers, and then save them as Combi patches. When a Combi patch is opened, all units in the created setup are instantly loaded, complete with sounds, settings and routings. The Combinator can house an unlimited number of Reason devices, which can all be combined, controlled and manipulated in any way. The Combinator's skinnable front panel holds four rotary controls and four buttons that can all be assigned to any function on any device in a combinator chain. The back of the Combinator reveals two connectors: the Combi input jacks that allow using Combinator as an effect unit. Combinator devices are the most commonly used device for *song* creation due to the flexibility and also as they are easily 'compacted' for easier viewing and arrangement (visually). Typically each combinator is used as an individual 'instrument' with its own EQ and effects within the unit and accompanied by a 6:2 Mixer and CV Merger/Splitter (see below). this allows greater control of the basic parameters of the patch and allows more manipulation to create the ideal sound without complicated re-routing as the editing is done within the Combinator (pre- combinators output).[25]

- *Spider Audio & CV Merger & Splitter* – The Spider Audio utility has two purposes: to merge and to split audio. Spider CV is exactly the same kind of utility as Spider Audio, but here the splitting and merging is performed on CV and gate signals.[26]

- *Matrix Pattern Sequencer* – This is an analog style sequencer with a maximum of 32 steps per pattern and is the part of Reason to use for ReBirth style sequences. The Matrix has 32 patterns and each can be freely sized regardless of what time signature has been chosen in the sequencer. The Resolution selector allows playback of the pattern in a range between 1/2 notes to 1/128th notes. The playback resolution is independent of the sequencer, and the display shows the 32 steps and a little graphic keyboard on the left hand side will tell what notes are being played. A switch left of the graphical keyboard gives access to 5 octaves within the programming interface. Moving the mouse over the lower part of the display will allow change of velocity levels.[27]

- *RPG-8 Monophonic Arpeggiator* – This contains a pattern section for muting selected notes in an arpeggio and a large display showing values and positions, and the 'Single Note Repeat' function engages the arpeggiator only when two or more simultaneous notes are held down. The 'Manual' mode will arpeggiate notes strictly in the order they were input for realtime arpeggio control.[28]

- *ReGroove Mixer* – This applies its timing magic non-destructively and in realtime, letting users adjust its settings as music plays. Users can lock all tracks together, or can apply different settings to up to 32 musical elements in a song. Each of the groove channels feature controls for groove amount, slide and shuffle and more detailed settings. The Reason soundbank comes with a selection of groove patches, created from analyzed recordings of real musicians as well as classic groovy tracks.[29]

2.21.3 ReFills

ReFills compress samples, loops and instrument patches into single files for simple sharing between users, and for selling commercial sample and patch libraries.

Official ReFills

Propellerhead Software has released the following ReFills for Reason:

- Reason Disco School
- Reason Soul School - includes Reason Soul Keys Refill
- Reason Strings
- ElectroMechanical - Available as a free download or relatively cheap CD to registered users of Reason 3.0 or later. Features the following keyboards:
  - Fender Rhodes Mk I Stage 73
  - Fender Rhodes Mk II Stage 73
  - Wurlitzer EP100
  - Wurlitzer EP200
  - Hammond Organ Model A
  - Hohner Clavinet D6
  - Hohner Pianet T
- Reason Drum Kits
- Reason Pianos - Features the following pianos:
  - Yamaha C7 grand piano
  - Steinway D grand piano
  - Steinway K upright piano
- Salazar Brothers Reggaeton ReFill

- Jason McGerr Sessions - Features drumming by Jason McGerr of Death Cab for Cutie.
- Abbey Road Keyboards - Recorded at Abbey Road Studios - Discontinued.[30] Features the following instruments:
    - Steinway upright piano
    - Challen Studio piano
    - Hammond RT-3
    - Mannborg Harmonium
    - Schiedmayer Celeste
    - Mellotron M400
    - Premier Tubular Bells
- Reason Electric Bass - Features the following electric bass guitars, played by Sven Lindvall and recorded by Niklas Flyckt:
    - Fender Jazz Bass
    - Fender Precision Bass
    - Fender Precision Bass played with a pick
    - Gibson EB-0
    - Gibson Les Paul
    - Kay Hollowbody
    - Music Man StingRay 5
    - Rickenbacker 4001

2.21.4 Demo songs

These demo songs show a few examples of what can be done with Reason. [31]

Propellerhead Software has released these demo songs:

- - Olivia Broadfield — Early Hours
    - Atom — Outside In
    - Anosou — Rack Disco
    - Anosou — Mountain
    - Josh Mobley & Blackjack — What's the Reason
    - Magnus Frykberg — 700 Dreams
    - Chaka Blackmon — Purple Ribbons
    - Abiram Brizuela — Evolution
    - Nora — Recall
    - BLKMGK — Power
    - Cntrl — Metamorph
    - JB — Bajo Caida
    - Qua z mo — I Just Wanna Be
    - Van Goghs — A Simple Song

[32]

2.21.5 References

[1] "Propellerhead - Reason 8 - Malström Graintable Synthesizer". Propellerhead. Retrieved 2015-02-25. *Graintable synthesis is neither granular nor wavetable synthesis but a combination of the best of both methods. ... The basis of a Graintable is a sampled sound, which has been pre-processed ... the result is a perfect set of periodic waveforms that, ... can be manipulated in a variety of ways. The Graintable can be treated as a wavetable: ...*

[2] "Propellerhead - Reason 8 - Thor Polysonic Synthesizer". Propellerhead. Retrieved 2015-02-25. *Wavetable oscillator / Wave table synthesis produces a characteristic sound that is rich and crisp. Features 32 selectable wavetables with variable position and x-fade.*

[3] Reason 6 - Neptune

[4] Reason 6 - Alligator

[5] Reason 6 - Pulveriser

[6] Reason 6 - The Echo

[7] Reason 5 Live Sampling preview

[8] Reason 5 Dr. Octo Rex preview

[9] Reason 5 Kong Drum Synthesizer preview

[10] Reason 5 Blocks preview

[11] "Propellerhead Releases Reason 6, Reason Essentials and Balance – Press – Propellerhead". Retrieved 28 September 2014.

[12] "Propellerhead". Retrieved 28 September 2014.

[13] "Propellerhead releases inspiring upgrades to Reason and Reason Essentials – Press – Propellerhead". Retrieved 28 September 2014.

[14] "Propellerhead - Reason - Subtractor". Propellerhead. Retrieved 2009-08-08.

[15] "Propellerhead - Reason - Thor Polysonic Synthesizer". Propellerhead. Retrieved 2009-08-08.

[16] "Propellerhead - Reason - Malstrom Graintable Synthesizer". Propellerhead. Retrieved 2009-08-08.

[17] "Propellerhead - Reason - NN-19 Digital Sampler". Propellerhead. Retrieved 2009-08-08.

[18] "Propellerhead - Reason - NN-XT Advanced Sampler". Propellerhead. Retrieved 2009-08-08.

[19] "Propellerhead - Reason - Dr.REX Loop Player". Propellerhead. Retrieved 2009-08-08.

[20] "Propellerhead - Reason - Redrum Drum Computer". Propellerhead. Retrieved 2009-08-08.

[21] "Propellerhead - Reason - MClass Mastering Suite". Propellerhead. Retrieved 2009-08-07.

[22] "Propellerhead - Reason - RV7000 Advanced Reverb". Propellerhead. Retrieved 2009-08-07.

[23] "Propellerhead - Reason - Matrix". Propellerhead. Retrieved 2009-08-07.

[24] "Propellerhead - Reason - BV512 Digital Vocoder". Propellerhead. Retrieved 2009-08-07.

[25] "Propellerhead - Reason - The Combinator". Propellerhead. Retrieved 2009-08-08.

[26] "Propellerhead - Reason - Spider Audio & Spider CV". Propellerhead. Retrieved 2009-08-08.

[27] "Propellerhead - Reason - Matrix". Propellerhead. Retrieved 2009-08-08.

[28] "Propellerhead - Reason - RPG-8 Arpeggiator". Propellerhead. Retrieved 2009-08-08.

[29] "Propellerhead - Reason - ReGroove Mixer". Propellerhead. Retrieved 2009-08-08.

[30] "Propellerhead - Your account - User login". Retrieved 28 September 2014.

[31] "Propellerhead - Reason - Demo Songs". Propellerhead. Retrieved 2015-10-01.

[32] "Propellerhead - Reason - Demo Songs". Propellerhead. Retrieved 2015-10-01.

2.21.6 External links

- Official website
    - Discovering Reason - Official tutorials
- Rackwiki - Community based wiki for all related topics
- Reason mixes, some reviewed here
- Reviews by Sound on Sound magazine: Version 1, v2, v2.5, v3, v4
- IT Reviews – Further independent product review of v4
- LearnReason - The number one free Reason Tutorial Site
- ReasonForums - The number one Forum Community - Powered by Learn Reason
- ReasonStation - Unofficial support community and tips
- Reason tutorial - an unofficial Reason tutorial for beginners
- Reason Resource - Reason tips, tricks, and tutorials, unupdated since 2007
- Reason France - reason News, tips, tutorials ...
- Reasonexperts - Reason tutorials
- The german Reason resources website - (Tutorials, Projects, Screencasts, ReFills and more)
-

2.22 Renoise

Renoise is a digital audio workstation (DAW) based upon the heritage and development of tracker software. Its primary use is the composition of music using sound samples, soft synths, and effects plug-ins. It is also able to interface with MIDI and OSC equipment. The main difference between Renoise and other music software is the characteristic vertical timeline sequencer used by tracking software.

2.22.1 History

Renoise was originally written from the code of another tracker called NoiseTrekker, made by Juan Antonio Arguelles Rius (Arguru). The then unnamed Renoise project was initiated by Eduard Müller (Taktik) and Zvonko Tesic (Phazze) during December 2000. The development team planned to take tracking software into a new standard of quality, enabling tracking scene composers to make audio of the same quality as other existing professional packages, while still keeping the proven layout that originated with Soundtracker in 1987.[1][2] By early 2002 stable versions (such as 1.27) were available. Over the years the development team has grown to distribute the tasks of testing, administrative, support and web duties among several people.[3]

2.22.2 Features

Renoise currently runs under recent versions of Windows (DirectSound or ASIO), Mac OS X (Core Audio) and Linux (ALSA or JACK).[4] Renoise has a long list of features, including full MIDI and MIDI sync support, VST 2.0 plugin support, ASIO multi I/O cards support, integrated sampler and sample editor, internal real-time DSP effects with unlimited number of effects per track, master and send tracks, full automation of all commands, Hi-Fi wav/aiff rendering (up to 32-bit, 96 kHz), Rewire support, etc.

Supported sample formats

WAV, AIFF, FLAC, Ogg, MP3, CAF

Supported effects standards

VSTi, AU, LADSPA, DSSI

Renoise also features a Signal Follower and cross-track routing.[5] The Signal Follower analyzes the audio output of a track and automates user-specified parameters based on the values it generates. Cross-track routing sends the automation of any Meta Device to any track. Computer Music magazine considered the combination of these two features to "open up some incredibly powerful control possibilities", and demonstrated how the signal triggered by a drum loop could control the filter cutoff frequency on a bass sound.[5]

Renoise includes many features such as an arranging tool called the "pattern matrix", full cross-track modulation routing, built-in effects including a signal-follower metadevice that allows sidechain functionality, automatic softsynth-to-sample instrument rendering, and improved MIDI mapping.[6]

2.22.3 Versions

Renoise is available as either a demo or a commercial version. The demo version excludes rendering to .WAV, ASIO support in Windows (DirectSound only) and a few other features. Also, the demo version has nag screens. The commercial version includes high quality WAV rendering (up to 32 bit 96 kHz) and ASIO support. The commercial version is notably cheaper than competitive digital audio workstations (DAWs) such as Ableton Live and Propellerhead Reason while meeting many of the same needs.

2.22.4 Development

The Renoise development team works with the Renoise user community online to pool ideas for new features. By registering, a user is permitted to download beta versions of the software and can contribute to the bug testing and feature improvement phase before the final release.

With the introduction of Lua scripting in version 2.6, users can expand Renoise. They are encouraged to share their work on the centralized Renoise Tools page.[7]

On 22 December 2013, Renoise 3 entered beta stage[8] and the final 3.0 version was released on 11 April 2014.

The beta version[9] of Renoise 3.1[10] was released on 9 October 2015.

XRNS file format

The XRNS file format is native to Renoise. It is based on the XML standard, and is readable in a normal text editor. This open XML-based file format also makes it possible for anyone to develop 3rd party applications and other systems in order to manipulate file content.

3rd party tools

A project for creating PHP scripts utilities for needed advanced edit tasks has been set at SourceForge: XRNS-PHP project

In August 2007, a functional XRNS2MIDI script was published in version 0.11 by Renoise team member Bantai. It enables Renoise users, via an external frontend, to convert native songs into regular MIDI files (.mid) and thus exporting their work for use in conventional piano-roll sequencers such as Cubase or Reason.[11]

Since version 2.6, it is possible to extend Renoise capabilities by writing plugins in the Lua programming language. A specific tools site has been created to showcase these. Almost any aspect of the program, except realtime audio data mangling, can be scripted using the native Renoise Lua API.

2.22.5 See also

- List of music software

2.22.6 References

[1] MusicRadar Staff (2009-04-02). "Renoise Software Renoise 2.0". *Music tech reviews*. MusicRadar.com. Retrieved 2011-02-20. *A great tracker that everyone can and should try*

[2] "Taktik and Phazze interview". No Error. 2002-08-03. Archived from the original on 2002-08-03. Retrieved 2011-02-20.

[3] "Renoise - Credits".

[4] "Renoise for Linux". Linux Journal. Retrieved 2008-02-04.

[5] "Totally Trackers: Hot cross fun". *Computer Music* (Future Publishing) (152): p. 76. June 2010.

[6] "What's new in Renoise 2.5". Renoise.com.

[7] "Renoise 2.6 Could Set New Bar for Control, Customization, Openness". Create Digital Music.

[8] "Renoise 3.0 release notes".

[9] "Renoise 3.1 Beta".

[10] "Release Note For Renoise 3.1".

[11] "XRNS2MIDI: Translates Renoise songs into MIDI format". XRNS-PHP.

2.22.7 External links

- Renoise Homepage
- Renoise Tutorials
- Renoise Resources
- Renoise featured artists

2.23 Software bug

To report a MediaWiki error on Wikipedia, see Wikipedia:Bug reports.

A **software bug** is an error, flaw, failure, or fault in a computer program or system that causes it to produce an incorrect or unexpected result, or to behave in unintended ways. Most bugs arise from mistakes and errors made by people in either a program's source code or its design, or in frameworks and operating systems used by such programs, and a few are caused by compilers producing incorrect code. A program that contains a large number of bugs, and/or bugs that seriously interfere with its functionality, is said to be *buggy* or defective. Reports detailing bugs in a program are commonly known as bug reports, defect reports, fault reports, problem reports, trouble reports, change requests, and so forth.

Bugs trigger errors that can in turn have a wide variety of ripple effects, with varying levels of inconvenience to the user of the program. Some bugs have only a subtle effect on the program's functionality, and may thus lie undetected for a long time. More serious bugs may cause the program to crash or freeze. Others qualify as security bugs and might for example enable a malicious user to bypass access controls in order to obtain unauthorized privileges.

The results of bugs may be extremely serious. Bugs in the code controlling the Therac-25 radiation therapy machine were directly responsible for some patient deaths in the 1980s. In 1996, the European Space Agency's US$1 billion prototype Ariane 5 rocket had to be destroyed less than a minute after launch, due to a bug in the on-board guidance computer program. In June 1994, a Royal Air Force Chinook helicopter crashed into the Mull of Kintyre, killing 29. This was initially dismissed as pilot error, but an investigation by *Computer Weekly* uncovered sufficient evidence to convince a House of Lords inquiry that it may have been caused by a software bug in the aircraft's engine control computer.[1]

In 2002, a study commissioned by the US Department of Commerce' National Institute of Standards and Technology concluded that "software bugs, or errors, are so prevalent and so detrimental that they cost the US economy an estimated $59 billion annually, or about 0.6 percent of the gross domestic product".[2]

2.23.1 Etymology

Use of the term "bug" to describe inexplicable defects has been a part of engineering jargon for many decades and predates computers and computer software; it may have originally been used in hardware engineering to describe mechanical malfunctions. For instance, Thomas Edison wrote the following words in a letter to an associate in 1878:

> It has been just so in all of my inventions. The first step is an intuition, and comes with a burst, then difficulties arise — this thing gives out and [it is] then that "Bugs" — as such little faults and difficulties are called — show themselves and months of intense watching, study and labor are requisite before commercial success or failure is certainly reached.*[3]*

The Middle English word *bugge* is the basis for the terms "bugbear" and "bugaboo", terms used for a monster.[4] Baffle Ball, the first mechanical pinball game, was advertised as being "free of bugs" in 1931.[5] Problems with military gear during World War II were referred to as bugs (or glitches).[6]

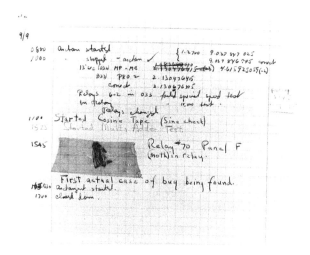

A page from the Harvard Mark II electromechanical computer's log, featuring a dead moth that was removed from the device

The term "bug" was used in an account by computer pioneer Grace Hopper, who publicized the cause of a malfunction in an early electromechanical computer.[7] A typical version of the story is given by this quote:[8]

> In 1946, when Hopper was released from active duty, she joined the Harvard Faculty at the Computation Laboratory where she continued her work on the Mark II and Mark III. Operators traced an error in the Mark II to a moth trapped in a relay, coining the term *bug*. This bug was carefully removed and taped to the log book. Stemming from the first bug, today we call errors or glitches in a program a *bug*.

Hopper was not actually the one who found the insect, as she readily acknowledged. The date in the log book was September 9, 1947,[9][10] although sometimes erroneously reported as 1945.[11] The operators who did find it, including William "Bill" Burke, later of the Naval Weapons Laboratory, Dahlgren, Virginia,[12] were familiar with the engineering term and, amused, kept the insect with the notation "First actual case of bug being found." Hopper loved to recount the story.[13] This log book, complete with attached moth, is part of the collection of the Smithsonian National Museum of American History.[10]

The related term "debug" also appears to predate its usage in computing: the Oxford English Dictionary's etymology of the word contains an attestation from 1945, in the context of aircraft engines.[14]

2.23.2 History

The concept that software might contain errors dates back to Ada Lovelace's 1843 notes on the analytical engine, in which she speaks of the possibility of program "cards" for Charles Babbage's analytical engine being erroneous:

> ... an analysing process must equally have been performed in order to furnish the Analytical Engine with the necessary *operative* data; and that herein may also lie a possible source of error. Granted that the actual mechanism is unerring in its processes, the *cards* may give it wrong orders.

2.23.3 Prevalence

In software development projects, a "mistake" or "fault" can be introduced at any stage during development. Bugs are a consequence of the nature of human factors in the programming task. They arise from oversights or mutual misunderstandings made by a software team during specification, design, coding, data entry and documentation. For example, in creating a relatively simple program to sort a list of words into alphabetical order, one's design might fail to consider what should happen when a word contains a hyphen. Perhaps, when converting the abstract design into the chosen programming language, one might inadvertently create an off-by-one error and fail to sort the last word in the list. Finally, when typing the resulting program into the computer, one might accidentally type a "<" where a ">" was intended, perhaps resulting in the words being sorted into reverse alphabetical order.

Another category of bug is called a *race condition* that can occur when programs have multiple components executing at the same time, either on the same system or across multiple systems interacting across a network. If the components interact in a different order than the developers intended, it may break the logical flow of the program. These bugs can be difficult to detect or anticipate, since they may not occur during every execution of a program.

More complex bugs can arise from unintended interactions between different parts of a computer program. This frequently occurs because computer programs can be complex — millions of lines long in some cases — often having been programmed by many people over a great length of time, so that programmers are unable to mentally track every possible way in which parts can interact.

2.23.4 Mistake metamorphism

There is ongoing debate over the use of the term "bug" to describe software errors.[15] One argument is that the word "bug" is divorced from a sense that a human being caused the problem, and instead implies that the defect arose on its own, leading to a push to abandon the term "bug" in favor of terms such as "defect", with limited success.

In software engineering, *mistake metamorphism* (from Greek *meta* = "change", *morph* = "form") refers to the evolution of a defect in the final stage of software deployment. Transformation of a "mistake" committed by an analyst in the early stages of the software development lifecycle, which leads to a "defect" in the final stage of the cycle has been called 'mistake metamorphism'.[16]

Different stages of a "mistake" in the entire cycle may be described as "mistakes", "anomalies", "faults", "failures", "errors", "exceptions", "crashes", "bugs", "defects", "incidents", or "side effects".[16]

2.23.5 Prevention

The software industry has put much effort into finding methods for preventing programmers from inadvertently introducing bugs while writing software.[17][18] These include:

Programming style While typos in the program code are often caught by the compiler, a bug usually appears when the programmer makes a logic error. Various innovations in programming style and defensive programming are designed to make these bugs less likely, or easier to spot. In some programming languages, so-called typos, especially of symbols or logical/mathematical operators, actually represent logic errors, since the mistyped constructs are accepted by the compiler with a meaning other than that which the programmer intended.

Programming techniques Bugs often create inconsistencies in the internal data of a running program. Programs can be written to check the consistency of their own internal data while running. If an inconsistency is encountered, the program can immediately halt, so that the bug can be located and fixed. Alternatively, the program can simply inform the user, attempt to correct the inconsistency, and continue running.

Development methodologies There are several schemes for managing programmer activity, so that fewer bugs are produced. Many of these fall under the discipline of software engineering (which addresses software design issues as well). For example, formal program specifications are used to state the exact behavior of programs, so that design bugs can be eliminated. Unfortunately, formal specifications are impractical or impossible for anything but the shortest programs, because of problems of combinatorial explosion and indeterminacy.

In modern times, popular approaches include automated unit testing and automated acceptance testing (sometimes going to the extreme of test-driven development), and agile software development (which is often combined with, or even in some cases mandates, automated testing). All of these approaches are supposed to catch bugs and poorly-specified requirements soon after they are introduced, which should make them easier and cheaper to fix, and to catch at least some of them before they enter into production use.

Programming language support Programming languages often include features which help programmers prevent bugs, such as static type systems, restricted namespaces and modular programming, among others. For example, when a programmer writes (pseudocode) LET REAL_VALUE PI = "THREE AND A BIT", although this may be syntactically correct, the code fails a type check. Depending on the language and implementation, this may be caught by the compiler or at run-time. In addition, many recently invented languages have deliberately excluded features which can easily lead to bugs, at the expense of making code slower than it need be: the general principle being that, because of Moore's law, computers get faster and software engineers get slower; it is *almost always* better to write simpler, slower code than "clever", inscrutable code, especially considering that maintenance cost is substantial. For example, the Java programming language does not support pointer arithmetic; implementations of some languages such as Pascal and scripting languages often have runtime bounds checking of arrays, at least in a debugging build.

Code analysis Tools for code analysis help developers by inspecting the program text beyond the compiler's capabilities to spot potential problems. Although in general the problem of finding all programming errors given a specification is not solvable (see halting problem), these tools exploit the fact that human programmers tend to make the same kinds of mistakes when writing software.

Instrumentation Tools to monitor the performance of the software as it is running, either specifically to find problems such as bottlenecks or to give assurance as to correct working, may be embedded in the code explicitly (perhaps as simple as a statement saying PRINT "I AM HERE"), or provided as tools. It is often a surprise to find where most of the time is taken by a piece of code, and this removal of assumptions might cause the code to be rewritten.

2.23.6 Debugging

Main article: Debugging

Finding and fixing bugs, or "debugging", has always been a major part of computer programming. Maurice Wilkes, an early computing pioneer, described his realization in the late 1940s that much of the rest of his life would be spent finding mistakes in his own programs.[19] As computer programs grow more complex, bugs become more common and difficult to fix. Often programmers spend more time and effort finding and fixing bugs than writing new code. Software testers are professionals whose primary task is to find bugs, or write code to support testing. On some projects, more resources can be spent on testing than in developing the program.

Usually, the most difficult part of debugging is finding the bug in the source code. Once it is found, correcting it is usually relatively easy. Programs known as debuggers exist

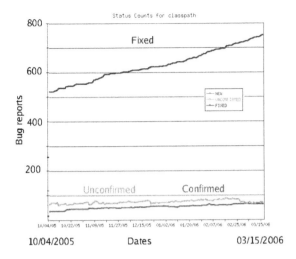

The typical bug history (GNU Classpath project data). A new bug submitted by the user is unconfirmed. *Once it has been reproduced by a developer, it is a* confirmed *bug. The confirmed bugs are later* fixed. *Bugs belonging to other categories (unreproducible, will not be fixed, etc.) are usually in the minority*

to help programmers locate bugs by executing code line by line, watching variable values, and other features to observe program behavior. Without a debugger, code can be added so that messages or values can be written to a console (for example with *printf* in the C programming language) or to a window or log file to trace program execution or show values.

However, even with the aid of a debugger, locating bugs is something of an art. It is not uncommon for a bug in one section of a program to cause failures in a completely different section, thus making it especially difficult to track (for example, an error in a graphics rendering routine causing a file I/O routine to fail), in an apparently unrelated part of the system.

Sometimes, a bug is not an isolated flaw, but represents an error of thinking or planning on the part of the programmer. Such *logic errors* require a section of the program to be overhauled or rewritten. As a part of Code review, stepping through the code modelling the execution process in one's head or on paper can often find these errors without ever needing to reproduce the bug as such, if it can be shown there is some faulty logic in its implementation.

But more typically, the first step in locating a bug is to reproduce it reliably. Once the bug is reproduced, the programmer can use a debugger or some other tool to monitor the execution of the program in the faulty region, and find the point at which the program went astray.

It is not always easy to reproduce bugs. Some are triggered by inputs to the program which may be difficult for the programmer to re-create. One cause of the Therac-25 radiation machine deaths was a bug (specifically, a race condition) that occurred only when the machine operator very rapidly entered a treatment plan; it took days of practice to become able to do this, so the bug did not manifest in testing or when the manufacturer attempted to duplicate it. Other bugs may disappear when the program is run with a debugger; these are heisenbugs (humorously named after the Heisenberg uncertainty principle).

Debugging is still a tedious task requiring considerable effort. Since the 1990s, particularly following the Ariane 5 Flight 501 disaster, there has been a renewed interest in the development of effective automated aids to debugging. For instance, methods of static code analysis by abstract interpretation have already made significant achievements, while still remaining much of a work in progress.

As with any creative act, sometimes a flash of inspiration will show a solution, but this is rare and, by definition, cannot be relied on.

There are also classes of bugs that have nothing to do with the code itself. If, for example, one relies on faulty documentation or hardware, the code may be written perfectly properly to what the documentation says, but the bug truly lies in the documentation or hardware, not the code. However, it is common to change the code instead of the other parts of the system, as the cost and time to change it is generally less. Embedded systems frequently have workarounds for hardware bugs, since to make a new version of a ROM is much cheaper than remanufacturing the hardware, especially if they are commodity items.

2.23.7 Bug management

Bug management encompasses more than bug tracking, and there exists no industry-wide standard. Proposed changes to software – bugs as well as enhancement requests and even entire releases – are commonly tracked and managed using bug tracking systems or issue tracking systems. The items added may be called defects, tickets, issues, or, following the agile development paradigm, stories and epics. The systems allow or even require some type of categorization of each issue. Categories may be objective, subjective or a combination, such as version number, area of the software, severity and priority, as well as what type of issue it is, such as a feature request or a bug.

Severity of a bug

Given a bug is impairing a user scenario, one can easily see the impact the bug has. This impact can be tangible as tangible as of data loss, immediate losses in terms of money, or can be indirect – loss of goodwill or man hours, and eventually business. This impact is said to be the severity of a bug: "the impact a bug causes when encountered by users". Thus, severity, as a software metric does have a very precise meaning. Unfortunately, severity levels are not standardized in industry and are decided by each software producer, if they are even used. This is because impacts differ across the industry. A crash in a video game has a totally different impact than a crash in the browser, or real time monitoring system. Irrespective of that, crashes would be generally categorised high severity in the respective fields. For example, bug severity levels might be "crash or hang", "no workaround" (meaning there is no way the customer can accomplish a given task), "has workaround" (meaning there is a way for the user to recover and accomplish the task), "UI" or "visual defect" (for example, a missing image or displaced button or form element), or "documentation error". Some software publishers use more qualified severities such as "critical", "high", "low," "blocker," or "trivial".[20] The severity of a bug may be a separate category to its priority for fixing, and the two may be quantified and managed separately.

Priority of a bug

Given a bug, how fast it needs to get fixed is defined by the software metric priority. How the priority for fixing is used is decided internally by each software producer. Priorities are sometimes numerical and sometimes words, such "critical," "high," "low" or "deferred"; note that these can be similar or even identical to severity ratings when looking at different software producers. For example, a software company may decide that priority 1 bugs are always to be fixed for the next release, whereas "5" could mean its fix is put off – sometimes indefinitely.

Connection between priority and severity

If a flaw is found in an application which causes it to crash, yet the crash is so rare and takes, say, ten extremely unusual or unlikely steps to produce it, management may set its priority as "low" or even "will not fix." Thus it is easily seen that Priority is a function of probability of a bug to occur, and Severity (impact) of the bug. In specificity, priority is a strictly increasing function of both probability of the bug occurrence and severity. Given probability p = 1, the severity defines the priority. When p = 0, the bug, in all probability needs not to be fixed at all, however we can have a priority strictly proportional to the severity. In the same way, when Severity S=0 for a bug, we can have a priority strictly proportional to the probability.

One can axiomatize the Priority function as any function having above characteristics, for example this very simplified function works : $P(p,s) = B - \lceil kpS \rceil$ where p is the probability while S is the severity, with k a scaling constant, and to invert the value B is the base. The ceiling function is used to get the domain of priority to only integers. It also assigns priority-B to almost never occurring bugs. Industry standard practice is to use an inverted scale, so that highest priority are low numbers, example priority 0, priority 1, while lowest priority are bigger numbers, i.e. priority 3, priority 4... etc.

Software releases

It is common practice for software to be released with known bugs that are considered "non-critical" as defined by the software producer(s). While software products may, by definition, contain any number of unknown bugs, measurements during testing can provide an estimate of the number of likely bugs remaining; this becomes more reliable the longer a product is tested and developed. Most big software projects maintain two lists of "known bugs" – those known to the software team, and those to be told to users. The second list informs users about bugs that are not fixed in the current release, or not fixed at all, and a workaround may be offered.

A software publisher may opt not to fix a particular bug for a number of reasons, including:

- A deadline must be met and priorities are such that only those above a certain severity are fixed for the current software release.

- The bug is already fixed in an upcoming release, and it is not serious enough to warrant an immediate update or patch

- The changes to the code required to fix the bug are too costly, will take too long for the current release, or affect too many other areas of the software.

- Users may be relying on the undocumented, buggy behavior; it may introduce a breaking change.

- The problem is in an area which will be obsolete with an upcoming release; fixing it is unnecessary.

- It's "not a bug". A misunderstanding has arisen between expected and perceived behavior, when such misunderstanding is not due to confusion arising from design flaws, or faulty documentation.

The amount and type of damage a software bug can cause naturally affects decision-making, processes and policy regarding software quality. In applications such as manned space travel or automotive safety, since software flaws have the potential to cause human injury or even death, such software will have far more scrutiny and quality control than, for example, an online shopping website. In applications such as banking, where software flaws have the potential to cause serious financial damage to a bank or its customers, quality control is also more important than, say, a photo editing application. NASA's Software Assurance Technology Center managed to reduce the number of errors to fewer than 0.1 per 1000 lines of code (SLOC) but this was not felt to be feasible for projects in the business world.

A school of thought popularized by Eric S. Raymond as Linus's Law says that popular open-source software has more chance of having few or no bugs than other software, because "given enough eyeballs, all bugs are shallow".[21] This assertion has been disputed, however: computer security specialist Elias Levy wrote that "it is easy to hide vulnerabilities in complex, little understood and undocumented source code," because, "even if people are reviewing the code, that doesn't mean they're qualified to do so."[22]

2.23.8 Security vulnerabilities

Malicious software may attempt to exploit known vulnerabilities in a system–which may or may not be bugs. Viruses are not bugs in themselves–they are typically programs that are doing precisely what they were designed to do. However, viruses are occasionally referred to as such in the popular press. In addition, it is often a security bug in a computer program that allows viruses to work in the first place.

2.23.9 Common types of computer bugs

- Conceptual error (code is syntactically correct, but the programmer or designer intended it to do something else).

Arithmetic bugs

- Division by zero.
- Arithmetic overflow or underflow.
- Loss of arithmetic precision due to rounding or numerically unstable algorithms.

Logic bugs

- Infinite loops and infinite recursion.
- Off-by-one error, counting one too many or too few when looping.

Syntax bugs

- Use of the wrong operator, such as performing assignment instead of equality test. For example, in some languages x=5 will set the value of x to 5 while x==5 will check whether x is currently 5 or some other number. In simple cases often the compiler can generate a warning. In many languages, the language syntax is deliberately designed to guard against this error.

Resource bugs

- Null pointer dereference.
- Using an uninitialized variable.
- Using an otherwise valid instruction on the wrong data type (see packed decimal/binary coded decimal).
- Access violations.
- Resource leaks, where a finite system resource (such as memory or file handles) become exhausted by repeated allocation without release.
- Buffer overflow, in which a program tries to store data past the end of allocated storage. This may or may not lead to an access violation or storage violation. These bugs can form a security vulnerability.
- Excessive recursion which — though logically valid — causes stack overflow.
- Use-after-free error, where a pointer is used after the system has freed the memory it references.
- Double free error.

Multi-threading programming bugs

- Deadlock, where task A can't continue until task B finishes, but at the same time, task B can't continue until task A finishes.
- Race condition, where the computer does not perform tasks in the order the programmer intended.
- Concurrency errors in critical sections, mutual exclusions and other features of concurrent processing. Time-of-check-to-time-of-use (TOCTOU) is a form of unprotected critical section.

Interfacing bugs

- Incorrect API usage.

- Incorrect protocol implementation.

- Incorrect hardware handling.

- Incorrect assumptions of a particular platform.

- Incompatible systems. Often a proposed "new API" or new communications protocol may seem to work when both computers use the old version or both computers use the new version, but upgrading only the receiver exposes backward compatibility problems; in other cases upgrading only the transmitter exposes forward compatibility problems. Often it is not feasible to upgrade every computer simultaneously—in particular, in the telecommunication industry[23] or the internet.[24][25][26] Even when it is feasible to update every computer simultaneously, sometimes people accidentally forget to update every computer—the Knight Capital Group#2012 stock trading disruption involved one such incompatibility between the old API and a new API.

Performance bugs

- Too high computational complexity of algorithm.

- Random disk or memory access.

Teamworking bugs

- Unpropagated updates; e.g. programmer changes "myAdd" but forgets to change "mySubtract", which uses the same algorithm. These errors are mitigated by the Don't Repeat Yourself philosophy.

- Comments out of date or incorrect: many programmers assume the comments accurately describe the code.

- Differences between documentation and the actual product.

2.23.10 Well-known bugs

Main article: List of software bugs

A number of software bugs have become well-known, usually due to their severity: examples include various space and military aircraft crashes. Possibly the most famous bug is the Year 2000 problem, also known as the Y2K bug, in which it was feared that worldwide economic collapse would happen at the start of the year 2000 as a result of computers thinking it was 1900. (In the end, no major problems occurred.)

2.23.11 In popular culture

- In Robert A. Heinlein's 1966 novel *The Moon Is a Harsh Mistress*, computer technician Manuel Davis blames a real bug for a (non-existent) failure of supercomputer Mike, presenting a dead fly as evidence.

- In the 1968 novel *2001: A Space Odyssey* (and its corresponding 1968 film adaptation), a spaceship's on-board computer, HAL 9000, attempts to kill all its crew members. In the followup 1982 novel, *2010: Odyssey Two*, and the accompanying 1984 film, *2010*, it is revealed that this action was caused by the computer having been programmed with two conflicting objectives: to fully disclose all its information, and to keep the true purpose of the flight secret from the crew; this conflict caused HAL to become paranoid and eventually homicidal.

- The 2004 novel *The Bug*, by Ellen Ullman, is about a programmer's attempt to find an elusive bug in a database application.

- The 2008 Canadian film *Control Alt Delete* is about a computer programmer at the end of 1999 struggling to fix bugs at his company related to the year 2000 problem.

2.23.12 See also

- Anti-pattern

- Software rot

- Bug bounty program

- Glitch removal

- ISO/IEC 9126, which classifies a bug as either a *defect* or a *nonconformity*

- Orthogonal Defect Classification

- Racetrack problem

- RISKS Digest

- Software defect indicator

- Software regression

2.23.13 Notes

[1] Prof. Simon Rogerson. "The Chinook Helicopter Disaster". Ccsr.cse.dmu.ac.uk. Retrieved September 24, 2012.

[2] "Software bugs cost US economy dear". Web.archive.org. June 10, 2009. Retrieved September 24, 2012.

[3] Edison to Puskas, 13 November 1878, Edison papers, Edison National Laboratory, U.S. National Park Service, West Orange, N.J., cited in Thomas P. Hughes, *American Genesis: A History of the American Genius for Invention,* Penguin Books, 1989, ISBN 0-14-009741-4, on page 75.

[4] Computerworld staff (September 3, 2011). "Moth in the machine: Debugging the origins of 'bug'". *Computerworld*.

[5] "Baffle Ball". Internet Pinball Database. (See image of advertisement in reference entry)

[6] "Modern Aircraft Carriers are Result of 20 Years of Smart Experimentation". *Life*. June 29, 1942. p. 25. Retrieved November 17, 2011.

[7] *FCAT NRT Test*, Harcourt, March 18, 2008

[8] "Danis, Sharron Ann: "Rear Admiral Grace Murray Hopper"". ei.cs.vt.edu. February 16, 1997. Retrieved January 31, 2010.

[9] "Bug", *The Jargon File*, ver. 4.4.7. Retrieved June 3, 2010.

[10] "Log Book With Computer Bug", National Museum of American History, Smithsonian Institution.

[11] "The First "Computer Bug"", Naval Historical Center. But note the Harvard Mark II computer was not complete until the summer of 1947.

[12] IEEE Annals of the History of Computing, Vol 22 Issue 1, 2000

[13] James S. Huggins. "First Computer Bug". Jamesshuggins.com. Retrieved September 24, 2012.

[14] Journal of the Royal Aeronautical Society. 49, 183/2, 1945 "It ranged ... through the stage of type test and flight test and 'debugging' ..."

[15] "News at SEI 1999 Archive". *cmu.edu*.

[16] *Testing Experience* (Germany: testingexperience): 42. March 2012. ISSN 1866-5705. Missing or empty |title= (help) (subscription required)

[17] Huizinga, Dorota; Kolawa, Adam (2007). *Automated Defect Prevention: Best Practices in Software Management*. Wiley-IEEE Computer Society Press. p. 426. ISBN 0-470-04212-5.

[18] McDonald, Marc; Musson, Robert; Smith, Ross (2007). *The Practical Guide to Defect Prevention*. Microsoft Press. p. 480. ISBN 0-7356-2253-1.

[19] Maurice Wilkes Quotes

[20] "5.3. Anatomy of a Bug". *bugzilla.org*.

[21] "Release Early, Release Often", Eric S. Raymond, *The Cathedral and the Bazaar*

[22] "Wide Open Source", Elias Levy, *SecurityFocus*, April 17, 2000

[23] K. Kimbler. "Feature Interactions in Telecommunications and Software Systems V" p. 8.

[24] Mahbubur Rahman Syed. "Multimedia Networking: Technology, Management and Applications: Technology, Management and Applications". p. 398.

[25] Chwan-Hwa (John) Wu, J. David Irwin. "Introduction to Computer Networks and Cybersecurity". p. 500.

[26] RFC 1263: "TCP Extensions Considered Harmful" quote: "the time to distribute the new version of the protocol to all hosts can be quite long (forever in fact). ... If there is the slightest incompatibly between old and new versions, chaos can result."

2.23.14 Further reading

- Allen, Mitch, May/Jun 2002 "Bug Tracking Basics: A beginner's guide to reporting and tracking defects" *The Software Testing & Quality Engineering Magazine*. Vol. 4, Issue 3, pp. 20–24.

2.23.15 External links

- Picture of the "first computer bug" at the Wayback Machine (archived January 12, 2015)

- The First Computer Bug! – an email from 1981 about Adm. Hopper's bug

2.24 Sonic artifact

In sound and music production, **sonic artifact**, or simply **artifact**, refers to sonic material that is accidental or unwanted, resulting from the editing or manipulation of a sound.

2.24.1 Types

Because there are always technical restrictions in the way a sound can be recorded (in the case of acoustic sounds) or designed (in the case of synthesised or processed sounds), sonic errors often occur. These errors are termed artifacts (or sound/sonic artifacts), and may be pleasing or displeasing. A sonic artifact is sometimes a type of digital artifact, and in some cases is the result of data compression (not to be confused with dynamic range compression, which also may create sonic artifacts).

Often an artifact is deliberately produced for creative reasons. For example to introduce a change in timbre of the original sound or to create a sense of cultural or stylistic context. A well-known example is the overdriving of an electric guitar or electric bass signal to produce a clipped, distorted guitar tone or fuzz bass.

Editing processes that deliberately produce artifacts often involve technical experimentation. A good example of the deliberate creation of sonic artifacts is the addition of grainy pops and clicks to a recent recording in order to make it sound like a vintage vinyl record.

Flanging and distortion were originally regarded as sonic artifacts; as time passed they became a valued part of pop music production methods. Flanging is added to electric guitar and keyboard parts. Other magnetic tape artifacts include wow, flutter, saturation, noise, and print-through.

It is valid to consider the genuine pops and clicks that are audible when a vintage vinyl recording is played back or recorded onto another medium as sonic artifacts, although not all sonic artifacts must contain in their meaning or production a sense of "past", more so a sense of "by-product".

In the Nyquist–Shannon sampling theorem, inadequate sampling bandwidth creates a sonic artifact known as an *alias*, and the resulting distortion of the sound is termed *aliasing*. Examples of aliasing can be heard in early music samplers since they could record audio at bit rates and sampling frequencies below the Nyquist rate, considered desirable by some musicians.[1] Aliasing is a major concern in the analog-to-digital conversion of video and audio signals.

In the creation of computer music and electronic music in the past decade, particularly in glitch music, software is used to create sonic artifacts of all stripes. They are also the primary focus of the practice of circuit bending: making sounds from products that were unintended by the makers of the circuitry.

2.24.2 See also

- Data compression
- Digital artifact
- Dynamic range compression
- Glitch (music)
- Compression artifact
- Sampling (information theory)
- Signal (information theory)
- Window function
- Circuit bending
- Sound reproduction
- Noise music

2.24.3 References

[1] "E-mu SP-12". VintageSynth.com. 2009. Retrieved 2009-12-21.

2.25 SuperCollider

This article is about the programming language. For other uses, see Supercollider.

SuperCollider is an environment and programming language originally released in 1996 by James McCartney for real-time audio synthesis and algorithmic composition.[2][3]

Since then it has been evolving into a system used and further developed by both scientists and artists working with sound. It is an efficient and expressive dynamic programming language providing a framework for acoustic research, algorithmic music, and interactive programming.[4]

Released under the terms of the GNU General Public License in 2002, SuperCollider is free software. The most recent major release (3.6.5) was released in November 2013.[5]

2.25.1 Architecture

Starting with version 3, the SuperCollider environment has been split into two components: a server, *scsynth*; and a client, *sclang*. These components communicate using OSC (Open Sound Control).[4]

SC Language combines the object oriented structure of Smalltalk and features from functional programming languages with a C family syntax.[4]

The *SC Server* application supports a simple C plugin API making it easy to write efficient sound algorithms (unit generators), which can then be combined into graphs of calculations. Because all external control in the server happens via OSC, it is possible to use it with other languages or applications.[4]

The SuperCollider synthesis server (*scsynth*)

SuperCollider's sound generation is bundled into an optimised command-line executable (named *scsynth*). In most cases it is controlled from within the SuperCollider programming language, but it can be used independently. The audio server has the following features:[4]

- Open Sound Control access
- Simple ANSI C plugin API
- Supports any number of input and output channels, including massively multichannel setups[6]
- Gives access to an ordered tree structure of synthesis nodes which define the order of execution
- Bus system which allows to dynamically restructure the signal flow
- Buffers for writing and reading
- Calculation at different rates depending on the needs: audio rate, control rate, demand rate

Supernova, an independent implementation of the Server architecture,[7] adds multi-processor support through explicit parallel grouping of synthesis nodes.

The SuperCollider programming language (*sclang*)

The SuperCollider programming language is a dynamically typed, garbage-collected, single inheritance object-oriented and functional language similar to Smalltalk,[3] with a syntax similar to Lisp or the C programming language. Its architecture strikes a balance between the needs of realtime computation and the flexibility and simplicity of an abstract language. Like many functional languages, it implements functions as first class objects, which may be composed. Functions and methods can have default argument values and variable length argument lists and can be called with any order of keyword arguments. Closures are lexical, and scope is both lexical and dynamic. Further features typical of functional languages are supported, including closure creation via partial application (explicit currying), tail call optimization, list comprehensions, and coroutines. Specifics include the implicit expansion of tuples and the stateless pattern system. Its constant time message lookup and real time garbage collection allows large systems to be efficient and to handle signal processing flexibly.[4]

By supporting methods of reflective, conversational, and literate programming, SuperCollider makes it relatively easy to find new sound algorithms[8] and to develop custom software as well as custom frameworks. With regards to domain specific knowledge, it is both general (e.g., it allows to represent properties such as time and pitch in variable degrees of abstraction) and copious of example implementations for specific purposes.[4]

GUI system

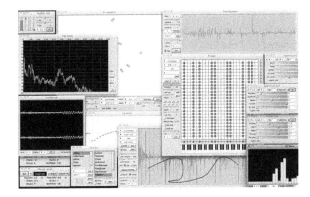

Screenshot of SuperCollider running the ixiQuarks GUI tools.

The SuperCollider language allows users to construct cross-platform graphical user interfaces for applications. The standard class library with user interface components may be extended by a number of available frameworks. For interactive programming, the system supports programmatic access to rich text code files. It may be used to generate vector graphics algorithmically.[9]

2.25.2 Interfacing and system support

Clients

Because the server is controlled using Open Sound Control (OSC), a variety of applications can be used to control the server. SuperCollider language environments (see below) are typically used, but other OSC-aware systems can be used such as Pure Data.[4]

"Third-party" clients for the SuperCollider server exist, including rsc3, a Scheme client, hsc3, based on Haskell, ScalaCollider,[10] based on Scala, and Overtone, based on Clojure.[11] These are distinct from the development environments mentioned below because they do not provide an interface to SuperCollider's programming language, instead they communicate directly with the audio server and provide their own approaches to facilitating user expression.[4]

2.25. SUPERCOLLIDER

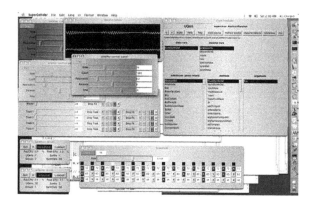

Screenshot of SuperCollider on Mac OS X with various user-generated GUI elements.

Supported operating systems

SuperCollider runs under Mac OS X, Linux, Windows and FreeBSD. The Windows version, however, tends to lag behind the others since most development is based on Mac and Linux. For each of these operating systems there are multiple language-editing environments and clients that can be used with SuperCollider (see below).[4]

It has also been demonstrated that SuperCollider can run on Android[12] and iOS.[13]

Editing environments

Screenshot of SuperCollider Vim on puredyne linux.

SuperCollider code is most commonly edit and used from within its own cross platform IDE (Linux, Mac, Windows).

Other development environments with SuperCollider support include:

- Emacs (Linux, Mac, Windows)[14]
- Vim (Linux, Mac)
- Atom (Linux, Mac, Windows)[15]
- gedit (Linux, Windows)
- Kate (Linux)[16]

2.25.3 Code examples

// print "Hello world!" "Hello world!".postln;
// play a mixture of an 800 Hz sine tone and pink noise { SinOsc.ar(800, 0, 0.1) + PinkNoise.ar(0.01) }.play;
// modulate a sine frequency and a noise amplitude with another sine // whose frequency depends on the horizontal mouse pointer position { var x = SinOsc.ar(MouseX.kr(1, 100)); SinOsc.ar(300 * x + 800, 0, 0.1) + PinkNoise.ar(0.1 * x + 0.1) }.play;
// list iteration: multiply the elements of a collection by their indices [1, 2, 5, 10, −3].collect { |elem, idx| elem * idx };
// factorial function f = { |x| if(x == 0) { 1 } { f.(x-1) * x } };

2.25.4 Live coding

As a versatile dynamic programming language, SuperCollider can be used for live coding, i.e. performances which involve the performer modifying and executing code on-the-fly.[17] Specific kinds of proxies serve as high level placeholders for synthesis objects which can be swapped in and out or modified at runtime. Environments allow sharing and modification of objects and process declarations over networks.[18] Various extension libraries support different abstraction and access to sound objects, e.g. dewdrop_lib[19] allows for the live creation and modification of pseudo-classes and -objects.

2.25.5 See also

- List of music software
- Comparison of audio synthesis environments

2.25.6 References

[1] asynth. "SuperCollider". Retrieved 20 June 2015.

[2] J. McCartney, SuperCollider: A new real time synthesis language, in Proc. International Computer Music Conference (ICMC'96), 1996, pp. 257–258.

[3] J. McCartney, Rethinking the computer music language: SuperCollider, Computer Music Journal, 26 (2002), pp. 61–68.

[4] Scott Wilson; David Cottle; Nick Collins (2011). *The SuperCollider Book*. The MIT Press. ISBN 978-0-262-23269-2.

[5] SuperCollider. "SuperCollider » SuperCollider". Retrieved 20 June 2015.

[6] "SuperCollider mailing lists". Retrieved 20 June 2015.

[7] T. Blechmann, supernova, a multiprocessor-aware synthesis server for SuperCollider, Proceedings of the Linux Audio Conference, Utrecht 2010.

[8] J. Rohrhuber, A. de Campo and Renate Wieser. Algorithms Today. Notes on Language Design for Just in Time Programming. In *Proceedings of the International Computer Music Conference*, Barcelona, 2005.

[9] The vector graphics interface is provided by the Pen class. Various examples can be found in Audiovisuals with SC, blog by Fredrik Olofsson, 02.05.2009 (updated 11.05.2012)

[10] Rutz, H. H. (2010). "Rethinking the SuperCollider Client...". *Proceedings of SuperCollider Symposium*. Berlin. CiteSeerX: 10.1.1.186.9817.

[11] "Systems interfacing with SC". Retrieved 20 June 2015.

[12] SuperCollider Android project on GitHub

[13] Tiny Music System - Cylob Blog, 04.11.2009

[14] "SuperCollider with emacs: scel". Retrieved 20 June 2015.

[15] "supercollider". *Atom*. Retrieved 20 June 2015.

[16] "jleben/Scate". *GitHub*. Retrieved 20 June 2015.

[17] Collins, N., McLean, A., Rohrhuber, J. & Ward, A. (2003), Live Coding Techniques for Laptop Performance, *Organised Sound* 8(3): pp 321-30. doi:10.1017/S135577180300030X

[18] J. Rohrhuber and A. de Campo. Waiting and uncertainty in computer music networks. In *Proceedings of the International Computer Music Conference*, Miami, 2004.

[19] One of the numerous user contributed libraries known as "Quarks", and published in the SuperCollider Quarks repository.

2.25.7 External links

- Official SuperCollider home page
- The SuperCollider Swiki
- SuperCollider users mailing list
- Workshop on SuperCollider by Nick Collins
- SuperCollider Online Help

Cover of Luigi Russolo's L'arte dei rumori, *published in book form in 1916.*

2.26 The Art of Noises

Not to be confused with Art of Noise.

The Art of Noises (Italian: *L'arte dei Rumori*) is a Futurist manifesto, written by Luigi Russolo in a 1913 letter to friend and Futurist composer Francesco Balilla Pratella. In it, Russolo argues that the human ear has become accustomed to the speed, energy, and noise of the urban industrial soundscape; furthermore, this new sonic palette requires a new approach to musical instrumentation and composition. He proposes a number of conclusions about how electronics and other technology will allow futurist musicians to "substitute for the limited variety of timbres that the orchestra possesses today the infinite variety of timbres in noises, reproduced with appropriate mechanisms".[1]

The Art of Noises is considered to be one of the most important and influential texts in 20th century musical aesthetics.[2]

2.26.1 The evolution of sound

Russolo's essay explores the origins of man made sounds.

"Ancient life was all silence"

Russolo states that "noise" first came into existence as the result of 19th century machines. Before this time the world was a quiet, if not silent, place. With the exception of storms, waterfalls, and tectonic activity, the noise that did punctuate this silence were not loud, prolonged, or varied.

Early sounds

He notes that the earliest "music" was very simplistic and was created with very simple instruments, and that many early civilizations considered the secrets of music sacred and reserved it for rites and rituals. The Greek musical theory was based on the tetrachord mathematics of Pythagoras, which did not allow for any harmonies. Developments and modifications to the Greek musical system were made during the Middle Ages, which led to music like Gregorian chant. Russolo notes that during this time sounds were still narrowly seen as "unfolding in time."[3] The chord did not yet exist.

"The complete sound"

Russolo refers to the chord as the "complete sound,"[3] the conception of various parts that make and are subordinate to the whole. He notes that chords developed gradually, first moving from the "consonant triad to the consistent and complicated dissonances that characterize contemporary music."[3] He notes that while early music tried to create sweet and pure sounds, it progressively grew more and more complex, with musicians seeking to create new and more dissonant chords. This, he says, comes ever closer to the "noise-sound."[3]

Musical noise

Russolo compares the evolution of music to the multiplication of machinery, pointing out that our once desolate sound environment has become increasingly filled with the noise of machines, encouraging musicians to create a more "complicated polyphony"[3] in order to provoke emotion and stir our sensibilities. He notes that music has been developing towards a more complicated polyphony by seeking greater variety in timbres and tone colors.

Noise-Sounds

Russolo explains how "musical sound is too limited in its variety of timbres."[3] He breaks the timbres of an orchestra down into four basic categories: bowed instruments, metal winds, wood winds, and percussion. He says that we must "break out of this limited circle of sound and conquer the infinite variety of noise-sounds,"[3] and that technology would allow us to manipulate noises in ways that could not have been done with earlier instruments.

Future sounds

Russolo claims that music has reached a point that no longer has the power to excite or inspire. Even when it is new, he argues, it still sounds old and familiar, leaving the audience "waiting for the extraordinary sensation that never comes."[4] He urges musicians to explore the city with "ears more sensitive than eyes,"[4] listening to the wide array of noises that are often taken for granted, yet (potentially) musical in nature. He feels these noises can be given pitch and "regulated harmonically," while still preserving their irregularity and character, even if it requires assigning multiple pitches to certain noises.

> *The variety of noises is infinite. If today, when we have perhaps a thousand different machines, we can distinguish a thousand different noises, tomorrow, as new machines multiply, we will be able to distinguish ten, twenty, or thirty thousand different noises, not merely in a simply imitative way, but to combine them according to our imagination.* [5]

2.26.2 Six Families of Noises for the Futurist Orchestra

Russolo sees the futurist orchestra drawing its sounds from "six families of noise":[6]

1. Roars, Thunderings, Explosions, Hissing roars, Bangs, Booms

2. Whistling, Hissing, Puffing

3. Whispers, Murmurs, Mumbling, Muttering, Gurgling

4. Screeching, Creaking, Rustling, Buzzing,[7] Crackling, Scraping [7]

5. Noises obtained by beating on metals, woods, skins, stones, pottery, etc.

6. Voices of animals and people, Shouts, Screams, Shrieks, Wails, Hoots, Howls, Death rattles, Sobs

Russolo asserts that these are the most basic and fundamental noises, and that all other noises are only associations and combinations of these.

2.26.3 Conclusions

Russolo includes a list of conclusions:

1. Futurist composers should use their creativity and innovation to "enlarge and enrich the field of sound"[6] by approaching the "noise-sound."

2. Futurist musicians should strive to replicate the infinite timbres in noises.

3. Futurist musicians should free themselves from the traditional and seek to explore the diverse rhythms of noise.

4. The complex tonalities of noise can be achieved by creating instruments that replicate that complexity.

5. The creation of instruments that replicate noise should not be a difficult task, since the manipulation of pitch will be simple once the mechanical principles that create the noise have been recreated. Pitch can be manipulated through simple changes in speed or tension.

6. The new orchestra will not evoke new and novel emotions by imitating the noises of life, but by finding new and unique combinations of timbres and rhythms in noise, to find a way to fully express the rhythm and sound that stretches beyond normal un-inebriated comprehension.

7. The variety of noise is infinite, and as man creates new machines the number of noises he can differentiate between continues to grow.

8. Therefore, he invites all talented musicians to pay attention to noises and their complexity, and once they discover the broadness of noise's palette of timbres, they will develop a passion for noise. He predicts that our "multiplied sensibility, having been conquered by futurist eyes, will finally have some futurist ears, and . . . every workshop will become an intoxicating orchestra of noise."[4]

2.26.4 Musicians/Artists influenced by *The Art of Noises*

- Pierre Schaeffer[2]
- Pierre Henry[2]
- Art of Noise[8]
- Adam Ant[9]
- Einstürzende Neubauten[2]
- Test Dept[2]
- DJ Spooky[2]
- Dywane Thomas, Jr.[10]
- The Sufis
- Francisco López[2]
- Panayiotis Kokoras
- Intonarumori[11]
- R. Henry Nigl[12]
- Material[13]
- Jean-Luc Hervé Berthelot[14]
- Spiral-Shaped Mind
- Marinos Koutsomichalis
- Luciano Chessa
- The New Blockaders
- Radium Audio

2.26.5 See also

- Experimental music
- Experimental musical instrument
- *Musica Futurista: The Art of Noises*
- Noise music

Bibliography

- Luigi Russolo, *L'Art des bruits*, textes réunis et préfacés par Giovanni Lista, bibliographie établie par Giovanni Lista, L'Age d'Homme, Lausanne, 1975
- Luciano Chessa: Luigi Russolo, Futurist. Noise, Visual Arts, and the Occult. University of California Press, 2012
- Giovanni Lista, *Luigi Russolo e la musica futurista*, Mudima, Milan, 2009, ISBN 978-88-96817-00-1
- Giovanni Lista, *Journal des Futurismes*, Éditions Hazan, Paris, 2008
- Giovanni Lista, *Le Futurisme : création et avant-garde*, Éditions L'Amateur, Paris, 2001

2.26.6 External links

- The Art of Noises at the Wayback Machine (archived March 5, 2010)
- The Art of Noises - unknown.nu

2.26.7 References

[1] Warner, Daniel; Cox, CChristoph (2004). *Audio Culture: Readings in Modern Music*. London: Continiuum International Publishing Group LTD. pp. 10–14. ISBN 0-8264-1615-2.

[2] (Warner & Cox 2004, p. 10)

[3] (Warner & Cox 2004, p. 11)

[4] Warner & Cox 2004, p. 12

[5] Luigi Russolo (1916). "The Art of Noises (English translation)". Archived from the original on 2010-11-27. Retrieved 2010-11-27.

[6] Warner & Cox 2004, p. 13

[7] The original Italian *ronzii* and *crepitii* are most easily translated with *humming* and *rubbing* respectively, but the connotations these words have in the English language do not fit well with the other sounds in this group; for this reason, alternative translations give more fitting *buzzing* and *scraping*.[5]

[8] Morley, Paul (2002-07-26). "Techno: the early years". *The Guardian*. Retrieved 2008-01-13.

[9] "Ant Influences". *Car Trouble*. Retrieved 2008-01-13.

[10] "MonoNeon Bassist, Composer" gruvgear.com.

[11] "Intonarumori". Retrieved 2008-01-14.

[12] "Shout Art".

[13] "Material - *Intonarumori*" at Discogs. Retrieved 2008-01-14.

[14] Jean-Luc Hervé Berthelot (French)

Chapter 3

Text and image sources, contributors, and licenses

3.1 Text

- **Glitch (music)** *Source:* https://en.wikipedia.org/wiki/Glitch_(music)?oldid=687403271 *Contributors:* Kurt Jansson, Lexor, CatherineMunro, Angela, Sugarfish, Pema~enwiki, Denis Barthel, Hyacinth, Omegatron, Owen, Twang, Altenmann, MilkMiruku, Magic Window, Alerante, DocWatson42, St3vo, Lvr, Beland, Mike Rosoft, Discospinster, Rich Farmbrough, STGM, Chadparker, Shanes, Barcex, Giraffedata, DragonGuyver, Ardric47, Gargaj, Keenan Pepper, Snowolf, Ringbang, Awk~enwiki, Ketiltrout, Quiddity, Intgr, RussBot, Chaser, Asmadeus, Aeusoes1, Mikeblas, LodeRunner, Zwobot, Slicing, Esprit15d, WesleyDodds, Sardanaphalus, SmackBot, Krovisser, Robotonic, Jagged 85, Matveims, Evanreyes, Gilliam, Fuzzform, Darktremor, Tsca.bot, T sCale, Mwtoews, Vickei, Ian Spackman, Gatesofawesome!, IronGargoyle, Makyen, Csmills, Dreftymac, Aeternus, Nina phunsta, Matthew Meta, Tawkerbot2, Filelakeshoe, Dto, Phantasy Phanatik, Jack's Revenge, Doceddi, J Milburn, Jozef Ahmed, Cyrus XIII, BFD1, Lighthead, Epistemophiliac, Peinwod, AndrewHowse, Gogo Dodo, Omicronpersei8, Treachjuris, Electroclass, T-1, Featheredserpent, Zeroday, Alphasixzero, Aboyle, Doktor Who, Jhsounds, WWB, Kaini, Andrzejbanas, JAnDbot, Hemingrubbish, Matthew Fennell, Freshacconci, JamesBWatson, Jackdark, Sambenito, JoyZipper, MartinBot, Origin29, P4k, Foetusized, Kemonoid, Fclass, Overcow, Countrymike, Erodecay, A4bot, Djcampblood, Ridernyc, Von9, Personline, Eight Suns, Rachmiel, MostAwesomeDude, Jotsko, Room429, Llcch, Parsifal, Gozombie, Newfarout, Ramsilver, That-boy-joe, Chphe, Peasantswithfeathers, I ate jelly, Panserbjorne51, Lars Ingebrigtsen, Foxj, Sefranklin11, Mild Bill Hiccup, N8sound, Doughouse, Rhododendrites, Bluefoz, ChrisHodgesUK, Miami33139, Happypoems, Semitransgenic, Pzqk, XLinkBot, Placesense, RichLow, Awfulcopter, Addbot, Sard112, Percivl, CanadianLinuxUser, Aryder779, Tassedethe, Prop A Gandah, Lightbot, Jarble, Luckas-bot, Yobot, TaBOT-zerem, Feteti, Gongshow, Silenceisgoldie, Sponge69, AnomieBOT, Valueyou, Hairhorn, JackieBot, Piano non troppo, RayvnEQ, Materialscientist, Nitarbell, ArthurBot, Sscochaa, Mix-sit, Measles, Karlzt, J04n, Sabrebd, ▯▯▯, Black Gold, FrescoBot, Sock, Beep21, Gartist, Pinethicket, Jonesey95, ViB, Tim1357, Kokoshky, Thisispain, Nrku, ThePhantasos, Hiddenstranger, RA0808, Aldarrof, ZéroBot, Andrew H. Goldberg, Fixblor, Lacon432, Dimitaru, SporkBot, Chocolatejoe, Marcusgabler, Dustzone, Conkern65, Therewillbehotcake, ClueBot NG, Shifted28, CactusBot, Spoken Bird, Frietjes, Ruriko inoyuki, Djstoneyj, Konekta, Wbm1058, BG19bot, Ettepuop, Heinzinsky, Pasicles, Vvven, MenkinAlRire, BattyBot, Miszatomic, Karshkarsh92, Myxomatosis57, EuroCarGT, Tuccio9719, Laiyxs, Angstost, GlitterDream, Pinecone23777, LuaIsEpic, Kingfelixmusic, Murderer & Victim, Wywin, Ede3724, Xanatos451, Myconix, Lilxxxwill, EDM4life, Padrino 007, Vandvl, CalMillbo, Dpandaking, Fixuture, Autumn harvest thrives, Geraldkrasner, Kaystay, EdmDistrict, Xavier917, Mcmaddo, Glennderp, Thewatertribe, Chiptronica, Mrsexyfiedman, Nerologicalstatic, ManMega5551, Grassman0, Kroponzipir, Underblue, RetroMaya, Villanueva100, Crazedragon, Dprent and Anonymous: 438

- **Ableton Live** *Source:* https://en.wikipedia.org/wiki/Ableton_Live?oldid=687208409 *Contributors:* Timo Honkasalo, Ellmist, Lexor, Crenner, Pnm, Ping, Glenn, Jubal, Johnleemk, Phildobbin, Sunray, Codernaut, Mushroom, Micru, Dsmdgold, Tim Pritlove, Ukexpat, Kevyn, Grm wnr, 6am, Bneely, Pavel Vozenilek, Martpol, Zenohockey, Shanes, Taarten, Stesmo, Eo, HelgeG, APPER, Protobob, CyberSkull, J Heath, Deadworm222, Forderud, Woohookitty, Jakobschmid, Scott.wheeler, Bluemoose, Junjk, FlaBot, JdforresterBot, TheDJ, Pelago, Superandrew, Vincent Jacobs, Irishguy, Jbible, Rynne, Jimmyjrg, Kim.o, Sebbi, Veinor, SmackBot, Temptinglip, Reedy, Fractal3, ProveIt, Ohnoitsjamie, Sigvard, Imaginaryoctopus, Zvar, Hanspoldoja, Lpgeffen, DJAM, Antodresa, Kuru, Wickethewok, Saxbryn, Kvng, Hu12, Aeternus, Turkeynutz, Filelakeshoe, Doceddi, Nosajthing, Ioripresent, Dgw, Anamexis, Shinysuitman, Spishco, Adam Singer, Digitaldischarge, Cydebot, Ntsimp, Guriboy, Wolfeboy100, Lbertybell, Omicronpersei8, Trev M, Thijs!bot, JAJW17, T-1, ItsNotUs, Jimmy666, Salavat, Xone464, AntiVandalBot, Sinewaves23, Kyorei, Rumandraisin, Erwin85Bot, Martin lindhe, Danger, Kerdek, Maslin, Kuteni, 100DashSix, MegX, Thezer0ist, Andypayne, Jimjamjak, Esanchez7587, Martin Roos, FisherQueen, Wani.., Simonm1000, Dylan anglada, PurpleHz, Balleyne, Frankn12345, KylieTastic, TreasuryTag, Djnghtcrwlr, Jcsunderman, DarkShroom, TXiKiBoT, A4bot, Binbago, Andy Dingley, Danelectro40, W4chris, EwokiWiki, Free Software Knight, Smilesfozwood, Lightmouse, NBS, Skusek, Silvergoat, Goodguy100, ImageRemovalBot, ClueBot, Bravo November, Binksternet, Wikievil666, Excirial, Ginbot86, DumZiBoT, XLinkBot, Tarheel95, Hutchan, Tomcosm, Dayyanb, Airplaneman, Kbdankbot, Addbot, Chanyi, Download, Guffydrawers, Jarble, LivingAndLearning, Openmindopen, 23pokrzywa, Sqgl, Mastazi, FrescoBot, Rockn-ice, Lonaowna, I dream of horses, NSU Spray, Meaghan, Manu887, Dude1818, MatWall, Jesse V., DASHBot, Honey Haq, Ctyonahl, Jamesbondaaa, ZéroBot, Aportnoy, MiniKellek, H3llBot, SzaZo, PopeButtercockXIV, Gepree, Atlantictire, Theterp88, ClueBot NG, AlternativeElectronics, BG19bot, Deep1212, A3poify, Daleallens, Matthewp1998, Nowvsnow, Cammsaul, JeffBaxter, Kennydaf, Maxymtkacz, Funk N., MidnightRequestLine, Epicgenius, Bookinglive, Pdecalculus, Wifsy, Iidxer, ImmersiveIEDMatt, Saadahmad, Alexisthegamer, Vorpzn, Tkdisko, Exoromusic, Kaspar-

3.1. TEXT

Bot and Anonymous: 288

- **AudioMulch** *Source:* https://en.wikipedia.org/wiki/AudioMulch?oldid=631261943 *Contributors:* Hyacinth, Tremolo, Junkyardprince, Gadfium, Ross bencina, SmackBot, Dl2000, Woodshed, KipperPhaeton, Hbent, R'n'B, TXiKiBoT, Free Software Knight, Ddxc, Addbot, Ronhjones, Download, Piano non troppo, DSisyphBot, GirlMadchen, DePitts, Auxpin, Aportnoy, Garamond Lethe and Anonymous: 26

- **Bidule** *Source:* https://en.wikipedia.org/wiki/Bidule?oldid=617746379 *Contributors:* Bearcat, Micru, Nkocharh, Woohookitty, Rjwilmsi, GünniX, Bgwhite, Colonies Chris, T-borg, KipperPhaeton, Msnicki, Rcrath, HairyWombat, Colonp, XLinkBot, Addbot, Luckas-bot, Rtyq2, Aoidh, FuFoFuEd, Jersmi and Anonymous: 3

- **ChucK** *Source:* https://en.wikipedia.org/wiki/ChucK?oldid=677846081 *Contributors:* William Avery, Twilsonb, Michael Hardy, Angela, Guaka, Omegatron, Twang, Bearcat, Rholton, Auric, Gewang, Micru, Amxitsa, Gronky, Danakil, RJHall, Adrianward, Mdd, Blx~enwiki, Fadereu, Zawersh, Uncle G, Scott.wheeler, MattGiuca, Sujith, Ruud Koot, MarSch, Ian Pitchford, Wavelength, RussBot, Gaius Cornelius, Black Falcon, Ninly, Neier, SmackBot, Reedy, Mcld, Thumperward, Zvar, Cybercobra, JonathanWakely, Dreftymac, HenningThielemann, Msnicki, T-1, Isilanes, Jhsounds, Jojopp, Slacka123, .anacondabot, Yaxu, Renick, TXiKiBoT, Micropolygon, Hrafn, Johnanth, HairyWombat, Vvneagleone, Kl4m-AWB, SF007, Semitransgenic, Nettings, Dthomsen8, Addbot, Mortense, Yobot, Martin Homuth-Rosemann, Edrowland, Quebec99, Xqbot, Citation bot 1, Minimac, RjwilmsiBot, John of Reading, H3llBot, Palosirkka, Helpful Pixie Bot, BG19bot, FuFoFuEd, Kwhipke1, AllenZh, François Robere, GLG GLG and Anonymous: 34

- **Circuit bending** *Source:* https://en.wikipedia.org/wiki/Circuit_bending?oldid=678504857 *Contributors:* Tregoweth, Sugarfish, Bogdangiusca, Hyacinth, Omegatron, Carnildo, Alan Liefting, Esk, Gzornenplatz, Bobblewik, Beland, MakeRocketGoNow, Zondor, Freakofnurture, Antaeus Feldspar, Cmdrjameson, Screeble, Ardric47, Pearle, CyberSkull, Andrewpmk, ReyBrujo, HenkvD, Feezo, Jeffrey O. Gustafson, K-flow, Tabletop, Graham87, Rjwilmsi, Yamamoto Ichiro, FlaBot, Ianthegecko, RexNL, Intgr, YurikBot, CambridgeBayWeather, Msikma, Dialectric, Grafen, Misza13, Phaedrus86, Jesusjonez, TheMadBaron, GraemeL, Searchforthenewland, Garion96, Bentmonkeycage, McGeddon, Ssbohio, Chris the speller, Mr Beige, Bluebot, Snori, Robth, Krallja, Gohst, Wickethewok, Alpha Omicron, Re mo, Mets501, Hu12, OnBeyondZebrax, Eastlaw, Cyrusc, Ekans, Clackbeetle, Xdugef, Alaibot, Thijs!bot, Bllix, T-1, Ego138, Tiny.ian, Guy Macon, Holotone, Kaini, Sophie means wisdom, JamesBWatson, Potar, Wayn3w, Maurice Carbonaro, Elugelab, SmithBlue, TheBendersPad, NegativeChild, RJASE1, Tsom, Broadbot, Delfy~enwiki, DrRek, Lucironic, Joseph Banks, ClueBot, Arakunem, Circuitben, Alexbot, Semitransgenic, JB8256, Mchaddock, Thebetatesters, XLinkBot, Ugh3n, Addbot, Leszek Jańczuk, Luter80, Kick52, Lightbot, AnomieBOT, Duktepemahn, Gartist, DarrenGuitarGuy, InformationGuardian, DSP-user, Intellec7, ClueBot NG, Catlemur, HMSSolent, YokoBeatdown, Hericlesa5, Madnessfan34537, Pdecalculus, Xeletron, Wikigeek244, Andrewdubber and Anonymous: 189

- **Clicks & Cuts Series** *Source:* https://en.wikipedia.org/wiki/Clicks_%26_Cuts_Series?oldid=628555251 *Contributors:* Zundark, Twang, David Edgar, Recury, Rjwilmsi, Crystallina, Anth a narchy, Lainagier, Bluebot, Stefan2, Aeons, FairuseBot, W guice, Alaibot, Andrzejbanas, Waacstats, Sodom122, Rockfang, Marcusgabler, Zettt~enwiki, BG19bot and Anonymous: 5

- **Crash (computing)** *Source:* https://en.wikipedia.org/wiki/Crash_(computing)?oldid=688399124 *Contributors:* Derek Ross, Arvindn, Edward, GRAHAMUK, Dysprosia, Roadmr, Jake Nelson, Joy, BenRG, Wile E. Heresiarch, Rsduhamel, Curps, Home Row Keysplurge, Andycjp, CryptoDerk, Dwedit, Neale Monks, Bluefoxicy, Freakofnurture, Night Gyr, Sum0, Danakil, Nabla, R. S. Shaw, CyberSkull, Yamla, Woohookitty, Uncle G, Splintax, MattGiuca, RzR~enwiki, GregorB, Kbdank71, Guinness2702, Ligulem, SchuminWeb, Querswpoia, Pinecar, YurikBot, Eraserhead1, Barefootguru, Mipadi, Msikma, Jpbowen, Moe Epsilon, Mtu, Deville, Arthur Rubin, CWenger, Shawnc, DisambigBot, SmackBot, Ccox@adobe.com, Fuzzyslob, Commander Keane bot, Plague006, Thumperward, Miguel Andrade, Philip Howard, JonHarder, Mr.Z-man, Piroroadkill, TechPurism, Hermione99~enwiki, Ohconfucius, Harryboyles, Nwwaew, Lee Carre, CmdrObot, Linguofreak, Meno25, Sonic3, ST47, Dotman557, Kozuch, UberScienceNerd, Thijs!bot, Pcu123456789, WhiteCrane, Kathovo, I do not exist, DataMatrix, Catgut, Nopira, Wilsonsamm, Erkan Yilmaz, Maurice Carbonaro, Cactus26, Flyer22 Reborn, Wiknerd, B.duck, ImageRemovalBot, ClueBot, Alvarokr, M4gnum0n, Anon lynx, Thingg, Ginbot86, DumZiBoT, XLinkBot, Kintaro, Dthomsen8, Armiris, Addbot, Legobot, Fraggle81, Materialscientist, Xqbot, Daemorris, Nasa-verve, Sex was great, 1a2c, FrescoBot, Pinethicket, Lotje, Mean as custard, Dalba, EmausBot, ClueBot NG, MelbourneStar, Primergrey, Widr, Novioboy, Wbm1058, Hissifriikki, Chmarkine, Fylbecatulous, BattyBot, ChrisGualtieri, Codename Lisa, Mogism, Corn cheese, Dhirajyadav, Epicgenius, Kristen.hess, Efftronics, DilkROM, Tsajed, Tetrabyte, Pauldavidmena, CotyledonCIC, Fraudulent frog, Gabrini, Olaeliseusdavid, Susansm, Jr8825, AncientPotato, Jaspet, Melody Lavender, Solvings, Kaqfa, Leexiong, Sammysammysammy, Johnnythorn10, HeatherLEvans, Manaq al rabie trading est, PapaDelta123, Raj Agarwal IV, Past Bedtime, CornellfOo, Unicornlover05, HandSolo-Bro, BestHealthGuide, Exzarus, Apeybaby87, Texasrunner95, Sanjeevchandrav, Jayeshbhapkar, Yolanda.Stacy, Camocaze, Jimsmithyapple, Alice macaire, JasonB926, Babylonlady, Rockyourteeth, Cheesedude23, Rebecca Woliver, Amortias, Ghalykamel and Anonymous: 82

- **Data compression** *Source:* https://en.wikipedia.org/wiki/Data_compression?oldid=687099972 *Contributors:* Damian Yerrick, Tobias Hoevekamp, LC~enwiki, Lee Daniel Crocker, Zundark, The Anome, Tarquin, Tbackstr, Taw, BenBaker, Wayne Hardman, Dachshund, Enchanter, Rade Kutil, Jlinton, FvdP, Edward, Bdesham, Patrick, Michael Hardy, Kwertii, Norm, Dcljr, (, Paul A, Minesweeper, Ahoerstemeier, ZoeB, Nanshu, J-Wiki, Glenn, Nikai, Andres, Hike395, Emperorbma, Novum, Berteun, Timwi, David Latapie, Dysprosia, AC, Rvalles, Furrykef, Tero~enwiki, Thue, Quoth-22, Pakaran, Rogper~enwiki, Robbot, Fredrik, Vespristiano, Moondyne, Psychonaut, Nurg, Meduz, Tim Ivorson, Rholton, Tobias Bergemann, Matthew Stannard, Giftlite, DavidCary, Haeleth, Frencheigh, Sietse, Eequor, Humberto (usurped), Jackol, Wacco, Wmahan, Bact, Pcarbonn, OverlordQ, Elektron, Hellisp, Grunt, Archer3, RedWordSmith, Lone Isle, EugeneZelenko, Discospinster, Rich Farmbrough, Smyth, Ericamick, Antaeus Feldspar, Byrial, Pavel Vozenilek, Nchaimov, Hhielscher, Bender235, Evice, Brian0918, Livajo, Pt, Miraceti, Phil websurfer@yahoo.com, Marcok, Spoon!, Fuxx, Shoujun, Cwolfsheep, Redquark, Photonique, Haham hanuka, Benbread, Varuna, Beyondthislife, Jic, Nsd, XB-70, Rick Sidwell, 2mcm, Jheald, SteinbDJ, Pierremenard, Pinball22, Uncle G, BillC, Armando, Pol098, Ruud Koot, Matt Mahoney, GregorB, Gimboid13, Marudubshinki, Pawnbroker, Arunib, Jshadias, Rjwilmsi, Plainsong, Tangotango, Dar-Ape, Duomillia, Ysangkok, Ewlyahoocom, Wikisurfer1, Bmicomp, JM.Beaubourg, Chobot, DVdm, Flashmorbid, Roboto de Ajvol, Wavelength, Borgx, Hairy Dude, J. M., Ihope127, RattleMan, ONEder Boy, Mikeblas, Super Rad!, StuRat, Arthur Rubin, Jaranda, DmitriyV, Bill, SmackBot, Jrlinton, CapitalSasha, Brianski, Kurykh, Thumperward, Oli Filth, George Church, Nbarth, Onorem, PsychoCola, Calbaer, Hateless, HarisM, Hgilbert, Daniel.Cardenas, Chungc, Paul Arzul, Superdosh, Nick Green, Wavy G, Darktemplar, Bezenek, Simon G Best, Warinthepocket, Beetstra, Dicklyon, Ryulong, Kvng, Lee Carre, WilliamJE, Dreftymac, Dockingman, Amakuru, Beno1000, Esurnir, Dlohcierekim, Chris55, Ghaly, GFellows, FleetCommand, CmdrObot, Zarex, Kaine I, Zack3rdbb, Requestion, SelfStudyBuddy, Cydebot, JFreeman, Capmaster, John254, Apantomimehorse, Stealth17, AntiVandalBot, Uselesswarrior, Sebastian85, JAnDbot, CosineKitty, Arch dude, Austinmurphy,

Hut 8.5, SiobhanHansa, Magioladitis, Mclean007, Realg187, Swpb, Crazytonyi, Thermal0xidizer, Rfellows, JJ Harrison, DerHexer, Kgfleischmann, Qe2eqe, Wre2wre, MartinBot, Jim.henderson, Rettetast, Speck-Made, Tgeairn, RockMFR, J.delanoy, Numbo3, Ayecee, Yonidebot, Parsondatas, Brolsma, Naniwako, Mikael Häggström, Ontarioboy, Hailangsea~enwiki, Bonadea, Joeinwap, R00723r0, J ham3, VolkovBot, Jeff G., Gvcormac, Jimmaths, Philip Trueman, Yugsdrawkcabehr, Lollipop Lady, Orgads, Mvineetmenon, Ocolon, Ydriuf, Jackfork, Haseo9999, Yk Yk Yk, Wasted Sapience, Seraphiel, AlleborgoBot, Jimmi Hugh, Logan, Rlwpx, SieBot, Digwuren, Bentogoa, Galileo seven, Jimthing, Travelingseth, Oxymoron83, Melcombe, TheHoax, Martarius, ClueBot, Justin W Smith, Dynamicimanyd, Gigacephalus, Adrianwn, Flyingbox, Wintools, Alla tedesca, Mecagon, Davis685, AlanM1, Qae, Dthomsen8, ErkinBatu, Dekart, RyanCross, Addbot, Mortense, Fgnievinski, Elsendero, Fluffernutter, MrOllie, Robert.Harker, Nate Wessel, CiasoMs, Slicer Mirkwood, Legobot, Luckas-bot, Yobot, Legobot II, Pcap, Imeson, Jeffz1, AnomieBOT, Piano non troppo, Materialscientist, MorgothX, Citation bot, Obersachsebot, Xqbot, TinucherianBot II, TechBot, I am Me true, GrouchoBot, Kotarosan, IShadowed, Shadowjams, FrescoBot, Balajiganapathi, I dream of horses, Jandalhandler, LiberatorG, Chrisbridson, SchreyP, Thái Nhi, Akrolsmir, Samir000, Jonkerz, Comet Tuttle, Dinamik-bot, Marcus256, Jhiltenb, LightStarch, EmausBot, Eekiv, Bulat Ziganshin, ZéroBot, Elungtrings, Josve05a, Shuipzv3, Luigi742, Cymru.lass, Donner60, Bomazi, BioPupil, TYelliot, ResearchRave, ClueBot NG, BarrelProof, Helpful Pixie Bot, Wbm1058, Alex Ratushnyak, AussieStorBlog, Walk&check, MusikAnimal, MrBill3, Scp890, Aisteco, Comfr, BattyBot, Grammar-master, ChrisGualtieri, Tagremover, Cherunglee, Sonarclawz, Iflyingwolf, Cwobeel, Jogfalls1947, TwoTwoHello, Lugia2453, Gari Legarda, Cmlefevre, Ginsuloft, Audiospotnow, Jianhui67, Anggadtm, Minhluan29051991, Monkbot, Thibaut120094, Haosjaboeces, Ziggy.coyer, Omerhazer, KasparBot, Vgenapl, Kumar525, Nirmal Diaz, Nvmemory and Anonymous: 347

- **Distortion** *Source:* https://en.wikipedia.org/wiki/Distortion?oldid=681138698 *Contributors:* The Anome, Mrwojo, Patrick, RTC, Kku, Ixfd64, Jdforrester, Andrewa, Iain, Glenn, Kricke, Paulnasca, Charles Matthews, Omegatron, Rogper~enwiki, RedWolf, Everyking, Dmmaus, Comics, Brother Dysk~enwiki, Bornintheguz, Guanabot, Chairboy, Acjelen, Hooperbloob, Alansohn, Neonumbers, Cdc, Lkinkade, Tbc2, Dysepsion, BD2412, Lgreen, Tzeck~enwiki, Rjwilmsi, DeadlyAssassin, SMC, Utuado, Srleffler, Antilived, Kopper65, Roboto de Ajvol, YurikBot, RussBot, Bhny, Toffile, Grubber, Rohitbd, Aaron Brenneman, Rbarreira, Brandon, Witger, Sebleblanc, Elkman, Light current, DerekL, Jonas Viper, Deville, Wonderactivist, Zeppelin4life, Selkem, KnightRider~enwiki, SmackBot, Fireman biff, Steve carlson, Hydrogen Iodide, Jcbarr, Arniep, Evanreyes, Gilliam, SchfiftyThree, A. B., Gracenotes, Pretzels, Tamfang, Onorem, MichaelBillington, Just plain Bill, NeilUK, 16@r, Dicklyon, Kvng, Blehfu, Gveret Tered, Xcentaur, Requestion, Neelix, Cydebot, Bassistphysicist, Roger Roger, Cancun771, Msebast~enwiki, Thijs!bot, Bllix, Marek69, WillMak050389, CharlotteWebb, Nick Number, JackTinWNY, Davewho2, Time3000, Y2kcrazyjoker4, Tornvmax, MichaelSHoffman, EagleFan, MartinBot, Jim.henderson, R'n'B, Mange01, Trusilver, STBotD, Funandtrvl, Amikake3, Oshwah, Asarlaí, Daisydaisy, Miko3k, GlassFET, Nagy, Scarian, AlexWaelde, Rocknrollsuicide, Faradayplank, Wsosfr, Anchor Link Bot, Dave Saunders, ClueBot, Binksternet, Postmortemjapan, Keraunoscopia, J.blackstone, Addbot, Simmonsghost, Tide rolls, Yobot, Nis Sigurdsson, MarcoAurelio, The Lamb of God, Dudeiluvwritin, Kjinho213, Outdepth, Nasa-verve, Nedim Ardoğa, Maitchy, Wifione, LittleWink, Merlion444, Vrenator, Theo10011, DexDor, AndyHe829, Eekerz, DesbWit, Atlantictire, ClueBot NG, Gareth Griffith-Jones, JordoCo, MerlIwBot, CitationCleanerBot, Mediran, JRC321, Doubaer, Revolution1221 and Anonymous: 127

- **Electronica** *Source:* https://en.wikipedia.org/wiki/Electronica?oldid=684038697 *Contributors:* Bryan Derksen, The Anome, Andre Engels, Mjb, Greg Godwin, Michael Hardy, TOGoS, Lexor, Ixfd64, Lquilter, Tregoweth, TUF-KAT, JonMoore, Hyacinth, Fredrik, LGagnon, Twiin, Tobias Bergemann, Alan Liefting, Alerante, MMBKG, Zigger, Ssd, Mboverload, Siroxo, Chowbok, SarekOfVulcan, Karol Langner, Phil1988, Mindspillage, Rich Farmbrough, Andros 1337, Pointblank~enwiki, Night Gyr, Brian0918, El C, Bookofjude, Longhair, Giraffedata, Espoo, Bob rulz, Alansohn, Ashley Pomeroy, RoySmith, Slugokramer, Versageek, Recury, Kenyon, Megan1967, C3o, Woohookitty, Sir Lewk, Arru, Frankie1969, Phlebas, LimoWreck, Lzygenius, BD2412, Rjwilmsi, Koavf, Sdornan, Chsf, Krash, FlaBot, SchuminWeb, Margosbot~enwiki, Intgr, Planetneutral, Chobot, Sherool, DVdm, Random user 39849958, Martin Hinks, Borgx, PiAndWhippedCream, Hede2000, Asmadeus, C777, Standarshy, Anomie, Aeusoes1, Ipsenaut, Syrthiss, ZhaoHong, Brat32, Nlu, Deeday-UK, Terryc, GraemeL, Sugar Bear, NiTenIchiRyu, WesleyDodds, ▯▯▯ robot, Sardanaphalus, SmackBot, Trance88, Jagged 85, Xblkx, ZS, Commander Keane bot, Betacommand, Talinus, Unint, Renamed user Sloane, TheLeopard, Tekhnofiend, John Reaves, MaxSem, KieferSkunk, Onorem, Fuhghettaboutit, GumTree, Matt Whyndham, SebastiaanPasma, Letslip, Ceoil, TenPoundHammer, SashatoBot, Minor edit~enwiki, Petr Kopač, Kuru, JackLumber, Paul ra, Wickethewok, 16@r, Beetstra, Publicus, Ryulong, Wwagner, Iridescent, Aeternus, Sporkmonger, Cyber Infinity, Feelfreetoblameme, Pontificake, Filelakeshoe, J Milburn, Denaar, CmdrObot, Wafulz, R9tgokunks, Sky-surfer, Harej bot, Neelix, Gregbard, Gogo Dodo, Accipio Mitis Frux, DumbBOT, FastLizard4, Thijs!bot, Epbr123, Barticus88, Hit bull, win steak, Dasani, Malrase, Commonwest, Klausness, Dawnseeker2000, Doktor Who, Rsocol, Sluzzelin, JAnDbot, Poga, Matthew Fennell, MegX, SteelersFan UK06, Appraiser, Zarino, Bodominjarvi, JMBryant, Tabac~enwiki, EagleFan, Shadiac, Megalodon99, Edmradio, Qabbalah, Cybersonik, MartinBot, Poeloq, R'n'B, Samuel.hinch@hotmail.com, Akronym, Virtualinvasion, J.delanoy, Djripley, All Is One, Neon white, Thechickenisbad, Thomas Larsen, Wiz-Pro3, Vanishdoom, Gonzalo M. Garcia, Satanical Eve, Zenbeats, Aibot (usurped), King Lopez, VolkovBot, CWii, Zavoloka music, Gamebhai, TXiKiBoT, Qxz, Ziounclesi, Parsifal, IL7Soulhunter, Hexebart, Newheadrecords, AlleborgoBot, Ennuified, Zonuleofzinn, SieBot, Chillywillycd, Malcolmxl5, Gary.van.domselaar, Alchemyhouse, Skarhawk, Nite-Sirk, Happysailor, Flyer22 Reborn, Allmightyduck, Gunmetal Angel, Reorgart~enwiki, StaticGull, Susume-eat, ClueBot, Binksternet, Wikisound1, Geeanderthol, Arakunem, Rubioblanca, Mild Bill Hiccup, Krusell.rowe, Roxport, DragonBot, Tikilounge, Human.v2.0, Ianjones600, Yoakamae, A poked anus, SoxBot III, Semitransgenic, Pzqk, PK2, Salamibears58, Mifter, Mindworkapparatus, RichLow, The Neutral Zone, Addbot, Sard112, Dan56, Binary TSO, Elmondo21st, Rejectwater, TeleTubbie ZOO, The Shadow-Fighter, Chzz, Debresser, Albertrocker, Tassedethe, Numbo3-bot, Mansour Said, Yobot, Gongshow, AnomieBOT, Materialscientist, El Perso - The Original, Citation bot, Kamikazebunnies, Xqbot, Mlpearc, Heslopian, Doctorx0079, Sabrebd, Jugdev, FrescoBot, Hyju, Bakartkung, Tetraedycal, Picto9000, Citation bot 1, Daggors, Olliepayne, SpacemanSpiff, Kjnelan, Tinton5, Smells like content, FoxBot, Jedi94, VEO15, Jonjonjohny, Sam Pedefmc, Tbhotch, Bento00, Chrisbkoolio, Hiddenstranger, JCRules, RenamedUser01302013, Aaa89, Huxley808, DubStepRoolz, Tobeprecise, VictorianMutant, Special Cases, ClueBot NG, CactusBot, O0goodiegoodieOo, Actcohen, Skomorokh's sock, DrDrake100, DeeRD, Frietjes, Cntras, Alanpreston1971, Bobberjoe, Helpful Pixie Bot, BG19bot, TomPlatzWannabe, Rlp17, AwesomeCoffee, AwamerT, Thatemooverthere, DeanBaetz, N765, Mrmoustache14, Jeremy112233, Sotdh, Myxomatosis57, Khazar2, Jeggers24, Dexbot, SWAGCANNON, Mogism, Otávio Augusto Silva, Cosyn, Raggy600, Kaams, Chartbot, Hyperultra, Ï¿½, Synthwave.94, Bolshoyparen, Clark102, Etheldavis, Thewatertribe, Malmsimp, ManMega5551, Orduin, PrometheusNowUnbound, Hackerkr3k, Nelly Randelova, Andresbfarrera and Anonymous: 334

- **FL Studio** *Source:* https://en.wikipedia.org/wiki/FL_Studio?oldid=686565057 *Contributors:* Zundark, Infrogmation, EddEdmondson, Lexor, Nixdorf, Graue, Tregoweth, Kricxjo, CatherineMunro, Angela, Darkwind, Glenn, Guaka, Dysprosia, Furrykef, Hyacinth, Gypsum Fantastic, Maheshkale, UtherSRG, Acm, MSGJ, Everyking, Micru, Alensha, AlistairMcMillan, Sam Hocevar, HunterX, Rich Farmbrough, ES-

3.1. TEXT

kog, GeZe, Shanes, Bobo192, WikiJhoto, George.dickeson, Eritain, PJ, SPUI, Gargaj, Cammoore, Yuckfoo, Danhash, PullUpYourSocks, Dennis Bratland, Mel Etitis, Woohookitty, Thivierr, Aveilleux, Borb, Flamingspinach, Waldir, Marudubshinki, GSlicer, Amitparikh, Tintazul, FlaBot, Ian Pitchford, JdforresterBot, Tumble, Gurch, Sorvino, Jhuuskon, Imnotminkus, Bgwhite, ShadowHntr, Faseidman, YurikBot, Mukkakukaku, DavenH, Matt.lohkamp, Gillean666, Mikeblas, Mlouns, Misza13, DGJM, SFC9394, Tachs, Kewp, Nlu, Slicing, Hal Raglan, Jeff Silvers, KnightRider~enwiki, SmackBot, Elonka, Haza-w, Eskimbot, M fic, HipHopHead88, HalfShadow, Gilliam, Ohnoitsjamie, Daysleeper47, William sharkey, TimBentley, Mitchellandness1, RoachMcKrackin, DStoykov, Repetition, Ssx232, Colonies Chris, Pretzels, Whpq, Gohst, Peteforsyth, Salamurai, MadCow257, Dylananglada, Harryboyles, Euchiasmus, Heimstern, Sakamura, Needlenose, Ckatz, Makyen, Beetstra, NegativeCreep, TastyPoutine, NJA, Noleander, Johnxp, Hu12, MikeWazowski, Nitemare, Iridescent, Shoeofdeath, Kestudi, Martin Kozák, Schlagwerk, Fernvale, Devourer09, JForget, Unionhawk, Zyxoas, QuinnJL, Moorice~enwiki, Terrydandan, Future Perfect at Sunrise, Michaelas10, Greyleonard, DumbBOT, Omexis, Roger Roger, SummonerMarc, Thijs!bot, Ultimus, NaviJ11, AntiVandalBot, David136a, RapidR, Kerdek, Myanw, Ioeth, Leuko, MER-C, Hiphophead88, Andylindsay, Goldenglove, Cameron Green, Akuyume, Magioladitis, Nac~enwiki, Bongwarrior, MartinDK, Hatrickpatrick, Usien6, Nick Cooper, Jessicapierce, Esanchez7587, Glennforever, Arnesh, Hoodsta5109, Ztobor, Vicar in a Tutu, MartinBot, STBot, Anaxial, Oherman, CommonsDelinker, Toxikator, Dylan anglada, Itzcuauhtli, Michalkun, Josestefan, Weakmassive, Mitsura Tsuki, AntiSpamBot, Dalisene, MarvinQueer, KylieTastic, Daxx wp, STBotD, Campbellce, Natl1, NFX, BBilge, Spellcast, Treasury-Tag, Pokerstar717, Zidonuke, WatchAndObserve, Hqb, Anonymous Dissident, Trans Arctica, Sloggerbum, Drummgenius, Kamunt, McM.bot, Jamelan, Captain Toke, Spinningspark, Quantpole, Vitalikk, Coffee, James599, Alfif, Blackjays1, Rawfam05, Hxhbot, Xeltran, Realist2, XiaoGuang, Pagen HD, Mumble45, Zengakuren, ImageRemovalBot, Blazmarf, ClueBot, Binksternet, The Thing That Should Not Be, Keeper76, LabOx, Psypherium, Drmies, BNexxus, Auntof6, Estemshorn, Jusdafax, Rd3k, PixelBot, Iesorto, Rufusplant, Doctor It, LonerXL, Xkennysaysx, Razorflame, Dekisugi, Atlantaboizone3, Ddiakopoulos, BOTarate, ChrisHamburg, Thehelpfulone, Kst447, Fallacia83~enwiki, Edit-or-perish, KirbyAu, Nibi, Mi$taFamousBeatz123, Akustika83, Electrorocker, Ginbot86, UKWikiGuy, XLinkBot, Smurfenlars, Reallygoodbeats, Jayden Macauley, Jblock0708, Yorstrooly, Black Dollar7, Marcos314159, Gazimoff, Kbdankbot, Ponkedya, Addbot, Loogiesquared, Paper Luigi, MaxUSA, Hubschrauber729, D0762, Gsalvadi, Oroboros123, Download, CJmiester, EstendorLin, Tide rolls, Webfarer, Bconover93, 50blues, Megaman en m, Hiphoptutorial, Ben Ben, Luckas-bot, Yobot, Fraggle81, Berkay0652, Vanished user rt41as76lk, Vubble, Sg227, Nfxbeats, Thekingof2009, AnomieBOT, Hairhorn, IRP, Piano non troppo, DrinkThineCookies, Deepestdesire, Materialscientist, Summerbreeze2020, GB fan, Quebec99, Slicksurfer1898, Xqbot, Drilnoth, Ruzgfpegk, Andreasbjorklund, Bammeh2, Blecmen, Repsrule, Fancy steve, Prbori2008, Superdavedangerous, 23pokrzywa, Smallman12q, Shadowjams, Xmubzx, Dragonheartman, Prbori2009, FrescoBot, NickL88, Sky Attacker, Cjsnow1, I dream of horses, Montanaboy99, Maginks, Justme54s, Mpurplegirl, RedBot, Agong1, Withers94, Manu887, Cam493, PowerPatrick, Kabraxis~enwiki, Cowlibob, Audio02audio, Diannaa, Tbhotch, Jesse V., Griff505, FLBot, Simplyhaydn, Oliverlyc, FruityWIKI, WikitanvirBot, FLobotomy, Lnievescruz, Ajraddatz, Djicepack, Jojon8, Rayukk, Solarra, Tanner Swett, Werieth, Marlgryd, ∆, Digitalmusic, Editor017935, MainFrame, NTox, MoZ16, MusicLover650, ClueBot NG, Anotherkid01, Gareth Griffith-Jones, Xession, Gggbgggb, Widr, AlternativeElectronics, Curb Chain, Gamer-Actu, Comptonreal, Lowercase sigmabot, BG19bot, StingR, Boyboi87, Christhewriter, Break Me (Beatzz song), Aris621, FictionHerndon, Dontreader, BattyBot, Ljkx, Saltric, AllWright89, Guillermobazan, EagerToddler39, Yamada Taro, Codename Lisa, M Tee Kay, Bif Jefferson, Base32, AngelOriginal, Hairobics, Backendgaming, Knowledgent, Nancyinthehouse, Epicerminer, Knismogenic, JustBerry, My name is not dave, DBrown SPS, ErickOnasis, 2x4bit, HiphopProd, KidFan1234, Image-Line Software, MayconHVAM, Matmatpenguin, CV9933, Syafriza, The Hitmakers, Noahsirlouis, Tashi, Conno123009, Jdbeacom97, Nvargas2, Narquise10, Narquise11, DanZakWiki, FuxkYourExpectations and Anonymous: 706

- **Generative music** *Source:* https://en.wikipedia.org/wiki/Generative_music?oldid=683216838 *Contributors:* Zundark, Hyacinth, Francs2000, Twang, Micru, Mboverload, Neilc, Satori, Korodzik, Robin klein, Jaberwocky6669, Pearle, Woohookitty, SDC, Ian Pitchford, Esslk, Chobot, RussBot, Anomie, Rwxrwxrwx, 2over0, Ninly, SmackBot, CopperMurdoch, Pkirlin, Bluebot, John Reaves, Radagast83, Doodle77, Rainwarrior, ReneWooller, CmdrObot, Jefchip, Besieged, Marek69, Alphachimpbot, Kaini, Freshacconci, Yaxu, Thibbs, Minkar~enwiki, R'n'B, UnitedStatesian, Andy Dingley, Niceguyedc, Trivialist, Tomer 070, Addbot, Mortense, Download, Redheylin, Maltaser~enwiki, Lightbot, Yobot, Amirobot, Valueyou, LilHelpa, Avilches~enwiki, Miym, FrescoBot, Iminfo, Jonmc, Wikipelli, Whqitsm, Thejmc, Itztzin, Kam101WKP, CondenserCoil, Pdecalculus, Fbrzvnrnd, Machinesleet, PasquierPhilippe and Anonymous: 67

- **Jeskola Buzz** *Source:* https://en.wikipedia.org/wiki/Jeskola_Buzz?oldid=648342790 *Contributors:* GameGod, Graue, Zoicon5, Furrykef, Fredrik, Tom harrison, Micru, Decoy, LucasVB, Kevyn, Pearle, Geschichte, Gargaj, Deadworm222, Marasmusine, Woohookitty, Wojciech.aniszewski, Sblive~enwiki, BD2412, Bensin, FlaBot, Kibibu, Viznut, Peter S., Slicing, Blueapples, SmackBot, Lyran, Kuru, Wickethewok, Aeternus, CmdrObot, Bohan, NisseSthlm, Cydebot, Cyanphase, The machine512, Thijs!bot, Joachim Michaelis, Kaini, Andreas Toth, Thenagz, Rhododendrites, Chadshef, DumZiBOT, InternetMeme, XLinkBot, SilvonenBot, Addbot, Yobot, Fragaria Vesca, AnomieBOT, J04n, Paulbuchholz22, FrescoBot, Podlec, Xlorite, Iamokapi, WikitanvirBot, Shaddim, BattyBot, Hmainsbot1, Thechinamen and Anonymous: 73

- **Max (software)** *Source:* https://en.wikipedia.org/wiki/Max_(software)?oldid=686321186 *Contributors:* Michael Hardy, Crenner, Oyd11, Tregoweth, Ahoerstemeier, Glenn, Guaka, Nohat, Hyacinth, Omegatron, Morn, Twang, Robbot, Tlogmer, R3m0t, RedWolf, Mushroom, Lupin, Rev3rend, Jfdwolff, Micru, Bovlb, Gadfium, Antandrus, MacGyverMagic, Mozzerati, Joyous!, Arcataroger, Helohe, ElTyrant, Solitude, Danakil, CanisRufus, MBisanz, Bobo192, Smalljim, Minghong, ProbablyX, Mareino, CyberSkull, Ksnow, Kanito~enwiki, Yuckfoo, Nightstallion, Markaci, Scott.wheeler, Zeh, Junjk, JIP, RxS, Edison, Ketiltrout, Rjwilmsi, Tangotango, FayssalF, Titoxd, FlaBot, RexNL, OrbitOne, Esslk, Hairy Dude, RussBot, Oswellm, Chris Capoccia, Stephenb, Misza13, Ethan Pemble, Mysid, N-Bot, Ninly, Nae'blis, JLaTondre, Alex Ruddick, Tall Midget, SmackBot, Kellen, Pgk, Mcld, Davigoli, Eighthave, EncMstr, EdgeOfEpsilon, MaxSem, Can't sleep, clown will eat me, Roquestrew, VegaDark, Mwtoews, Wilt, Sparkleyone, Blahm, Kuru, Wickethewok, PseudoSudo, Slakr, Waggers, ILovePlankton, KsprayDad, Tommy Jarvis, Neurillon, Tawkerbot2, Doceddi, Fullofbeans, MisterMcJesus, Voyager5674, Cydebot, FabgrOOv, T-1, Gillesvanleeuwen, Klausness, Gioto, Rsocol, Jhsounds, Pawi~enwiki, ThezerOist, 20coconuts, A3nm, FisherQueen, Holykow, R'n'B, Cls-classic~enwiki, Lexein, Mikeygnyc, TXiKiBoT, Theconverseguy, 1904.CC, Jamelan, Scottywong, SieBot, Jerryobject, Markdask, Dala0, BrooklynBen, Xeltran, Pequeniosaltamontes, Szintenzenesz, Mattgirling, 718 Bot, Pointillist, Jigsaw dog, Toshikatsu okubo, Alexbot, Rhododendrites, Denseorg, Semitransgenic, XLinkBot, Addbot, Mabdul, Riley Wiki, Angelus1753, Yobot, Tempodivalse, AnomieBOT, Wtachi, Galoubet, Spada2, The Black Rabbit of Inlé, SkiAustria, Brunonar, WilliamTheaker, FrescoBot, Djkcel, EmausBot, Honey Haq, Surgesg, Tikitpok, Midas02, ClueBot NG, Cc21002, MelbourneStar, Henry Jester, Gluontronic, Ettepuop, Erin100280, Cheeze17, BeauDamion, Mikeco3181, Radiodef, Juanverdaguer, JulienGuil, Eliott paris, Pdecalculus, Vieque, Kldhoyt and Anonymous: 230

- **Microsound** *Source:* https://en.wikipedia.org/wiki/Microsound?oldid=675802967 *Contributors:* Hyacinth, Wahoofive, Gaius Cornelius, Yahya Abdal-Aziz, Mikeblas, SmackBot, Jerome Kohl, Addbot, Yobot, Solomon7968 and Anonymous: 6

- **Music software** *Source:* https://en.wikipedia.org/wiki/Music_software?oldid=685274077 *Contributors:* Bearcat, Ringbang, AlisonW, SmackBot, Chris the speller, Andreas Möllenkamp, Lenticel, XLinkBot, Trappist the monk, Zakawer, Nvagale, Jamietw, ClueBot NG, BattyBot, Isaac Guy, Writing101MSU, Thompson-devilias, Pdecalculus, Noyster, Ollybt, BobKas, Alchemea, Podecas and Anonymous: 4

- **Noise music** *Source:* https://en.wikipedia.org/wiki/Noise_music?oldid=685980020 *Contributors:* WojPob, William Avery, Camembert, Nairobiny, Greg Godwin, Michael Hardy, Tim Starling, Lexor, Graue, Delirium, Doom, TUF-KAT, Andrewa, Guaka, Furrykef, Hyacinth, Omegatron, Lypheklub, Topbanana, Secretlondon, Owen, Twang, Bearcat, Robbot, Yas~enwiki, TMC1221, RedWolf, Sbisolo, Neckro, MilkMiruku, GreatWhiteNortherner, Tobias Bergemann, Nagelfar, Somercet, Everyking, Guanaco, Mboverload, Antandrus, OverlordQ, Curtsurly, Humblefool, Idolcrash, Zondor, Gazpacho, D6, Justin Foote, Discospinster, Rich Farmbrough, WikiPediaAid, ESkog, Dpotter, CanisRufus, Mr. Strong Bad, Cpomeara, Trevj, Draconiszeta, Kx1186, Anthony Appleyard, Babajobu, Lightdarkness, Malo, HGB, Recury, Bookandcoffee, Woohookitty, GVOLTT, Jpers36, Bratsche, Aubin, Grammarbot, Ketiltrout, Koavf, Quiddity, Zozza~enwiki, Remurmur, Ucucha, FlaBot, CaseKid, YurikBot, Wavelength, Deeptrivia, Peter G Werner, RussBot, Anomie, Welsh, AmanitaMuscaria, Retired username, Xdenizen, PhilipO, Alex43223, Klutzy, Wknight94, Ninly, RickReinckens, MrBook, Whouk, Queenvictoria, Justyn1337, Sardanaphalus, Veinor, SmackBot, Bentmonkeycage, Kellen, Jagged 85, Eskimbot, Gorepriest, Amatulic, Chris the speller, Jprg1966, Colonies Chris, Sarasdano~enwiki, Darth Panda, Kotra, TheKMan, Cdh1984, Cyhatch, The-dissonance-reports, Llafeht, A.R., Bob Castle, KurtKocaine, Kabrewskee, Nishkid64, Harryboyles, Rabbitfighter, Ewegogetemtiger, Adrift*, Adj08, Ckatz, JHunterJ, Beetstra, Mr Stephen, Dicklyon, Lenn0r, Iridescent, Cls14, FairuseBot, HowardSelsam, The Haunted Angel, J Milburn, CmdrObot, PuerExMachina, Doctormatt, Cydebot, Gogo Dodo, Khatru2, R-41, Tawkerbot4, EqualRights, Inkington, Thijs!bot, Epbr123, Qwyrxian, Prehberg, Allquestions, Nick Number, AntiVandalBot, Shirt58, Leolapinos, Falconleaf, Sluzzelin, JAnDbot, MER-C, Albany NY, Rosemarymalign, Rhinowing, JosephNechvatal, Repku, Lelasson, VoABot II, Yarongolan, Nzeeman, Jerome Kohl, Artlondon, Mikehaley, Tatva, Hiplibrarianship, EagleFan, Kawaputra, Lororavachol, Spellmaster, Electronique, Crowdedhair, Alex LaPointe, CommonsDelinker, DandyDan2007, L337 kybldmstr, Monkeyatemydog, 5theye, Skier Dude, AntiSpamBot, Vanished user g454XxNpUVWvxzlr, SJP, M ward85, Kraanerg, Jderosier, VolkovBot, Steptb, Tomaat~enwiki, Hmasteraz, Peperzout, Rei-bot, Broadbot, Lesternighthawk, John aziz, K d f m, IL7Soulhunter, Creepyguy666, Edkollin, Munci, Sfmammamia, EmxBot, Diluvien, Nite-Sirk, Joseph Banks, Venomous9, Aspects, Tafenau, Cyfal, Mygerardromance, Godisaconcept, Kit.music, Jpereira net, ImageRemovalBot, Soporaeternus, ClueBot, Binksternet, The Thing That Should Not Be, Plastikspork, TheOldJacobite, CounterVandalismBot, Ktr101, Coralmizu, Peter.C, Kaiba, Puceron, SchreiberBike, ChrisHodgesUK, Aprilmonkey, DumZiBoT, Heathen Harvest Sage, Semitransgenic, XLinkBot, Delicious carbuncle, WikHead, ZooFari, Addbot, Guoguo12, Fyrael, Samuelmpmac, Innv, Aryder779, TeleTubbie ZOO, Redheylin, Charf, WikiStuffs, Tassedethe, Verbal, Lightbot, Zorrobot, SasiSasi, Jarble, Legobot, Luckas-bot, Ptbotgourou, Taxisfolder, Weeeeeew, AnomieBOT, Valueyou, Hairhorn, Piano non troppo, Deadsnob, Cyaniedthistles, Daskronikler, Nitarbell, Jchthys, Xqbot, 3family6, Control.valve, Measles, Sabrebd, WebCiteBOT, Ddrse5647, FrescoBot, Vehement, GreenZeb, Elbloggers, Senselessstudios, Tim1357, Kokoshky, Nadir80, E Echavarria, Lotje, Kommissar Hjuler, Edcitybest2009, Tonybraxton, AlemanI2.0, Calamity2009, Rivet138, Henchren, RjwilmsiBot, Piershaw, EmausBot, Mashaunix, TuHan-Bot, Fixblor, Wolfinruins, Nikulasczernak, Lexusuns, Isanuric, Delitist, CocuBot, Suiseisekiryu, Frietjes, Helpful Pixie Bot, Pjbdjk, Northamerica1000, Solomon7968, CitationCleanerBot, OCCullens, Cyberbot II, ChrisGualtieri, Drawordoodle, Myxomatosis57, Springsnow93, GentleCollapse16, Pinecone23777, Thedude242u2, Screenmet, Ilovetopaint, Tonio Romi, Autumn harvest thrives, Sophdoe, Nøkkenbuer and Anonymous: 321

- **Pure Data** *Source:* https://en.wikipedia.org/wiki/Pure_Data?oldid=688207456 *Contributors:* Fnielsen, Michael Hardy, Jll, Guaka, Furrykef, Omegatron, Bloodshedder, Twang, MrJones, Scyrma, Rev3rend, Micru, Utcursch, OwenBlacker, Ojw, Kate, Paul August, Gronky, Danakil, CanisRufus, MBisanz, Lycurgus, CyberSkull, Kocio, Marasmusine, Scott.wheeler, FlaBot, GreyCat, Spencerk, YurikBot, RussBot, NawlinWiki, Mokhov, Ejdzej, Jona, Ninly, JLaTondre, SmackBot, Kellen, Reedy, Eskimbot, BrN, Mcld, Andyvn22, Davigoli, Eighthave, Thumperward, Shift8, Tony fanta, Jefchip, DavidMcCabe, Thijs!bot, T-1, Isilanes, MJD86, Xb2u7Zjzc32, WhatamIdoing, Yaxu, Gwern, Tristan Chambers, Birczanin, VolkovBot, WOSlinker, Una Smith, Jamelan, Jerryobject, DancingHacker, Johnanth, ImageRemovalBot, Methossant, Kl4m-AWB, Mumiemonstret, Semitransgenic, Nettings, XLinkBot, Fastily, Dthomsen8, MystBot, Dwjbosman, Addbot, Mortense, Furiousgreencloud, StevenWilkin, Umlaeute, Omnipaedista, RibotBOT, FrescoBot, OgreBot, Lasukals, ChronoKinetic, Minimac, Mattwigway, Gf uip, Surgesg, Groovyamusement, Ledhed2222, Panoramedia, Drakeland, Helpful Pixie Bot, B0o-supermario, FuFoFuEd, 13bitdandy, BattyBot, GuitarExtended, Pdecalculus, Reduzent, Skwuent, Farsmuse, Sj 2000, RSMilward and Anonymous: 53

- **Raster-Noton** *Source:* https://en.wikipedia.org/wiki/Raster-Noton?oldid=687280735 *Contributors:* Denis Barthel, Robbot, Kipton, TearJohnDown, Pigman, Fram, SmackBot, AlexReynolds, Meno25, Lugnuts, Mattisse, Young Pioneer, AlexOvShaolin, Toutoune25, R'n'B, Overcow, Black Kite, Sparklism, Alexbot, Addbot, Ronhjones, Xqbot, FrescoBot, Hvonhahn, Starcheerspeaksnewslostwars, BG19bot, BattyBot, Dexbot, Freebirdthemonk II, Mcraciun and Anonymous: 12

- **Reaktor** *Source:* https://en.wikipedia.org/wiki/Reaktor?oldid=681942466 *Contributors:* Zimbres, Ringomassa, Academic Challenger, Mintleaf~enwiki, Micru, Gadfium, Ulrich Tausend, GreenReaper, Rich Farmbrough, Smyth, Surachit, Artur Nowak~enwiki, RJFJR, Senor ibex, PullUpYourSocks, JdforresterBot, Scott.wheeler, Rjwilmsi, Quiddity, JdforresterBot, Gurch, Intgr, Marminnetje, Anonymous editor, Stenun, SmackBot, Gabriel Roth, Frap, OrphanBot, TheEXIT, Dl2000, Hu12, Vanisaac, Stanlekub, Bohan, Lemmio, Thijs!bot, TAnthony, City-state, Leftblank, MartinBot, Rimwolf, Leopold B. Stotch, Bluhd, Gg bris, ImageRemovalBot, Mattgirling, Peterdines, BOTarate, Addbot, Persilrein, Jncraton, SpBot, Lightbot, Yobot, FrescoBot, Jimwmurphy, Full-date unlinking bot, H3llBot, Snotbot, Frietjes, AlternativeElectronics, Calzamor, Pdecalculus, Hacksandwich, KMCAudio and Anonymous: 41

- **Reason (software)** *Source:* https://en.wikipedia.org/wiki/Reason_(software)?oldid=686439886 *Contributors:* Andre Engels, ZoeB, Glenn, Chuljin, Hyacinth, Robbot, ZimZalaBim, Cyberia23, Zigger, Micru, Nwynder, Ary29, Two Bananas, Mastgrr, Reefer, CALR, Discospinster, Bender235, LordRM, Revolutionary, BalooUrsidae, Gargaj, Ferretgames, Mlessard, Jackliddle, Woutersmet, Danhash, SteinbDJ, PullUpYourSocks, Charon.sk, Nuno Tavares, Scott.wheeler, Tabletop, Bbatsell, Marudubshinki, GSlicer, BD2412, Rjwilmsi, Lockley, Binary, Nightfreak, The wub, MapsMan, Titoxd, FlaBot, JdforresterBot, Jmorgan, Bgwhite, Tone, Poorsod, Byron Vickers, Peter S., Ihope127, Pelago, NawlinWiki, Tastemyhouse, Cholmes75, Veezay~enwiki, Hosterweis, DerekL, Osmaker, Sebbi, Veinor, KnightRider~enwiki, SmackBot, Gabriel Roth, Eskimbot, Fractal3, Direktorxxx, Commander Keane bot, Headwes, Emufarmers, EncMstr, Jbachman, Feathers, Yorick8080, Aldaron, Lpgeffen, DietrichM, A.B.Dell, Wickethewok, Kvng, Hu12, Iridescent, Sameboat, Tommywommy117, J Milburn, JiriK, Betaeleven, BananaManCanDance, Kameraad Pjotr, Elektromekanik, Ripton, ShelfSkewed, Cydebot, Tdvance, EmmSeeMusic, Thijs!bot, JustAGal, Reasonmain, Nick Number, Dancanm, Prolog, Gert4gt, Kerdek, Kaini, JAnDbot, Molten tar, Sophie means wisdom, Jakce, Esanchez7587, JediLofty, Kcoutu, Galaxas0, KhaOS, Rettetast, R'n'B, AntiSpamBot, Professorchinese, NickR753, Pravda23, Naim312, Signalhead, Black Kite, TreasuryTag,

3.1. TEXT

Alkota, Amikake3, LeilaniLad, PGSONIC, Skjalg.skagen, PhilyG, MightyJordan, Danelectro40, Andrarias, Gmakaveli, Jerryobject, Tronikfunk, Babarr, ImageRemovalBot, Binksternet, Lonegroover, Rsmktng, Peter Banana, Auntof6, Gizard, DragonBot, FiendishDemon, Boydoesknow, Edit-or-perish, Arkarian01, XLinkBot, Vincenzo284, SP1R1TM4N, EnochLight, Kbdankbot, Tayste, Addbot, Pborten, Download, SpBot, Yobot, Fraggle81, AnomieBOT, DemocraticLuntz, Hairhorn, Barrydmann, Akathedrummer, LilHelpa, 23pokrzywa, Nighteater, Irish Techno Zombie, BillyFckwards, Ryansonicreality, BigChrill, Maginks, Manu887, JRGOdin, Alimony, JV Smithy, Jesse V., Djkcel, EmausBot, John of Reading, WikitanvirBot, Mornelmornel, Martinacain, GoingBatty, Clusternote, Wittenbergdoor, Erpert, Landofthesamp, Unreal7, Δ, L Kensington, Quantumor, Colejohnson66, Synthmanboy, ClueBot NG, Arteeni, Lonecretin, AlternativeElectronics, Yeshua Savant House, BG19bot, Blandrys, SodaAnt, MediaSVI, Mikemcatpt, N3WROYAL, JYBot, Codename Lisa, Profesjonalizm, Radiodef, Andrewreynolds1965, Smortypi, Bookinglive, Pdecalculus, ColeLoki, ScienEar, Uto500, Wakalaka123, Calvandavis and Anonymous: 323

- **Renoise** *Source:* https://en.wikipedia.org/wiki/Renoise?oldid=686040932 *Contributors:* EddEdmondson, Minesweeper, Darkwind, Glenn, Charles Matthews, Timwi, Zoicon5, Bloodshedder, Psychonaut, Twilek, Micru, Mboverload, Herzliyya, Camitommy, Gargaj, Stephan Leeds, Marasmusine, Vossanova, Bensin, YurikBot, RussBot, Peter S., Suva, Patto, SmackBot, Zvar, 4hodmt, Decept404, Wickethewok, A. Parrot, Aeternus, Cydebot, Mr mark dollin, Spartaz, Bantai~enwiki, OriginalJunglist, TreasuryTag, Davehi1, Norma Jeans Mortensen Ghost, Augmatic, Fratrep, Conner bw, Niceguyedc, Alexbot, Muhandes, JBLanteigne, Nettings, InternetMeme, Delt01, Kbdankbot, Addbot, Lightbot, Yobot, 4th-otaku, Akilaa, 23pokrzywa, FrescoBot, Kami68k, Manu887, Minimac, John of Reading, Teacherhax, ZéroBot, Trust me im not crazy, Shaddim, Pdecalculus, ScotXW, Monkbot, Bruncitier, Hakken, Gerirish and Anonymous: 80

- **Software bug** *Source:* https://en.wikipedia.org/wiki/Software_bug?oldid=684752141 *Contributors:* Damian Yerrick, AxelBoldt, CYD, Mav, Wesley, Bryan Derksen, Robert Merkel, Malcolm Farmer, Ed Poor, Kowloonese, Tommy~enwiki, Arvindn, PierreAbbat, Fubar Obfusco, SimonP, Hephaestos, Frecklefoot, Patrick, RTC, Michael Hardy, Kwertii, Kku, Liftarn, Tompagenet, Wapcaplet, TakuyaMurata, CG, Eric119, Alfio, Goatasaur, Ahoerstemeier, DavidWBrooks, Stan Shebs, Ronz, Nanshu, Baylink, Mark Foskey, Julesd, Jimregan, Evercat, Rl, Focus mankind~enwiki, GRAHAMUK, Emperorbma, Popsracer, Charles Matthews, Timwi, Ww, Dysprosia, Doradus, Greenrd, Markhurd, VeryVerily, Wazow~enwiki, Bevo, Shizhao, Khym Chanur, Raul654, Mpost89, David.Monniaux, Denelson83, Robbot, Enceladus, Rfc1394, Ancheta Wis, Matthew Stannard, DocWatson42, DavidCary, Fastfission, Taviso, Maha ts, Lakefall~enwiki, TerokNor, Alexf, Abu badali, Neilm, Sam Hocevar, Ojw, Kevyn, Andreas Kaufmann, Vbganesh, Corti, Mike Rosoft, Freakofnurture, AliveFreeHappy, Slady, Discospinster, Twinxor, Rich Farmbrough, Leibniz, Pmsyyz, Drano, ArnoldReinhold, Notinasnaid, Jasonq, Sperling, Paul August, ZeroOne, Moa3333, Kjoonlee, Danakil, Ylee, El C, Bobo192, Smalljim, Daf, Minghong, Haham hanuka, Jarich, Rolfmueller, V2Blast, Walter Görlitz, Atlant, Ashley Pomeroy, Joris Gillis, Knowledge Seeker, Danhash, RainbowOfLight, Drat, BlastOButter42, Gunter, Nuno Tavares, Woohookitty, Mindmatrix, Ben Liblit, Camw, Bluemoose, Eilthireach, Dovid, Gerbrant, MassGalactusUniversum, Cuchullain, BD2412, Qwertyus, Kbdank71, FreplySpang, Ahsen, Josh Parris, Isaac Rabinovitch, Leeyc0, Nick R, ScottJ, Yahoolian, Syced, FlaBot, Nivix, NavarroJ, SteveBaker, DoomBringer, Chobot, Pinecar, YurikBot, Wavelength, Borgx, Hairy Dude, Kafziel, Nmondal, RussBot, Witan, Hede2000, Hydrargyrum, Ptomes, Pseudomonas, NawlinWiki, -OOPSIE-, Benja, Aeusoes1, Korny O'Near, Ondenc, Irishguy, Rbarreira, Jpbowen, Gadget850, Richardcavell, Gtdp, Nikkimaria, Moogsi, KGasso, JLaTondre, David Biddulph, DisambigBot, Mhkay, Rwwww, GrinBot~enwiki, Devans00, AtomCrusher, SmackBot, Haymaker, Incnis Mrsi, Unyoyega, C.Fred, ChaseVenters, HalfShadow, Yamaguchi??, Ohnoitsjamie, Anwar saadat, TimBentley, @modi, Jopsen, IAmAI, Thumperward, Kevin Hanse, Russvdw, EncMstr, MabryTyson, Krallja, QuimGil, Scwlong, Audriusa, Can't sleep, clown will eat me, Yidisheryid, TKD, Normxxx, Cybercobra, Akulkis, Richard001, DMacks, Acdx, Ohconfucius, Lambiam, Serein (renamed because of SUL), Derek farn, Dak, Kuru, GVP Webmaster, 16@r, JHunterJ, Noah Salzman, Larrymcp, Cbuckley, Fredil Yupigo, Matt714, RARPSL, WhoSaid?, MeCalabi, SkyWalker, JForget, CRGreathouse, Kameraad Pjotr, Hsingh77, NaBUru38, Jaxad0127, El aprendelenguas, Chrisahn, Davnor, Cydebot, Dennette, Sweavo, Gogo Dodo, Dmacedo, DonFB, Guyinblack25, Bob Stein - VisiBone, Thijs!bot, Al Lemos, Trevyn, Marek69, Knalsite, Escarbot, DewiMorgan, Mentifisto, AntiVandalBot, Gioto, Bondolo, SFairchild, JAnDbot, MER-C, Martinkunev, Aubadaurada, Acroterion, LarryHughes, Magioladitis, Bongwarrior, VoABot II, Firealwaysworks, Cpl Syx, Oroso, Gwern, AVRS, MartinBot, Mage0, Robijn, Kostisl, R'n'B, Tgeairn, Erkan Yilmaz, Slash, J.delanoy, Mindgames11, Love Krittaya, Adavidb, Jesant13, Thaurisil, Laurusnobilis, Spyforthemoon, Robert Illes, Jigesh, Tarotcards, SJP, Jackaranga, Izno, Funandtrvl, PeaceNT, Wombleme, Technopat, A4bot, T-bonham, JhsBot, Maxim, Softtest123, Mouse is back, Forlornturtle, Strong Tower, JonnyJD, SieBot, PanagosTheOther, Bachcell, Gerakibot, Triwbe, JuWiki2, Colfer2, Boogster, SimonTrew, Cfinazzo, Pinkadelica, Martarius, ClueBot, Deanlaw, Processguy, Jan1nad, Eddiehu, Gohan2091, CounterVandalismBot, Kurumban, AnnLanders, Excirial, Lartoven, Swtechwr, Brianbjparker, Trinadh Kumar Bonam, PCHS-NJROTC, Callinus, Bonams, Squeedle, Fathisules, InternetMeme, Roxy the dog, Dezaxa, Dthomsen8, Shieber, Avoided, Srikant.sharma, Mitch Ames, Addbot, Conboy98, Ronhjones, MrOllie, Morning277, Favonian, ChenzwBot, Tassedethe, Tide rolls, Jarble, Fajardojosh, Bextrad, Luckas-bot, Yobot, TaBOT-zerem, Legobot II, Dfe6543, AnomieBOT, Rubinbot, Digulla, Piano non troppo, NabiKAZ, Lolschoolishorrible, Obersachsebot, Xqbot, Qatutor, TinucherianBot II, J04n, Cresix, Ikovalyov, Joaquin008, FrescoBot, Jumper32, Miklcct, BenzolBot, DivineAlpha, HamburgerRadio, Redrose64, Winterst, Gbolton, NinjaCross, Jusses2, RedBot, Merlion444, TobeBot, Trappist the monk, Vrenator, Hadger, Cowlibob, Reaper Eternal, Unique.kevin, Alph Bot, WildBot, EmausBot, Never give in, Arturotena, Rabbabodrool, KimBecker, K6ka, ZéroBot, Josve05a, Bamyers99, Callmeking87, L Kensington, MaGa, Wikiloop, Ego White Tray, MainFrame, ChuispastonBot, ClueBot NG, Mrkillno1, Bigmaxwell, G0gogcsc300, Gavin.perch, Helpful Pixie Bot, Kenyonhero, BG19bot, Softwrite, Raihantex, Biebs101, 23W, Minsbot, Proxyma, MeanMotherJr, Isarra (HG), Corn cheese, Shashank16392, TheFrog001, Eerfem, Missannafjmorris, Carrot Lord, MichelleLovesJustin, Hannohase, Johnfranciscollins, Monkbot, IagoQnsi, Fatso69, Stepbang, Jiten.meena, Sousasuza and Anonymous: 366

- **Sonic artifact** *Source:* https://en.wikipedia.org/wiki/Sonic_artifact?oldid=585933005 *Contributors:* Zundark, Twang, Ewlyahoocom, Rwalker, NickD, Kle0012, SmackBot, Lainagier, EncMstr, Oatmeal batman, Wizardman, OnBeyondZebrax, Peter M Dodge, CmdrObot, Yarnalgo, Thijs!bot, Binksternet, Addbot, Robert.Harker, AnomieBOT, Erik9bot, BattyBot, ChrisGualtieri, Metadox and Anonymous: 3

- **SuperCollider** *Source:* https://en.wikipedia.org/wiki/SuperCollider?oldid=679996652 *Contributors:* Michael Hardy, Pnm, GTBacchus, Delirium, Kragen, Guaka, Hyacinth, K1Bond007, Omegatron, Samsara, Fvw, Twang, Phil Boswell, Bearcat, Fredrik, Somercet, Ds13, Markhadman, Cynical, Miborovsky, Rich Farmbrough, Antaeus Feldspar, Pavel Vozenilek, Gronky, Danakil, Sietse Snel, RoyBoy, Smalljim, Polarscribe, CyberSkull, Snowolf, Zawersh, Deeahbz, Marudubshinki, MarSch, Nandesuka, FlaBot, GreyCat, Wavelength, Markhoney, Gardar Rurak, Gaius Cornelius, Black Falcon, Esprit15d, Audiolo, SmackBot, Elonka, Mcld, Thumperward, Colonies Chris, Frap, Jmlk17, Ergative rlt, Anjow, Atoll, Cheapmachines, Cydebot, T-1, KrakatoaKatie, Isilanes, Dylan Lake, Somasociety, Freshacconci, Yaxu, Gwern, MartinBot, Speck-Made, R'n'B, Rob Cranfill, Leopold B. Stotch, Micropolygon, Jesegel, EmxBot, HairyWombat, ImageRemovalBot, Kl4m-AWB, Nenano, SF007, DumZiBoT, Semitransgenic, Ariarielle, Nettings, Psytronikk, C.treppo, RichLow, Oriyn142, Addbot, Mortense, Dadaesque, WfrdHuis, Ustrasime,

Sooberkollydr, ChenzwBot, WikiDreamer Bot, Fiftyquid, Yobot, Marinok7, Maxens, AnomieBOT, Spotsroad, Joaomartinhomoura, VX, Gidoca, Brunonar, FrescoBot, Csediment, Seansay, Oracleofottawa, Shiny.Magnum, Minimac, Ledhed2222, ClueBot NG, Catlemur, Widr, Helpful Pixie Bot, BG19bot, FuFoFuEd, JOSmithIII, SoledadKabocha, Chaimara, Mathiasbredholt, Pdecalculus, Heyokha, Alex.friedrichs and Anonymous: 90

- **The Art of Noises** *Source:* https://en.wikipedia.org/wiki/The_Art_of_Noises?oldid=628063424 *Contributors:* Hyacinth, Bender235, El C, Red dwarf, Theostavrides, Rjwilmsi, Metropolitan90, RussBot, SmackBot, Neddyseagoon, Epictetus, Doceddi, Husond, Pkokoras74, Dsp13, Brandt Luke Zorn, Yonidebot, 5theye, GrahamHardy, Slysplace, EHonkoop, Kylemew, CharlesGillingham, Cyfal, Soporaeternus, Doughouse, Xic667, Arjayay, Semitransgenic, XLinkBot, Addbot, Lightbot, Jarble, Luckas-bot, Valueyou, Mauro Lanari, J04n, FrescoBot, Citation bot 1, Chrisdesign, Lotje, Marinos Ko, RjwilmsiBot, Helpful Pixie Bot, Jamesallen2, Sanvizc and Anonymous: 29

3.2 Images

- **File:1989_Kawasaki_Electronic_Digital_Guitar_by_Remco_circuit_bend_2.jpg** *Source:* https://upload.wikimedia.org/wikipedia/commons/a/ad/1989_Kawasaki_Electronic_Digital_Guitar_by_Remco_circuit_bend_2.jpg *License:* CC BY 2.0 *Contributors:* kawi2 *Original artist:* Greg Francke from Seattle, US
- **File:Ableton_Live_logo.png** *Source:* https://upload.wikimedia.org/wikipedia/en/b/bf/Ableton_Live_logo.png *License:* Fair use *Contributors:* Source: http://www.ableton.com/graphics, vectorized with Inkscape. *Original artist:* ?
- **File:Acap.svg** *Source:* https://upload.wikimedia.org/wikipedia/commons/5/52/Acap.svg *License:* Public domain *Contributors:* Own work *Original artist:* F l a n k e r
- **File:Ambox_important.svg** *Source:* https://upload.wikimedia.org/wikipedia/commons/b/b4/Ambox_important.svg *License:* Public domain *Contributors:* Own work, based off of Image:Ambox scales.svg *Original artist:* Dsmurat (talk · contribs)
- **File:Audio_a.svg** *Source:* https://upload.wikimedia.org/wikipedia/commons/2/2b/Audio_a.svg *License:* Public domain *Contributors:*
- 'A'_(PSF).png *Original artist:* 'A'_(PSF).png: Pearson Scott Foresman
- **File:AudiodatenkompressionManowarThePowerOfThySword.jpg** *Source:* https://upload.wikimedia.org/wikipedia/commons/3/3a/AudiodatenkompressionManowarThePowerOfThySword.jpg *License:* CC BY-SA 3.0 *Contributors:* Own work *Original artist:* Moehre1992
- **File:Bending.jpg** *Source:* https://upload.wikimedia.org/wikipedia/commons/b/bd/Bending.jpg *License:* CC BY-SA 2.5 *Contributors:* Own work - *Original artist:* Holotone / Holotone at en.wikipedia
- **File:Bidule.png** *Source:* https://upload.wikimedia.org/wikipedia/en/a/af/Bidule.png *License:* Cc-by-sa-3.0 *Contributors:*

  Own work

  Original artist:

  Rcrath (talk) (Uploads)
- **File:Blue_Screen_Phone.jpg** *Source:* https://upload.wikimedia.org/wikipedia/commons/4/47/Blue_Screen_Phone.jpg *License:* Public domain *Contributors:* en: Wikipedia *Original artist:* en:User:Edward
- **File:BuzzScreenshot.png** *Source:* https://upload.wikimedia.org/wikipedia/commons/d/d4/BuzzScreenshot.png *License:* CC-BY-SA-3.0 *Contributors:* Transferred from en.wikipedia to Commons by Quedel using CommonsHelper. *Original artist:* GameGod at English Wikipedia
- **File:CSIRAC.jpg** *Source:* https://upload.wikimedia.org/wikipedia/commons/f/fb/CSIRAC.jpg *License:* BSD *Contributors:* Transferred from en.wikipedia to Commons. *Original artist:* The original uploader was Dysprosia at English Wikipedia
- **File:ChucK_logo2.jpg** *Source:* https://upload.wikimedia.org/wikipedia/commons/6/6a/ChucK_logo2.jpg *License:* CC-BY-SA-3.0 *Contributors:* Transferred from en.wikipedia to Commons by Martin Homuth-Rosemann. *Original artist:* The original uploader was Gewang at English Wikipedia
- **File:Classpath_bugs.png** *Source:* https://upload.wikimedia.org/wikipedia/commons/c/cf/Classpath_bugs.png *License:* CC-BY-SA-3.0 *Contributors:* Own work *Original artist:* Audriusa
- **File:Commons-logo.svg** *Source:* https://upload.wikimedia.org/wikipedia/en/4/4a/Commons-logo.svg *License:* ? *Contributors:* ? *Original artist:* ?
- **File:Computer_crash_airport.jpg** *Source:* https://upload.wikimedia.org/wikipedia/commons/6/64/Computer_crash_airport.jpg *License:* Public domain *Contributors:* Miguel Andrade's own work. *Original artist:* Miguel Andrade at English Wikipedia
- **File:DJ_Sasha_at_Arenele_Romane,_Bucharest_(2006)_(rear_view).jpg** *Source:* https://upload.wikimedia.org/wikipedia/commons/2/27/DJ_Sasha_at_Arenele_Romane%2C_Bucharest_%282006%29_%28rear_view%29.jpg *License:* CC BY-SA 2.5 *Contributors:* Taken on 8 July at Arenele Romane in Bucharest, Romania by Barbu Cristian. Courtesy of Red Light Management [1]. *Original artist:* . The original uploader was Wickethewok at English Wikipedia
- **File:Distorted_waveforms_square_sine.svg** *Source:* https://upload.wikimedia.org/wikipedia/commons/2/22/Distorted_waveforms_square_sine.svg *License:* Public domain *Contributors:* This file was derived from: Distorted waveforms square sine.png

  Original artist: User:NeilUK
- **File:Distortion_effect.ogg** *Source:* https://upload.wikimedia.org/wikipedia/commons/1/15/Distortion_effect.ogg *License:* Public domain *Contributors:* Transferred from en.wikipedia; transferred to Commons by User:FSII using CommonsHelper. *Original artist:* Original uploader was Paulnasca at en.wikipedia
- **File:Distortion_waveform.svg** *Source:* https://upload.wikimedia.org/wikipedia/commons/c/c6/Distortion_waveform.svg *License:* Public domain *Contributors:* ? *Original artist:* DesbWit at English Wikipedia

3.2. IMAGES

- **File:DripPiece-Maciunas.jpg** *Source:* https://upload.wikimedia.org/wikipedia/en/2/26/DripPiece-Maciunas.jpg *License:* Fair use *Contributors:*
George Brecht Events; A Heterospective, Robinson, Walter König
Original artist: ?
- **File:Edit-clear.svg** *Source:* https://upload.wikimedia.org/wikipedia/en/f/f2/Edit-clear.svg *License:* Public domain *Contributors:* The *Tango! Desktop Project*. *Original artist:*
The people from the Tango! project. And according to the meta-data in the file, specifically: "Andreas Nilsson, and Jakub Steiner (although minimally)."
- **File:FL_Studio_11_just_logo.png** *Source:* https://upload.wikimedia.org/wikipedia/en/6/69/FL_Studio_11_just_logo.png *License:* Fair use *Contributors:*
http://www.image-line.com/innovaeditor/assets/HomePageIcons_FLStudio_1.png *Original artist:*
Image Line
- **File:FL_Studio_12_User_Interface.png** *Source:* https://upload.wikimedia.org/wikipedia/commons/2/29/FL_Studio_12_User_Interface.png *License:* CC BY-SA 4.0 *Contributors:* Own work *Original artist:* Image-Line Software
- **File:Figure_rythmique_equivalence_noire_pointee.svg** *Source:* https://upload.wikimedia.org/wikipedia/commons/8/86/Figure_rythmique_equivalence_noire_pointee.svg *License:* CC-BY-SA-3.0 *Contributors:* self-made, with Inkscape, from LilyPond model *Original artist:* Christophe Dang Ngoc Chan (cdang)
- **File:Folder_Hexagonal_Icon.svg** *Source:* https://upload.wikimedia.org/wikipedia/en/4/48/Folder_Hexagonal_Icon.svg *License:* Cc-by-sa-3.0 *Contributors:* ? *Original artist:* ?
- **File:Free_Software_Portal_Logo.svg** *Source:* https://upload.wikimedia.org/wikipedia/commons/6/67/Nuvola_apps_emacs_vector.svg *License:* LGPL *Contributors:*
- Nuvola_apps_emacs.png *Original artist:* Nuvola_apps_emacs.png: David Vignoni
- **File:Futurist_pratella.jpg** *Source:* https://upload.wikimedia.org/wikipedia/commons/a/af/Futurist_pratella.jpg *License:* Public domain *Contributors:* ? *Original artist:* ?
- **File:Gnome-dev-cdrom-audio.svg** *Source:* https://upload.wikimedia.org/wikipedia/commons/b/b0/Gnome-dev-cdrom-audio.svg *License:* LGPL *Contributors:* http://ftp.gnome.org/pub/GNOME/sources/gnome-themes-extras/0.9/gnome-themes-extras-0.9.0.tar.gz *Original artist:* David Vignoni
- **File:Gnome-mime-sound-openclipart.svg** *Source:* https://upload.wikimedia.org/wikipedia/commons/8/87/Gnome-mime-sound-openclipart.svg *License:* Public domain *Contributors:* Own work. Based on File:Gnome-mime-audio-openclipart.svg, which is public domain. *Original artist:* User:Eubulides
- **File:Green_bug_and_broom.svg** *Source:* https://upload.wikimedia.org/wikipedia/commons/8/83/Green_bug_and_broom.svg *License:* LGPL *Contributors:* File:Broom icon.svg, file:Green_bug.svg *Original artist:* Poznaniak, pozostali autorzy w plikach źródłowych
- **File:H96566k.jpg** *Source:* https://upload.wikimedia.org/wikipedia/commons/8/8a/H96566k.jpg *License:* Public domain *Contributors:* U.S. Naval Historical Center Online Library Photograph NH 96566-KN *Original artist:* Courtesy of the Naval Surface Warfare Center, Dahlgren, VA., 1988.
- **File:IxiQuarks.jpg** *Source:* https://upload.wikimedia.org/wikipedia/en/f/f0/IxiQuarks.jpg *License:* CC-BY-SA-3.0 *Contributors:*
http://www.ixi-audio.net/content/download/ixiquarks/img/ixiQuarks2.jpg *Original artist:*
SooperKollydr
- **File:Kraakdoos_(Cracklebox).jpg** *Source:* https://upload.wikimedia.org/wikipedia/commons/d/d1/Kraakdoos_%28Cracklebox%29.jpg *License:* CC BY 2.0 *Contributors:* originally posted to **Flickr** as Dorkbot CPH *Original artist:* Sascha Pohflepp
- **File:LandMap_Max_patcher.jpg** *Source:* https://upload.wikimedia.org/wikipedia/commons/0/0e/LandMap_Max_patcher.jpg *License:* CC BY 2.5 *Contributors:* Own work *Original artist:* Alexis Chazard et Gwenola Wagon
- **File:Live_8_Screenshot.png** *Source:* https://upload.wikimedia.org/wikipedia/en/7/7c/Live_8_Screenshot.png *License:* Fair use *Contributors:* Myself
Original artist: ?
- **File:Luigi_Russolo_ca._1916.gif** *Source:* https://upload.wikimedia.org/wikipedia/commons/8/8c/Luigi_Russolo_ca._1916.gif *License:* Public domain *Contributors:* From en.wikipedia. [1] *Original artist:* ?
- **File:Magtape1.jpg** *Source:* https://upload.wikimedia.org/wikipedia/commons/8/83/Magtape1.jpg *License:* CC-BY-SA-3.0 *Contributors:* Image by Daniel P. B. Smith.; *Original artist:* Daniel P. B. Smith.
- **File:Maplin_5600.jpg** *Source:* https://upload.wikimedia.org/wikipedia/commons/f/fe/Maplin_5600.jpg *License:* Public domain *Contributors:* ? *Original artist:* ?
- **File:Masami_Akita_5267969.jpg** *Source:* https://upload.wikimedia.org/wikipedia/commons/6/62/Masami_Akita_5267969.jpg *License:* CC BY 2.5 *Contributors:* No machine-readable source provided. Own work assumed (based on copyright claims). *Original artist:* No machine-readable author provided. Nomo assumed (based on copyright claims).
- **File:Max6.PNG** *Source:* https://upload.wikimedia.org/wikipedia/commons/9/90/Max6.PNG *License:* GFDL *Contributors:* Website *Original artist:* Cycling 74
- **File:Mediawiki.png** *Source:* https://upload.wikimedia.org/wikipedia/commons/6/64/MediaWiki_logo_without_tagline.png *License:* Public domain *Contributors:*

- The flower is Image:Tournesol.png *Original artist:* User:Anthere (flower) and User:Eloquence (combination, concept), reworked by User:Aka
- **File:Metal_machine_music.jpg** *Source:* https://upload.wikimedia.org/wikipedia/en/6/65/Metal_machine_music.jpg *License:* Fair use *Contributors:*
  The cover art can be obtained from RCA Records. *Original artist:* ?
- **File:NONPaganMuzak.jpg** *Source:* https://upload.wikimedia.org/wikipedia/en/2/26/NONPaganMuzak.jpg *License:* Fair use *Contributors:* ? *Original artist:* ?
- **File:Pd-helloworld.svg** *Source:* https://upload.wikimedia.org/wikipedia/commons/f/fe/Pd-helloworld.svg *License:* CC BY-SA 3.0 *Contributors:* Own work *Original artist:* Jancsika
- **File:Pd_example_2.png** *Source:* https://upload.wikimedia.org/wikipedia/commons/0/0e/Pd_example_2.png *License:* Public domain *Contributors:* Transferred from en.wikipedia; transferred to Commons by User:Clusternote using CommonsHelper. *Original artist:* Original uploader was Ledhed2222 at en.wikipedia
- **File:Pd_example_3.svg** *Source:* https://upload.wikimedia.org/wikipedia/commons/7/7b/Pd_example_3.svg *License:* BSD *Contributors:* SVG converted from the PostScript output of the software *Original artist:* Miller Puckette
- **File:Pdobjects.svg** *Source:* https://upload.wikimedia.org/wikipedia/commons/9/94/Pdobjects.svg *License:* CC BY-SA 3.0 *Contributors:* Own work *Original artist:* Jancsika
- **File:Placa-audioPC-925.jpg** *Source:* https://upload.wikimedia.org/wikipedia/en/1/19/Placa-audioPC-925.jpg *License:* PD *Contributors:* ? *Original artist:* ?
- **File:Pure_Data_with_many_patches_open_(showing_netpd_project).png** *Source:* https://upload.wikimedia.org/wikipedia/commons/f/f8/Pure_Data_with_many_patches_open_%28showing_netpd_project%29.png *License:* CC BY-SA 3.0 *Contributors:* This is a screenshot of a netpd session *Original artist:* Reduzent
- **File:Puredyne-supercollider-eee.png** *Source:* https://upload.wikimedia.org/wikipedia/commons/6/62/Puredyne-supercollider-eee.png *License:* CC BY-SA 3.0 *Contributors:* User:Mcld *Original artist:* goto10 collective (puredyne), SuperCollider developers, Jack Control developers
- **File:Question_book-new.svg** *Source:* https://upload.wikimedia.org/wikipedia/en/9/99/Question_book-new.svg *License:* Cc-by-sa-3.0 *Contributors:*
  Created from scratch in Adobe Illustrator. Based on Image:Question book.png created by User:Equazcion *Original artist:* Tkgd2007
- **File:RN-Twenty.jpg** *Source:* https://upload.wikimedia.org/wikipedia/en/a/a9/RN-Twenty.jpg *License:* Fair use *Contributors:*
  Photo of the CD block (creator of this digital version is irrelevant as the copyright in all equivalent images is still held by the same party) Copyright held by the record company or the artist. Claimed as fair use regardless.
  Original artist: ?
- **File:Raster-Noton_logo.png** *Source:* https://upload.wikimedia.org/wikipedia/en/e/e2/Raster-Noton_logo.png *License:* PD *Contributors:*
  www.raster-noton.net
  Original artist:
  Martin Craciun
- **File:RasterNoton-ByetoneLive.png** *Source:* https://upload.wikimedia.org/wikipedia/commons/6/6e/RasterNoton-ByetoneLive.png *License:* CC BY 2.5 *Contributors:* Transferred from en.wikipedia to Commons. Transfer was stated to be made by User:Denis Barthel. *Original artist:* The original uploader was AlexReynolds at English Wikipedia
- **File:RasterNoton-NotoLive.png** *Source:* https://upload.wikimedia.org/wikipedia/commons/0/01/RasterNoton-NotoLive.png *License:* CC BY 2.5 *Contributors:* Transferred from en.wikipedia to Commons. Transfer was stated to be made by User:Denis Barthel. *Original artist:* The original uploader was AlexReynolds at English Wikipedia
- **File:Reaktor_Logo.jpg** *Source:* https://upload.wikimedia.org/wikipedia/en/f/f5/Reaktor_Logo.jpg *License:* Fair use *Contributors:*
  The logo may be obtained from Reaktor.
  Original artist: ?
- **File:Reason-Software-Logo.svg** *Source:* https://upload.wikimedia.org/wikipedia/en/5/5d/Reason-Software-Logo.svg *License:* Fair use *Contributors:*
  The logo is from the http://www.propellerheads.se/products/reason/dsp_frameset_reasonversion4.cfm website. *Original artist:* ?
- **File:Reason_7.0_screenshots.png** *Source:* https://upload.wikimedia.org/wikipedia/en/f/fb/Reason_7.0_screenshots.png *License:* Fair use *Contributors:* Using Reason myself *Original artist:* Propellerhead Software AB
- **File:Renoise_2.6.png** *Source:* https://upload.wikimedia.org/wikipedia/commons/d/da/Renoise_2.6.png *License:* GFDL *Contributors:* http://www.renoise.com/board/index.php?showtopic=26675&st=0&gopid=209721&#entry209721
  Original artist: conner_bw
- **File:Setups_@_One_Step_Beyond_at_Museum_of_Natural_History_2010-09-09.jpg** *Source:* https://upload.wikimedia.org/wikipedia/commons/6/62/Setups_%40_One_Step_Beyond_at_Museum_of_Natural_History_2010-09-09.jpg *License:* CC BY-SA 2.0 *Contributors:* setups *Original artist:* ghostdad
- **File:Sharp.svg** *Source:* https://upload.wikimedia.org/wikipedia/commons/a/a6/Sharp.svg *License:* Public domain *Contributors:* ?'s file *Original artist:* ?
- **File:Solitude.png** *Source:* https://upload.wikimedia.org/wikipedia/commons/5/52/Solitude.png *License:* GPLv2 *Contributors:* Transferred from en.wikipedia to Commons. *Original artist:* The original uploader was Davigoli at English Wikipedia

- **File:Sonic1991b.jpg** *Source:* https://upload.wikimedia.org/wikipedia/commons/8/89/Sonic1991b.jpg *License:* CC BY-SA 3.0 *Contributors:* Transferred from en.wikipedia to Commons by Channel_R using CommonsHelper. *Original artist:* Channel R at English Wikipedia
- **File:SuperCollider_screenshot2.jpg** *Source:* https://upload.wikimedia.org/wikipedia/en/5/51/SuperCollider_screenshot2.jpg *License:* ? *Contributors:* ? *Original artist:* ?
- **File:Symbol_book_class2.svg** *Source:* https://upload.wikimedia.org/wikipedia/commons/8/89/Symbol_book_class2.svg *License:* CC BY-SA 2.5 *Contributors:* Mad by Lokal_Profil by combining: *Original artist:* Lokal_Profil
- **File:Symbol_list_class.svg** *Source:* https://upload.wikimedia.org/wikipedia/en/d/db/Symbol_list_class.svg *License:* Public domain *Contributors:* ? *Original artist:* ?
- **File:Symbol_template_class.svg** *Source:* https://upload.wikimedia.org/wikipedia/en/5/5c/Symbol_template_class.svg *License:* Public domain *Contributors:* ? *Original artist:* ?
- **File:Tellus_13_cover.jpg** *Source:* https://upload.wikimedia.org/wikipedia/en/2/26/Tellus_13_cover.jpg *License:* Fair use *Contributors:* Joseph Nechvatal' blog at post.thing.net/node/2302 *Original artist:* Cover art by Joseph Nechvatal
- **File:The_Art_of_Noises.gif** *Source:* https://upload.wikimedia.org/wikipedia/en/7/7c/The_Art_of_Noises.gif *License:* Fair use *Contributors:* http://www.thereminvox.com/article/articleview/116 *Original artist:* ?
- **File:Vista-multimedia.png** *Source:* https://upload.wikimedia.org/wikipedia/commons/7/7b/Vista-multimedia.png *License:* GPL *Contributors:* ? *Original artist:* ?
- **File:Whitenoisesound.ogg** *Source:* https://upload.wikimedia.org/wikipedia/commons/6/66/Whitenoisesound.ogg *License:* Public domain *Contributors:* ? *Original artist:* ?
- **File:Wikibooks-logo-en-noslogan.svg** *Source:* https://upload.wikimedia.org/wikipedia/commons/d/df/Wikibooks-logo-en-noslogan.svg *License:* CC BY-SA 3.0 *Contributors:* Own work *Original artist:* User:Bastique, User:Ramac et al.
- **File:Yamaha_PSR-6_circuit_bended_@_Dorkbot_Helsinki_2007.jpg** *Source:* https://upload.wikimedia.org/wikipedia/commons/a/ac/Yamaha_PSR-6_circuit_bended_%40_Dorkbot_Helsinki_2007.jpg *License:* CC BY 2.0 *Contributors:* originally posted to **Flickr** as IMG_4262.JPG *Original artist:* Aleksi Pihkanen

3.3 Content license

- Creative Commons Attribution-Share Alike 3.0